GW01186237

Reverse Speech
Hidden Messages in Human Communication

by David John Oates

Resources for Creative Personal and Social Change

Knowledge Systems, Inc.
7777 W. Morris Street • Indianapolis, IN 46231 • USA

KNOWLEDGE
SYSTEMS, INC.

Copyright © 1991 by David John Oates

All rights reserved. No part of this work may be reprinted in any form or by any means without permission in writing from the publisher. Knowledge Systems, Inc., publisher of this book, has done so in order to place before the reading public what, at this time, appears to be a very interesting new discovery with respect to oral communications controlled by the human mind. Of course, functioning solely as publisher, Knowledge Systems, Inc., is not in a position to and has not sought to verify any of the author's data or conclusions. It therefore disclaims any representations herein and does not in any manner warrant the validity of the same.

Published by Knowledge Systems, Inc., 7777 West Morris Street, Indianapolis, IN 46231. Phone: (317) 241-0749, fax (317) 248-1503.

Cover design by Ilona Staples.

Reverse Speech™ is the term used to describe the phenomenon of Glossolanostics: The analysis of reversed unconsciously acquired verbal messages built into the sounds of human speech. Reverse Speech is a trademark and service mark owned by David John Oates. For more information about Reverse Speech, contact Reverse Speech Research, Inc., P.O. Box 181862, Dallas, TX 75218-9998. Phone: (214) 324-3216, fax (214)324-1191.

Library of Congress Cataloging-in-Publication Data

Oates, David John, 1955-
       Reverse Speech : Hidden messages in human communication
/ by David John Oates
              p.   cm.
       Includes bibliographical references and index.
       ISBN 0-941705-18-8 : $29.95
       1. Oral communication—Psychological aspects. 2. Backward masking. 3. Subliminal perception. I. Title
BF637.C45027   1991
153.6—dc20   91-26525
                                                         CIP

Dedicated to
Timothy Pascoe

Thank you so very much
for all your help

With Special Acknowledgment to Kathleen Hawkins

The book you're about to read is the result of seven years of research by primarily one person. Like many researchers, however, I wanted to present my findings clearly in the easiest to read, most understandable way for the lay person as well as the academic community. One of my highest priorities was to make the information of Reverse Speech accessible to everyone, not just to a select group of academicians, scientists, or government officials.

I enlisted the expertise of professional writer, Kathleen Hawkins, who is the author of several popular books, audio-cassette learning programs, and more than 200 articles. Much of the credit for the way this book is presented goes to her.

I approached many writers with the task of transforming my research material into book form. Kathleen was the only one who thoroughly understood the concept, grasped the vision as I perceived it, and in her brilliant and creative manner, subsequently turned my research notes into a comprehensive and well-ordered masterpiece. She has spent over a year studying my material, reorganizing it, and writing and rewriting, until this book came into being.

Thank you, Kathleen, for creating the means through which everyone can have access to, and understand, the many complexities of the Reverse Speech technology.

Thanks also to:

All those who assisted in the development and research of Reverse Speech and to those who gave their financial and moral support. I would like to specially thank:

Greg Albrecht, who assisted for most of 1987, by documenting some of the very first reversals discovered in human speech and for helping with the initial theoretical development.

Kathy Oates, for her patience, strength, and support.

Becky Thompson, the first student to ever graduate from the Reverse Speech training course and who has since pursued Reverse Speech with fervor.

Paul Von Stroheim and John Suess, two of my personal mentors since 1988, who have contributed many insights that led to successful directions of research.

John Marszalek, Carolyn Rozeboom, Samela Harris, Brian Vickery, Jeff Smiley, John Hampel, the late Peter Thomas, James Rossiter, Tom Haynes, Brad Walton and the rest of the gang.

For my children—Michael, Symone, and Jaye.

Life can only be understood backwards, but it must be lived forwards.

—Søren Kierkegaard

The discipline of linguistics can be likened to a pathway which is being cut through the dark and mysterious forest of language. Different parts of the forest have been explored at different times so we can depict the path as a winding one.

—Jean Atchinson, *Teach Yourself Linguistics*

Four legs and two voices. A most delicate monster! His forward voice, now, is to speak well of his friend; His backward voice is to utter foul speeches and to detract.

If all my wine in my bottle will recover him, it will help his other voice.

Come! Amen! I will pour some into thy other mouth.

—Shakespeare, *The Tempest*, Act II, Scene II

Contents

Preface

David Oates has introduced an understanding of human communication that, in every likelihood, is a major breakthrough of the century. With his characteristically rigorous, scientific, and meticulous approach, he has developed the technology to demonstrate and apply Reverse Speech toward the improvement of human life.

Reverse Speech analysis and its corresponding technology are a major discovery of specifically how human beings communicate with each other at a deep level far beyond ordinary awareness. Mr. Oates has taken a bold, important step in the advancement of human communication.

Profound Discovery

"Backward masking" or "backmasking" was first noticed when the Beatles became popular and teenagers began to talk about hidden messages in some of their music.

Religious fundamentalists created further interest by stating that certain songs contained negative, subliminal phrases and commands, commercial suggestions, and other cryptic messages discernable only when the music was played backwards.

Now, Oates has proven that reversals are indeed present in music and, *much more significantly*, he has discovered that *reversals exist naturally in all human speech*, no matter what the subject and no matter who is talking. *Any* recorded human speech, when played backwards, contains reversals that appear as intelligible forward phrases amid the backward gibberish. In addition, these reversals are not just random words—they actually communicate to anyone who will listen. They verify, negate, or expand upon the subject that is being discussed.

Naturally occurring speech reversals go far beyond the early attempts at intentional backmasking in rock music. Reverse Speech is an entirely different issue. In this book, David discusses at length the revolutionary discovery that:

1. **Human speech has two distinctive and complementary functions and modes.** The Overt Mode is spoken forward and constructed by conscious cognitive processes. The Covert Mode, spoken simultaneously with the Overt Mode, is a reversal of the forward speech sounds, and is constructed by automatic cognitive processes.

2. **These two modes of speech are dependent upon each other.** They form an integral part of communication. In the dynamics of interpersonal communication, both modes of speech communicate the total psyche of a person—conscious as well as unconscious.

3. **The process of language development in children starts backward before it does forward.** Children first develop the Covert Mode of communication and then, as Overt speech begins, these two modes gradually combine into one, forming a bi-level communication process.

Speech reversals, which the listener must carefully glean from surrounding backward gibberish, occur on the average of once every 15 seconds, with the number of reversals increasing when the conversation is casual and/or emotionally charged.

A serious and methodic researcher, Oates cites many examples in which the unconscious mind:

- Expands, in reverse, on what speakers are saying in their forward speech;
- Contradicts or verifies, in reverse, what speakers are saying;
- Engages in "self-talk," in reverse that attempts to resolve a speaker's inner, personal conflicts;
- Responds directly to others' reversals, thus explaining, at least in part, the very nature of human intuition.

Dynamic Transformations

The applications of this new technology are so far reaching that the very nature of human communication as we know it may be changed.

Reverse Speech has already been used effectively in a wide variety of professions including psychotherapy, police work, sales and marketing, personality development and counseling of children, advertising, relationship counseling, law, and business negotiations—all of which are discussed in this book.

The benefits of Reverse Speech have become remarkably clear to me in my own work as a psychotherapist, a trainer, a designer of therapeutic programs, and as a consultant to legal and management professionals. Accordingly, I expect Reverse Speech, when used by properly trained and compassionate individuals, to make a lasting and a significant contribution to the field of communication and to the transformation of human beings.

—Dan Mitchell, Ph.D.
Psychotherapy Trainer and Consultant
Dallas, Texas

Introduction

Imagine knowing what the people in your life—your spouse, children, friends, co-workers, or colleagues—are *really* thinking.

Imagine how useful a technology would be that reveals what's going on in the minds of politicians when they say, "No new taxes," or that helps investigators solve crimes and enables therapists to quickly access the unconscious mind of their clients to bring about positive changes.

Imagine hearing your *own* unconscious mind communicate with you in *words* to give you valuable insight into the previously-hidden realms of your own psyche.

Now, by using Reverse Speech analysis, all this is possible.

Listening at the Keyhole

David Oates, the founder and developer of Reverse Speech technology gives us the opportunity to actually listen in on the unconscious mind as it communicates to us and others in its small, sometimes sing-song voice. Like a child that adults have previously ignored, it's been speaking all these years, talking virtually to itself and to the unconscious minds of others, while we go about our daily business.

During conversations, the unconscious mind cries out, in reverse, for help or attention. It comments on what's being said forward; it speaks in poetry, metaphors, and archetypes, and sometimes, swears. It's least vocal during rehearsed speeches and most vocal during emotionally-charged conversations.

Freud began to chart the unconscious mind; Jung went further in revealing how it speaks to us through dreams and archetypal images. David Oates now provides us with a technology for directly listening in on what the unconscious is saying.

How You Can Benefit from Reverse Speech Analysis

Anyone who wants to better understand himself or herself or who wants to communicate more effectively can benefit from Reverse Speech analysis. It crosses all boundaries of race, nationality, financial status, religion, and profession.

There are four ways that you can become involved with Reverse Speech: as a client, as a Reverse Speech analyst, as a professional who teams up with an analyst, or as someone who simply wants to be better informed and entertained by reading a good book on the subject.

You might want to explore your own reversals with a trained Reverse Speech analyst in order to:

- Let your unconscious mind guide, instruct, and inspire you;
- Overcome any damaging effects of repressed emotions such as grief, anger, anxiety, fear, guilt, loneliness, hurt, or sadness;
- Feel a deeper connection with humanity and a greater sense of belonging;
- Be more comfortable with your life and more "at home" with yourself;
- Better understand other people; and
- Increase your personal and professional effectiveness.

As a client, you'll find that Reverse Speech is the ultimate adventure: fun, enlightening, and serious business. Hearing the voice of your unconscious mind for the first time can be unsettling. It may communicate with a rich and surprising blend of poetry and profanity, simple words, and mysterious metaphors. It reveals the true nature, the depth, and the innate intelligence of your own psyche.

It can also be disquieting to reach that more honest part of yourself for the first time as it communicates its needs, strengths and desires. Reverse Speech has the potential to unite your conscious and unconscious mind and repair the divided Self.

You can become a Reverse Speech analyst yourself (details in Appendix I), in which case you'll still go through the above self-discovery process. Since Reverse Speech can be applied to all professions, the career opportunities for qualified analysts are endless. You may simply choose to team up with a Reverse Speech analyst. Well-trained professionals such as therapists, educators, or police investigators who work together with qualified Reverse Speech analysts to interpret reversals achieve impressive results. By working together, each brings their particular knowledge and expertise to the task at hand.

Enjoy a Good Book

You may simply want to learn something new or be entertained. If so, read this book as though it were a detective story and you're the investigator unraveling a mystery clue by clue—just as David Oates did when he first discovered Reverse Speech. Compare forward dialogue in the transcripts with what people say in reverse, and determine the motives, desires, shortcomings and, in some cases, the guilt or innocence of the speakers.

Explore the inner workings of the minds of the people in this book—and what a cast of characters it is: murderers and ministers, rock musicians and presidents, hostages, prisoners of war, babies, and couples thrashing out the particulars of their relationships. And, you get to listen in.

- You'll hitch a ride with psychiatrists during their therapy sessions, attorneys in the court room, and police officers on investigations.
- You'll meet Lindy Chamberlain, the woman whose baby was stolen by a wild dingo in the Australian outback and whose story was made into a Hollywood movie starring Meryl Streep.
- You'll eavesdrop on the private thoughts of some key players in the Persian Gulf crisis as they fervently searched for solutions and tried to prevent the inevitable war.
- And, you'll discover what certain politicians, personalities, celebrities, and religious leaders are *really*

saying by reading the reversals of people such as Neil Armstrong on the moon, Jimmy Swaggart, Lee Harvey Oswald, Steve Martin, and Donald Trump.

This book gives you a head start in understanding the history of Reverse Speech, how it operates, and its exciting possibilities. After reading this informative book, you're sure to join the growing number of scientists, researchers, investigators, and therapists who believe that Reverse Speech analysis will revolutionize the entire field of human communication.

Whether your journey into Reverse Speech is a curious adventure, a serious inroad to greater self-understanding or a viable, practical tool to use in your profession, you'll find hours of thought-provoking, perhaps life-changing, information in this book.

—*Kathleen Hawkins, M.A.*
Author and Training Consultant
National Management Institute
Dallas, Texas

Author's Note

In April 1984, a single event dramatically changed my life.

I was the director of a privately-funded halfway house for teenagers in Berri, a small, country town in South Australia. An evangelist from the United States had just conducted a crusade down in "the big smoke," South Australia's capital city, Adelaide, and was spreading the word that rock 'n' roll was the devil's music and contained backward satanic messages. The word traveled up the grapevine, tapes were distributed, and I had several frightened teenagers on my hands who claimed to have heard demons talking to them backwards on records. My initial reaction was amused skepticism, mixed with anger toward the evangelist for scaring the kids with such rubbish.

I calmed the kids down and went home that night to investigate and debunk the whole thing. I'd been an active amateur radio operator for the last ten years (VK5ADO) and an electronics and audio enthusiast. I rewired some equipment, found one of the suspect tracks and played it backwards. To my complete surprise, an intelligible phrase appeared to be there. Over the next months my curiosity increased significantly as I conducted numerous tests with many audio tracks both forward and backward.

In 1987, my curiosity turned to full-time research. With the assistance of my friend, Greg Albrecht, I spent all that year meticulously analyzing and documenting hundreds of hours of tapes. With overwhelming and irrefutable evidence of numerous backward messages in both music and speech, Greg and I became convinced that we'd discovered another form of communication.

I contacted academicians who discretely told me that I was crazy, investigators who told me that they'd contact me if they were interested, and people from the media who asked me who was I to make such outlandish claims?

Eventually, in November 1987, I self-published and distributed the book, *Beyond Backward Masking,* co-authored with Greg Albrecht. At that stage, the media covered the story and within six months, Reverse Speech had become a highly controversial topic.

I found myself with a new career, trying to understand what backward messages meant, verifying their existence, and talking to others about them. Various professionals started to work with this new phenomenon and to prove my theories.

Several significant events dispelled remaining doubts about the existence of the phenomenon.

1. Electroencephalogram tests verified that brain-wave activity changed while backward messages occurred.

2. Interviews conducted with strangers revealed details of people and events in their lives. In an interview with a television reporter in Brisbane, Australia, I found the reversal, **Steve was my bad brother.** The reporter did have a brother, Steve, with whom she'd been on bad terms for years. Only days before the interview they'd settled their differences, hence, her use of the past tense in the reversal.

3. Case studies conducted with psychotherapists revealed private facts in reverse. For example, in a case analyzed for an Australian psychotherapist as she put her client into a hypnotic trance I found the reversal, **Shamrock. You must bear him that, his memory.** When the therapist reviewed the session transcript, she acknowledged that "Shamrock" had special significance to the client who had given her a shamrock as a condolence when her son died. Its use as a reversal at the beginning of the trance induction re-articulated the client/therapist bond necessary for successful therapy.

4. In a police case I found accurate details in reverse about weapons that were used in a crime, facts that were not made public. In another case, I found in reverse the

location of hidden funds. The police found these assets exactly where the backward message said they were.

Since those early stages of research and with the resulting proofs, I've traveled and lectured extensively. I've worked successfully with psychotherapists, with the police, and with the public. Communication and the unconscious mind have become my constant focus. Now I find myself in a role that wasn't originally in my life plans—the role of someone presenting new theories about language, communication, and the nature of the unconscious mind.

For some, my ideas may seem unbelievable simply because they're new. Throughout history humanity has had difficulty accepting new discoveries and theories such as, the world is round and people can fly. Pioneers are considered great people now, and yet, when they first presented their ideas, many of these courageous people were ridiculed and rejected as cranks. New theories tend to threaten some of us because they challenge our fixed views of the world in which we live. But such is the nature of change.

I trust that as you read this book, you'll be receptive to the ideas presented. They're different and unusual. And, they may very well change civilization's concept of language, psychology, and the way we view the very make-up of the human psyche.

I wish you pleasant reading.

—*David John Oates*
Dallas, Texas

Process Notes

Reversals are symbolic in nature. The same word may have different meanings for different speakers. Likewise, examples of reversals and their interpretations in this book may be considered open to alternative interpretations, in spite of every effort to be completely accurate. Speech reversals are a new discovery that involve one of the more complex of natural phenomena—the human mind—and much research remains to be done. The interpretations and theories that I set forth in this book must be taken in this light.

I will not be responsible, nor will the publisher of this book be responsible, for the consequences of any counseling using speech reversals, any publication of reversals that a reader may claim to find, or any other work done based on information contained herein. Training in the identification, analysis, and use of speech reversals is available through the classes and seminars offered by the Reverse Speech Education and Research Institute.

Regarding the transcripts of interviews, portions of interviews, and my analysis of them, please note the following:

1. I've taken all transcripts from the extensive library that I started to compile in 1984. I haven't tampered with, or changed, the recordings in any way from the original recordings.

2. I've analyzed the recordings according to the criteria detailed in this book.

3. To protect the identity of people involved with the case studies, names, places, and some sections of the forward dialogue (but only the forward) have been changed. In

addition, releases were obtained from these people to publish their transcriptions in this book, even though their names were changed.

4. All reversals are quoted EXACTLY as they appeared during my research.

5. Since I often worked alone while researching and gathering the information in this book, a second or third opinion wasn't always available that might have helped me to decipher very fast or muffled reversals. On most occasions, however, participants listened to their own reversals and validated them.

6. I've put all reversed dialogue in **bold print**. Some reversals may be spasmodic in context. In these cases, I've separated them in the text with a slash mark (/). The forward dialogue that is responsible for the reversals is indicated by brackets: [ ].

Reverse Speech

1

The Discovery
of Reverse Speech

*'Tis strange but true; for Truth is always strange—Stranger
than fiction.* —Lord Byron (1788-1824) *Don Juan*

Communication—a simple word that describes one of the more complex functions of our nature as human beings.

All of us communicate with each other in a variety of ways. For example, I'm communicating now as I sit at my desk, typing on my computer. This is written communication: a series of symbols that anyone who has learned how to read can decipher.

Spoken language is another obvious form of communication which, when combined with our own personal speech patterns and emotional tones, becomes a unique expression of our individuality.

The overall process of communicating, however, involves using more than just the spoken word. A whole range of subtleties: facial expressions, body language, eye movements, and many other often unconscious signals are automatically constructed, sent, and received by the brain. Many of these diverse, complementary brain functions are not under our conscious control, such as Freudian slips, Meta-language, unintentional "backward masking," and Reverse Speech.

Communication is a tribute to our endless complexity as human beings and to our evolving natures, as well as an invitation to understand ourselves more thoroughly.

3

Have you ever made a "Freudian slip," said something embarrassing that you didn't mean to say? Or, maybe you've used an involuntary facial expression or a gesture to inadvertently express a feeling that slipped through your conscious guard.

Can you trust your own communicative signals to express what you really mean or, perhaps even more to the point, can you trust the signals that you receive from others? Often you need to depend on more than just what someone is telling you verbally. How can you more accurately know when people are lying to you or hiding pertinent facts?

People constantly, often unconsciously, check the signals they receive from others for truth or error. This checking or screening process is typically called "intuition" or "the sixth sense." How does this happen? What is it that makes people know, even "feel" that the signals they receive from others are valid—or invalid?

Meta-language

Some signals are obvious such as emotional emphasis or body language and yet, there's even more to the process of intuition. Some researchers suggest that another hidden form of communication exists that tells us what's true and what is not. This covert form of communication is called "meta-language"— a language that's changed in place or form, hidden behind our conscious language, existing in conjunction with, and even transcending, that which we communicate consciously.

Does this hidden or "meta-language" have a form that we can analyze, recognize consciously, or even use? Is it as simple as body language or as complex and esoteric as extrasensory perception? Or, is it a combination of them all?

Often the most complex and puzzling problems have simple solutions. Can this be the case with intuition? Can it be that humankind's quest for centuries to probe the human mind, to find the elusive doorway, to understand our nature and the hidden parts of our psyche also has a simple solution?

After years of carefully documented research, I've found that there definitely is a hidden form of communication that we can recognize, access, and analyze. A reliable way to gain entry into the inner parts of our minds lies in the very nature and structure of spoken language. We can explore our elusive psyches simply by playing a tape recording of human speech—backwards.

Backward Masking Discovered in Rock 'n' Roll

In the late 1960's, the famed Beatle, John Lennon, created a new recording technique when he accidentally spliced in the last part of the song "Rain" backward and then liked the effect.[1] It was the first of a series of bold experiments in the attempt to be original and to create special effects in The Beatles' music.

Shortly after, an American disk jockey, having received an anonymous tip, claimed to have discovered eerie, hidden backward messages on some of the Beatles' albums, which hinted that bass guitarist, Paul McCartney had been killed in an automobile accident. It sparked imagination and, for a time, caused a great deal of attention to be focused on the Beatles' album. Were there hidden messages? Was Paul McCartney really dead? If he was, who was impersonating him?

Since that time, these hidden backward messages, and others subsequently found in recordings by various musicians, have captured the media's attention and led people to speculate on the effects they have on people's behavior. For example, Charles Manson supposedly was driven to a crazed frenzy after allegedly hearing voices in the Beatles' music that told him to kill. Mark Chapman murdered Lennon in 1980, after also claiming to hear voices in the *Double Fantasy* album that told him to kill Lennon.

On April 28, 1982, CBS Evening News ran a story stating that 30 teenagers in Huntersville, North Carolina, had organized a mass rock record burning through their church led by a reformed rock musician turned minister. The devil was doing it, so they claimed—possessing the singers and manipulating their voices so that subliminally implanted backward messages could be placed on records to destroy the youth of America.[2]

Then, in a five-year legal process that concluded in 1990, heavy metal music was placed on trial in Reno, Nevada, following the death of two youths who killed themselves after listening repeatedly to a Judas Priest album. Attorneys for the boys' parents claimed that the album, *Stained Class*, was "backmasked" with subliminally implanted backward messages.

To many, backward masking seemed to be a gigantic hoax, yet the controversy just wouldn't go away. It's been taken so seriously by some sections of society that in 1982, the United States House of Representatives passed a bill calling for all suspect records to be labelled:

Warning: This record contains backward masking that makes a verbal statement which is audible when this record is played backward and which may be perceptible at a subliminal level when this record is played forward.[3]

The bill did not proceed through the Senate to become law, but the questions persisted. So what's this phenomenon of backward masking really all about? Is it all the product of overactive imaginations? Are rock musicians really inserting subliminal backward messages into their music? Is the devil involved? Or, is there something far deeper and much more profound to this whole concept—something so obvious that it has been overlooked by just about everyone?

Two types of backward masking are often confused: intentional and unintentional.

1. **Intentional backward masking** in which a recording studio or artist has spliced an additional recording backward onto the main, master track. This is a fairly easy, infrequent practice that some bands use for special effects or publicity gimmicks.

2. **Unintentional backward masking** in which the message has not been placed by recording techniques, but instead appears mysteriously among the gibberish.

Intentional Backward Masking

Intentional backward masking was the type that John Lennon created with the Beatles' song, "Rain." It's easy to recognize. When listening to the recording forward it can be heard as gibberish. When the record is played backward, the gibberish, or the additional soundtrack superimposed backward, becomes clearly understandable English. In the case of the song "Rain," strange sounding vocals at the end of the song become an intelligible reprise beginning with the drawn out word **Sunshine**.

The White Album

The "Paul-is-dead" conspiracy was also, to some extent, an example of intentional backward masking. Probably the most well-known case of this can be found on the song, "Revolution 9," from *The White Album*.

The eight-minute track is a surrealistic collection of disjointed sounds played both forward and backward. Listeners can hear many things on this track: radio broadcasts, sirens, applause, screams, laughter, a baby gurgling plus other sounds.

There are also concealed messages. An obvious one can be found approximately five minutes into the recording. It is forward and I could hear it only with the left track turned off. The ellipses indicate places I could not identify the words with confidence, even thought others claim to have heard more. It says:

> *So the wife called, and we better go to see a surgeon . . . Well, what were the prices, the prices have snowballed, no wonder it's closed . . . So any and all, we went to see the dentist instead, who gave him a pair of teeth, which wasn't any good at all. So instead of that he joined the bloody Navy and went to sea.*[4]

Further on in the track, a backward message can be heard under the pandemonium of loud screams and someone calling out, "rape." When reversed, the words, **Let me out, let me out**, can be heard. When this was discovered, some people claimed that it represented Paul McCartney calling out from his smashed up Aston Martin, which is where he supposedly "died."

Another backward message on this song, which added fuel to the fire, can be found when the phrase "number nine," repeated throughout the song, is played backward. The words become, **Turn me on dead man, turn me on dead man.** This phrase is not an engineered backward message, but rather the result of a phonetic oddity. It could be said to be coincidence, but, to my mind, this is hard to believe given the inventive mind of John Lennon and the theme of the track.

Yet again, toward the end of "Revolution 9," there appears to be another deliberate word reversal that's not as innocent as other hidden messages that the track contains. John Lennon calls out (forward) the meaningless sound, "Oomcha!" Played backward this says, **Satan.**

Also on *The White Album*, at the end of the song, "I'm So Tired," there's gibberish that, when played backward, says, **Paul is a dead man. Miss him, miss him, miss him.**

The Magical Mystery Tour

The *Magical Mystery Tour* album by the Beatles also contains hidden messages. One can be found at the end of the song, "Strawberry Fields." A faint voice seems to say (forward): "I buried Paul." When questioned about this message, John Lennon told *Rolling Stone* magazine that the words were "Cranberry sauce."[5]

The message is so faint that it's difficult to decide what was actually said. Nevertheless, a massive controversy erupted when this and other messages were uncovered. Paul had died, or so many believed, and the Beatles' record sales skyrocketed as avid fans searched for these "secret" messages.

Abbey Road

Further evidence that supported this rumor were tantalizing clues such as a photograph on the cover of *Abbey Road* that shows Paul walking barefoot across a road with the other Beatles. Why was he barefoot? Because that's how he was buried, or so the story goes. A white Volkswagon in the background of the album cover has on its number plate—28 IF—the age Paul McCartney would have been "IF" he had not "died." On the cover of the *Sergeant Pepper's* album, a floral design that represents a guitar was believed by many to really resemble—Paul?

Cloud Nine

An aftermath to this conspiracy controversy can be found in an album released many years later by George Harrison. *Cloud Nine* contains a hidden message at the end of the song, "When We Were Fab," which sings about the old Beatles' days. It is forward, quite faint, and says: "Paul isn't dead. The Beatles died."

Of course, Paul McCartney hadn't died and, although the Beatles have never openly admitted to inserting these messages on their albums, in my opinion the entire exercise was a carefully orchestrated marketing strategy designed to boost their failing career at the time. John Lennon had only recently created a massive backlash and sparked the desertion of fans when he said publicly that the Beatles were more popular than Jesus Christ.

Whatever the truth, a new hobby emerged among teenagers across the world: playing records backward. Unknowingly, the Beatles had opened quite a can of worms. In addition to these hidden messages having been discovered, other messages of an unplanned, "eerie" nature were found as well on the recordings of other artists.

As time went on, religious leaders claimed that the Beatles were inspired to experiment with backward masking by the teachings of early 20th Century occultist Aleister Crowley. The purpose, according to the fundamentalists, was to start a sinister trend that would later pollute society with subliminal messages. They point to the appearance of Crowley's face amid the many other faces on the cover of the *Sergeant Pepper's Lonely Heart's Club Band* album, as evidence of this claim.

Intentional Backward Masking by Other Groups

Since these initial experiments by the Beatles with backward masking, other groups have had fun with engineered backmasked messages. A few examples are:

1. *Face the Music*, by Electric Light Orchestra. The message can be found at the start of the album right at the beginning of the song "Fire on High." Played forward, it sounds like gibberish or a strange language. When reversed, a deep male voice booms out the words: **The music is reversible but time (is not). Turn back, turn back, turn back.** (The phrase "is not" is very faint.)

2. *The Wall*, by Pink Floyd. The message can be found at the end of the song "Good-bye Blue Sky" in a small section of the album entitled *Empty Spaces*. It's on the right track and reverses to say: **Congratulations. You have just discovered the secret message. Please send your answer to old pink, care of the funny farm.**

3. *Shout at the Devil*, by Motley Crüe. This album has a warning on the front cover that says: "THIS ALBUM MAY CONTAIN BACKWARD MESSAGES." The

message is: **Backward mask where you are. Oh, lost in error, Satan.**

4. *Kilroy Was Here,* by Styx. This album also has a warning on the front cover that says: "BY ORDER OF THE MAJORITY FOR MUSICAL MORALITY, THIS ALBUM CONTAINS SECRET MESSAGES." The message can be found at the start of the song "Heavy Metal Poisoning" and, when played backward, says: **Annuit Coeptis. Novus ordo seclorum.** This is the Latin inscription encircling the pyramid on the back on the U.S. dollar bill. Two possible translations are: (a) "Announcing the arrival of a new secret order of this age"; (b) "The established order of the ages looks favorably upon our endeavors."[6]

5. *Coup d'Etat,* by the Plasmastics. There's a backmasked message on this album that says: **Consensus programming is dangerous to your health. The brainwashed do not know they are brainwashed.**

6. *Piece of Mind,* by Iron Maiden. The backmasked message can be found just before the song "Still Life," and it says: **Messin' with things you don't understand.**

These examples are but a small selection of intentional backward masking. For the most part, they appear to be nothing more that a simple marketing exercise and the creation of special effects for recording. They are *not* a plot by rock 'n' roll artists to subliminally program their listeners.

Unintentional backward masking, however, is another story entirely.

Unintentional Backward Masking

Backward messages that are not intentional can be heard on other albums. These messages are not planned by the artist or by recording studio personnel. They appear randomly throughout many songs and make complete, intelligible and grammatically correct sentences. Their origin is a mystery and there's no technical explanation for their appearance, purpose, or source.

Their occurrence seems to be determined by the peculiar tonal makeup and phonetic construction of the forward lyrics. In other words, the lyrics and tune of the song are formed in such a way that they say two messages at the same time. One message can be heard forward and the other can be heard backward. These unintentional backward messages have caused even greater controversy.

"Stairway to Heaven"

The most famous of these examples can be found in the song "Stairway to Heaven," by Led Zeppelin. The song contains no deliberately engineered backward messages or superimposed soundtracks, but does contain examples of unintentional backward messages. These backward messages occur in the reversed phonetic structure of the lyrical sounds—in other words, by the exact way in which the words were structured and sung. I'll examine this song in detail in Chapter 10.

"Stairway to Heaven" is by no means an isolated example of backward messages that appear in songs with no conscious thought or design. Here are some examples from other well-known songs:

1. "Help," by the Beatles: **Now he uses marijuana. I kissed you once.**
2. "Black Knight," by Deep Purple: **Oh demon that's leading from Hell, we believe.**
3. "I Don't Know How to Love Him," in the rock opera *Jesus Christ Superstar*: On the reverse of the first forward lyrics—**He's the Saviour, loves me. He's the one.**[7]
4. "Burning Love," by Elvis Presley—**I wish to fade away.**
5. "Tops," by The Rolling Stones: **I love you said the devil.**
6. "It's About Time," by John Denver: **I believe Jesus died for sinners. / He died for sin. / All the more reason to thank you. / More and more I prefer you.**
7. "Soolaimon," by Neil Diamond: **Vietnam. We want peace. / Vietnam, on the loose.**

Communicating More Than . . .

Backward phrases appeared to be in every sound track I examined. Thus began a new career direction—researching communication in its many different forms. I soon realized what a creative and wonderful mechanism the unconscious mind is to make itself known in so many ways—in Freudian slips, meta-language, dreams, body language, and Reverse Speech. How curious it is that the unconscious mind "percolates" through the conscious mind to express a deeper, perhaps more honest part of ourselves, and gives us a hint that something grander, and maybe even more knowledgeable, exists in the realms of the human mind.

I was first alerted that something was going on behind the scenes when I began to study intentional backward masking. This led to my discovery of *unintentional* reversed messages, which appear so widely in music and human speech. They appeared so predictably, on such a regular basis, and with such grammatical precision, that I soon realized the chance of these reversals occurring by pure coincidence was astronomically high.

When I noticed that these reversals seemed to be *communicating*, I knew that something far deeper and previously unexplored was happening, a phenomenon that was explosive in its implications.

2

The Initial Research

To myself I seemed to have been only like a boy playing on the sea shore . . . whilst the great ocean of truth lay all undiscovered before me. —Sir Isaac Newton (1642-1727)

When I began to research the intriguing phenomenon of what I then called "naturally occurring backward masking," I had three objectives:

1. Define "backward masking";
2. Establish how backward messages occur; and
3. Verify the accuracy of backward messages.

As I met these objectives, I made a startling discovery that promised to redefine the very nature of human communication as we have known it.

Initially, a commonly accepted definition of "backward masking" was:

A message hidden in a song that can be discovered only when the sequence of music listening is reversed.[1]

This explanation was too broad, however, because I had already established that there were two different forms of backward masking: intentional and unintentional. I was concerned with the *unintentional* occurrence of this phenomenon and with redefining backward masking accordingly.

Establishing The Accuracy of Backward Lyrics

To many people, the idea that intelligible phrases can be heard when tapes are played backward seems incredulous. They

13

wonder if it's all in the mind, like seeing pictures in ink blots, or if it's just coincidental.

To test the accuracy of backward lyrics, I established strict procedures and criteria.

1. To remove as much bias as possible, I first listened to all the recordings *backward*. I found the reversals before I knew the subject matter of the forward soundtrack. After a tape was analyzed, I found the appropriate forward section and dubbed it, together with the suspected reversals, at three different speeds, onto a master reel.

2. I then analyzed them separately, meticulously ensuring that a suspected reversal actually existed. I particularly noted the syllable count, letters at the beginnings and endings of words, consonant and vowel sounds, and spaces between words. As time went on I noticed other factors, such as differences between the tonal quality of assorted backward messages, which I also took into account.

3. From that point, I gave each reversal a "Validity Factor" between one and five depending on certain "check points" that they met (see Chapter 7).

Once a large assortment of backward messages was collected, I conducted further tests to check their existence, which included establishing controlled, repeatable audibility tests. Over a period of time, I compiled tape recordings that contained examples of backward messages isolated from surrounding gibberish. I played the tape recordings for three groups of people, with each group being assigned a different task.

Group One: This group was given a written list that specified what each backward message was assumed to say. I asked them if they could also hear the same phrase. Most people in this group reported positive results.

Group Two: This group had a list of backward messages that didn't exist and were told to hear messages that weren't there. No one in this group was able to hear any of the "control phrases."

Group Three: This group received no list and was asked to tell me what they heard in the reversed soundtracks. Most of these people were able to accurately transcribe key words in the backward message after three listenings.

From these tests, I concluded that the reliability factor of interpretation was high. I could rule out imagination in most cases *providing* that all the "Check points," discussed in Chapter Seven were strictly followed.

Coincidence of Sound?

Next, I tested for coincidence of sound to determine if the backward phrases were a result of phonetic coincidences.

To do this, I tried to reproduce the backward phrases by verbally repeating the forward phrase into a tape recorder. Then I played the tape backward to see if the backward phrase was repeated.

Despite many attempts, also using other people, I wasn't able to reproduce most of the backward phrases accurately. I found that a few individual words seemed coincidental, but these were words only, not entire sentences. The coincidental words frequently reversed to say the same thing and I noted these for future reference.[2]

The majority of all backward phrases tested have *not* been phonetic coincidence. The reversals were determined, instead, by the phonetic construction of the forward speech sounds as they were said in the instant they were captured on tape. These sounds varied considerably depending on individual speech patterns and the emotional state of the speaker.

There were only two other obvious possible explanations remaining for their occurrence: intentional composition or occult manipulation.

Intentional Composition?

If the backward messages were intentionally created, then the lyrics and tune would have to have been deliberately composed in such a way that the sentence said something different when played backwards. Due to the extremely complicated and time consuming semantic difficulty of this task, I soon discounted this explanation. It seemed to be virtually impossible for so many musicians to compose so many songs that contained so many verifiable, grammatically correct, unintentional backward messages.[3]

Next, I explored the possibility of occult manipulation.

Occult Manipulation?

Another explanation was occult manipulation—that is, external spiritual forces had possessed the minds of singers so they said something in reverse as well as forward. This was a chilling prospect. Were the religious fundamentalists correct?

My first test of the occult manipulation theory was to analyze Gospel recordings and look for hidden backward messages. The reversals that I found are in are **bold print** below.

1. "More Than Wonderful," by Sandi Patti. **Jesus is God's son. God gives the armor.**
2. "My Heart's Desire," by Denise Williams. **Christ is God's son who died for me. Hallelujah.**
3. "Star of the Morning," by Leon Patillo. **Jesus, he's the Lord. And on the cross Jesus became Savior.**
4. "Rock That Makes Me Roll," by Stryper. **Jesus released the beast within me.**
5. "Only Jesus," by Dion. **Jesus, He is the Lord.**
6. "Steel Killer," by Saint. **World's deceiver, Master Satan. I shall shit on Satan.**

After I analyzed these religious songs and others, I noticed a trend. The backward messages in Gospel music often praised God or explained some theological truth. Why would *occult* forces possess the minds of Gospel artists in order to praise God? Why would *angelic* forces possess the minds of Gospel artists to praise God? Either presumption would indicate an intent to manipulate on the part of the powers of the universe that did not align with my experience.

Thus began an extensive review of research notes already compiled and I noticed that the majority of documented backward phrases related in some way to the forward lyrics or message of the song. For example, if the song was about love, then the backward messages were also about love. If the song was about the occult, the backward messages were about the occult. If the song was about God, the backward messages were about God.

After extensive analysis of the research, I finally discounted the possibility of occult manipulation.

Backward Messages in Speech

I then conducted a field test. To do this, I obtained permission to record a Pentecostal church service initially intending to research the phenomenon of "Glossolalia," or "speaking in tongues." My original research partner, Greg Albrecht, went with me. At the end of the service, one of the deacons spoke to us and the conversation was unintentionally recorded. When we analyzed this recording, the mystery deepened. We found clear backward messages on all the speakers.

First, we found a backward message on the preacher at the end of a section of singing (reversals in **bold print**).

> Preacher: "Yes, [all right. Praise the Lord. Something else] I just remembered..." **The singing, oooh it sounds terrible.**

Next, we found a backward message on the deacon during our conversation with him:

> Deacon: "What motivated you to [research methods of worship and religious practices]?" **I know, I believe, you are damned, both.**

To Greg and I, the reversal seemed to indicate that behind this seemingly innocent question, the deacon had other thoughts. Indeed, both of us had sensed that this man had ulterior motives which were then reflected in the backward message that we found.

Next, we found a backward message on me:

> David: "We feel that there's a lot of things going on that people don't know about. There's a lot of deception, [I'm not necessarily talking about your church,] you know." **There's sin on, er, this place.**

Notice that again the backward message reveals apparently more honest feelings than what was said forward. It was particularly interesting that the message occurred on the exact forward words that it did.

> Deacon: "You've been baptized by full immersion and all those sorts of things?" No reversal.
>
> David: "Yeah, I have. We've both been heavily involved, [er, in church groups] and, er drop-in centers and youth clubs." **We're not stupid.**
>
> (Once again, a cautious forward reply with the backward message reflecting my growing indignation concerning the Deacon's questioning.)
>
> Deacon: "How do you feel about the link between the Holy Spirit and speaking in tongues?" No reversal.
>
> David: "[I'm not too sure.] It was certainly quite a valid part of the early Christian's life." **Bullshit, I'm not.** An untruth spoken forward—quite definite views revealed in reverse.

Our analysis of this conversation turned my research in an entirely new direction. For the first time, I realized that *backward messages can be found in casual, conversational speech*. The amazing thing was that the messages seemed to reflect the actual thought processes of the speakers at the time.

I obtained recordings of famous speeches and media broadcasts and noticed that, as with music, the backward messages in speech related directly to what was spoken forward. In addition to this, the reversals often revealed extra information about the forward topic. Here are some examples:

1. Neil Armstrong stepping onto the moon: "That's one [small step for man]." **Man will space walk.**

2 A live commentary of the President Kennedy assassination: "Stand by please. [Parkland hospital, there has been a shooting.] Parkland hospital has been advised to stand by for a severe gun shot wound." **He's shot bad. Hold it. Try and look up.**

3. Lee Harvey Oswald being interviewed *prior* to the assassination. "The fact that [I did live for a time] in the Soviet Union gives me excellent qualifications to repudiate charges that Cuba and [The Fair Play for

Cuba Committee] is communist controlled." **Oswald angry. / Hear them. Wish to kill President**.

4. Australia's Prime Minister Bob Hawke after winning the 1987 Federal election responding to questions of how he'll celebrate: "[Ah, several cups of tea.]" **Used to smoke the best marijuana.**

5. Prince Andrew following the birth of his baby daughter in 1987, *before* he publicly announced her name: "It's very difficult to tell who she looks like, [but probably after her father and mother like most]." **My mum will love her. I love Beatrice**.

6. John Lennon being interviewed following the death of the Beatles' manager, Brian Epstein: "The Maharishi told us not to get overwhelmed [by grief] and whatever thoughts we have of [Brian, to keep them happy]." **Must not fear. / We can't be Beatles now.**

Summary of Findings

Many common patterns and trends were uncovered, which we will explore in depth. Here is a short list of those trends, compiled after analyzing hundreds of hours of tape recordings. The reversals:

- Confirmed existing claims that when listening to some rock 'n' roll records backward, certain reversed phonetic sounds formed meaningful and grammatically correct sentences. Reversed messages were found in most of the over 2,000 songs that were studied.
- Complemented, or related to, the theme of the song.
- Occurred in *all* normal human speech. (This *major* discovery is really the key to all that followed.)
- Often revealed the inner thoughts of the speakers. This was repeatedly verified by later questioning the speakers.
- Occurred as often as once every three seconds in highly-charged emotional states and usually once every 15 seconds in casual conversations. In prepared scripts or

monologue-style presentations, reversals can occur as little as once every five minutes.

- Seemed to be "more honest" than the forward communication.

- Seemed to fit in with body language, including the mouthing of words when videos of speakers are reversed.

- Appear in infants as early as four months of age—well before forward speech begins. At a later stage, these infants combine the two modes of speech, forward and backward, into one.

- Depend on conditions such as mood, emotion, accent, and voice inflections, with only minor dependence on the verbal content. They also frequently appear in pauses and stammerings.

It was also discovered that:

- A second, reversed conversation can exist in ordinary conversations. Speech reversals can directly communicate with each other as an unconscious reversed conversation. This indicates that backward messages can not only be transmitted but can also be perceived and understood.

- Rapid activity occurs between the left and right brain hemispheres at the point that the reversals occur, in addition to the different parts of the brain that are stimulated depending on the subject matter of the reversal. This brain activity is evidenced by EEG readings taken on subjects listening to sound-tracks known to contain reversals at precise intervals throughout the tape.

- The type and frequency of reversals could be accurately predicted depending on the nature of the forward speech.

- Many common patterns and themes emerge in backward messages, including a unique and consistent vocabulary, which is discussed later at length.

Theory of Reverse Speech and Speech Complementarity

The previous "explanations" for backward messages such as coincidence, intention, and occult manipulation were inadequate and not in keeping with any of the documented facts. These findings led to the formulation of the "Theory of Reverse Speech and Speech Complementarity."[4]

1. **Human speech has two distinctive and complementary functions and modes.**

   The Overt Mode is spoken forward and constructed by conscious cognitive processes. The Covert Mode, spoken simultaneously with the Overt Mode, is a reversal of forward speech sounds, and is constructed by automatic cognitive processes.

2. **These two modes of speech are dependent upon each other.**

   They form an integral part of communication. In the dynamics of interpersonal communication, both modes in combination communicate the total psyche of a person—conscious as well as unconscious.

3. **The process of language development in children starts backwards before it does forwards.**

   Children first develop the Covert Mode of communication and then, as Overt speech begins, these two modes gradually combine into one, forming a bi-level communication process.

In other words, as the brain constructs the sounds that form intelligible language, it constructs them in such a way that at least two verbal messages are communicated at the same time: one forward, which is constructed and heard consciously, and one in reverse, which is constructed and heard unconsciously and stems from deeper realms of the psyche.

Unintentional backward masking, which we find in music, is merely another form of this previously undiscovered function of the human mind.

Intentional backward masking is limited to music and describes *only* the deliberate insertion of backward messages in audio soundtracks. I've found it imperative, therefore, to create a more appropriate term to define this phenomenon: "Reverse Speech."

"Reverse Speech" Defined

"Reverse Speech" encompasses all forms of naturally-occurring, *unintentional* backward messages (speech reversals) that occur in human speech, either sung or spoken. "Reverse Speech" describes the unintentional occurrence of the phenomenon in all forms of speech. It is an innate human function similar to those of other senses.

By understanding the complex patterns found in Reverse Speech and by using precise methods to analyze audio-recordings played backwards, it is possible to accurately look into the inner mind and hear unspoken thoughts, facts, and emotions.

This research had taken me far beyond the study of simple, intentional backward masking. I'd met my original objectives, which were to define backward masking, establish how backward messages occur, and verify their accuracy. But, much more significantly, I'd discovered that reversed messages occur in *all* human speech, no matter who is talking, no matter what the subject.

The implications of these discoveries are profound. Reverse Speech holds the key to one of humanity's oldest dreams—to obtain an accurate and scientific means to access the marvelous, mysterious depths of the human mind.

3

The Source
of Reverse Speech

Human speech has two distinctive and complementary functions and modes. The Overt Mode is spoken forward and constructed by conscious cognitive processes. The Covert Mode, spoken simultaneously with the Overt Mode, is a reversal of the forward speech sounds and is constructed by automatic cognitive processes.
—The Process of Reverse Speech and
Speech Complementarity (Point #1)

Language is an outward projection of internal, mental processes that we use to frame and express our experiences. We've always known this to be true of our conscious, forward language, but what about Reverse Speech? I've found that it reflects to a greater extent both right- and left -brain functions and, as it does so, it seems to reveal a deeper part of the mind. It shows us the "other side" of language, so to speak, the previously hidden side.

By studying the different levels of consciousness with their many facets and rich images, as they reveal themselves through Reverse Speech, it is possible to unravel the mysteries of the human psyche—a monumental breakthrough in the exploration of the Self.

Hidden Codes of Language

The concept that language can carry messages that are unheard by the conscious mind is an old one. In fact,

23

communication that's below conscious perception is a constant part of daily life. In the early 1970's, two California researchers, John Grinder and Richard Bandler, developed a comprehensive model for understanding human thought, communication and behavior. Their model, Neurolinguistic Programming (NLP), is a remarkable integration of skills, techniques, and patterns that they gleaned from such diverse fields as psychology, linguistics, neurology, communications theory, cybernetics, and systems theory.

As the name implies, Neurolinguistic Programming addresses how the brain internally codes, organizes, and processes experiences with pictures, sounds, words and feelings.[1]

In their book, *The Structure of Magic*, Bandler and Grinder state that:

> *Language serves as a representational system for our experiences. Our possible experiences as humans are tremendously rich and complex. If language is adequately to fulfill its functions as a representational system, it must itself provide a rich and complex set of expressions to represent our possible experiences.*[2]

NLP teaches that language is more than communication. It is also a means of perception and contains within it the codes and patterns of mental processes. Only about seven percent of these perceptions, or codes and patterns, are delivered and received with the consciously spoken word.[3]

By far, the majority of communication takes place via other means that include tonality (tempo, tone, volume) and physiology (gestures, posture, breathing, facial expressions).

When discussing the phenomenon of Reverse Speech at a seminar in Australia, Grinder stated:

> *The notion that language can carry extra secondary and tertiary messages as well as the overt manifest content is well known . . . the fact that you can learn to hear the reversed form and extract the message from it is quite a revolutionary concept.*[4]

Just as the senses of sight, touch, smell, taste, and hearing, have always played a major role in perception, so has Reverse Speech even though its existence has only recently come to our attention. It has also played a significant role in the projection of the Self.

The Process of Communication

The human speech process is complicated and involves many variables. Educational theorist, Don Holdaway, states in his book, *The Foundations of Literacy*:

> The whole concert of speech activity proceeds at such a startling pace that only a fraction is under conscious control. The greatest burden of work is carried out in a delicately structured automatic performance by little understood processes in the nervous system.[5]

Spoken language is formed by a series of rapidly fluctuating sounds that the brain recognizes as intelligible information. Thoughts, conscious and unconscious, are converted into forms that can be understood by other people. This involves the construction of grammar, the development of progressive content, the expression of emotion and many other subtle units of information.

The process of communication is primarily automatic and involves little understood mental functions, many of which are beyond conscious control and have never been explored by linguists. The construction of simultaneously delivered speech reversals adds even more complexity to this process. This gave the developing research into Reverse Speech a mighty task: how does the brain construct forward *and* backward speech—at the same time? Here are some points to consider.

The Virtually Limitless Capacity of the Human Brain

The task of constructing forward and backward speech simultaneously is well within the capabilities of the human brain. Dr. David Samuels of the Weizmann Institute estimated that there are between 100,000 and 1,000,000 different chemical reactions occurring every minute within the brain. The brain has approximately 10,000,000,000 individual nerve cells and they can interact with each other in a multitude of ways. This gives the number of possible combinations of their usage conservatively at a figure of 10 followed by 800 zeros![6]

Dr. Pryotra Anokin of Moscow University has estimated that the functional capacity of the brain is:

> so great that writing it would take a line of figures in normal manuscript characters, more than 10.5 million kilometers in

*length! With such a number of possibilities, the brain has been
described as a keyboard on which hundreds of millions of
different melodies—acts of behavior or intelligence—can be
played.*[7]

The Brain's Capacity for Reverse Functions

It's already known that the brain is capable of reversible
functions. Light, for example, is reversed through the lens of the
eye before it is interpreted by the brain.

Dyslexia, another reversed function, is a condition associated
with people who, during the process of reading, may reverse
letters of words or even whole words themselves. They may read
'saw' as 'was,' 'b' for 'd,' 'p' for 'q,' etc. Words can sometimes
appear as a mirror-image (eg: 'OIL' may be written as 'ʇIO').

In rare cases, dyslexics can even reverse words in actual
speech. This phenomenon has also been observed in some forms
of hypnosis, where people have been known to speak backward
while in trance, with no conscious knowledge of how they did
this.

I personally experienced one such incident during a series of
experimental trance sessions, that were conducted in order to
contact parts of the mind responsible for the formation of speech
reversals (see Chapter 13). I was in deep trance and the hypnotist
wanted to obtain reassurance from my unconscious mind that all
was proceeding as it should be.

> Hypnotist: "Would the unconscious mind be prepared
> now to provide David with that reassurance?"
> David: (immediate response, softly) "[Yeah, okay.] Yeah."
> (soft laugh) "EGERI."

In direct response to the hypnotist's question, I first delivered
a very clear, genuine reversal on, "Yeah, okay," that said, **I agree.**
This was immediately followed by my meaningless sound,
"EGERI," a phonetic pronunciation of the previous reversal, I
agree. An amazing feat to be performed with no conscious
collusion on my part!

None of these reversed functions intentionally alter the
information that's being communicated. People simply interpret
information, or deliver it, from another perspective—

unconsciously, in reverse. By playing speech backwards it is possible to consciously hear information that was always there, but which was delivered and received unconsciously.

Common Understandings Emerge

These ideas and experiences gave me the first two of five points considered in this chapter, toward understanding the mental processes involved in the occurrence of Reverse Speech.

One

Reverse Speech is well within the computing power of the brain.

Two

Reverse Speech is unconscious in nature. Automatic brain functions are involved in the delivery and interpretation of reversals.

Three

Reverse Speech is performed within the overall speech process. It's an intricate part of spoken language.

Four

Reversals increase in ease and frequency the more emotional a speaker becomes.

Five

Reversals become more metaphoric the more emotional a speaker becomes.

Point One is fairly apparent, statistically speaking. It is important, however, to rehearse this 'obvious' understanding as an essential foundation for the following points.

Point Two is equally foundational. Even though Reverse Speech is unconscious in nature, the subject matter of Reverse Speech relates to the subject matter of the forward speech, or complements it, thus the term, "Speech Complementarity."

This complementarity can be seen in the many reversals of music and speech that I've documented in previous chapters. In the example from commentary on the Kennedy motorcade, the reversal, **He's shot bad,** occurred at the precise point that the commentator realized there had been a shooting.

The following is another example of speech complementarity from a section of conversation with a man at a roadside stall who made and sold cushions:

> MAN: "I am 33 years old, (pause), [I've only just had] a birthday recently, (pause), and I'm here today at the market to sell some cushions . . . you can put quite a few together and make a bed . . . they've got nice silks on them, corduroys and they're filled with wool. They're quite solid and heavy . . . [I'd like to sell some] more cushions . . . hopefully we can produce enough to have a, er, reasonable sort of lifestyle, um, and maybe a trip overseas occasionally." **Watch the youth / I cover them with silver.**

Note the connections these reversals have with the forward dialogue. The first one occurred as a quick insert into the conversation and shows unconscious concern regarding the man's age, **Watch the youth** (just discussed forward). The second reversal described his cushions in greater detail, **I cover them with silver** (which this man did—shiny silver stitching that crisscrossed the fabric).

I also found examples of speech complementarity when some old Country and Western songs were analyzed such as Hank William's song, "I Saw the Light." In the tradition of authentic Gospel songs, the forward lyrics portray his search for truth in the midst of a life filled with despair. After aimless wandering through a sin-filled life, he finds Jesus and the title of the song becomes part of the repeated refrain, "I saw the light." In reverse, the song says:

> **Ah, the Lord sought me. / Ask the old rascal.**
>
> **No more sin, God no more night.**
>
> **Ah the Lord sought me, ah the Lord sought, ah the Lord sought me.**

The song, viewed both forward and backward, depicts two complementary theological perspectives:

1. One is a person's decision to follow Christ or, as Hank sings, "I saw the light."
2. Paradoxically, God simultaneously seeks the individual, it is the Lord's choice or, as Hank sings in reverse: **Ah, The Lord sought *me*.**

Here is part of a session conducted with a man who was talking about life in general and his current relationship:

> MAN: "I'm about to move and buy a property and refurbish it, (pause), bit of a risk, don't know whether [to do it or not] . . . I can't figure out what to do about my girlfriend. She doesn't stimulate me at all, but she's um, I admire the way she [polishes her body]."
> **But still run with it / She's boring.**

Like the previous examples, the reversals relate to the forward dialogue and give additional information.

Thus, Speech Complementarity gives another clue concerning the process involved in the formation of Reverse Speech.

THREE

Reverse Speech is performed within the overall speech process. It is one with spoken language, an intricate part of forward speech.

Differing reversed sounds occur in a predictable fashion depending on the nature of the conversation. An experienced researcher can recognize the nature of the forward conversation just by listening to the sounds of tapes run backwards.

To the uninitiated ear, tapes played backward appear to be a jumble of meaningless sounds with little form or rhythm. Researchers new to the field of Reverse Speech usually find only a few reversed phrases of low clarity. Sometimes, they even interpret gibberish. With practice, however, they become familiar with the sounds and begin to recognize what is imagination and what is genuine. They begin to locate the true reversals, which appear in varying levels of clarity or tone and fade in and out of the gibberish.

Sometimes these reversals are strong, powerful, and clear, with perfect phonetic construction. They stand out unmistakably from the gibberish and have a definite rhythmic tonal flow that's pleasant and natural to the ear.

Other times, the reversals are disjointed and robotic, containing the semblance of phonetic construction, but are "mechanical sounding" with no tonality. They sound like computer-generated speech.

Once I became familiar with the tonal flow of tapes being run backward, I noticed the following:

- In rehearsed dialogues speech reversals have a definite, mechanical sound that increases in proportion to how prepared or rehearsed the speaker is. In scripted media broadcasts, for example, the mechanical sound is intense. The occurrence of reversals is extremely low, about one reversal every one or two minutes of dialogue.

- In casual conversations when someone speaks in a thoughtful, prepared fashion or reiterates something that he or she has said many times before, the reversals still sound fairly mechanical, although not as intensely mechanical as in scripted broadcasts. Likewise, the less prepared a speaker is, the higher the number of reversals.

- In casual conversations that flow smoothly with little forethought, the reversals have a definite smooth, sing-song sound, with an average of one reversal for every 15 seconds of conversation.

- In emotionally charged conversations reversals are smooth and remarkably clear and occur on the average of one reversal every two or three seconds.

These trends were so accurate that I could tell what section of the conversation was the most spontaneous and what section was the most contrived—merely by listening to the sound of reversals at intervals throughout the conversation.

This was also evident in music. Songs that had been recorded in a studio tended to contain mechanical sounding reversals, whereas songs that were performed at live concerts tended to contain sing-song reversals. I also noticed that melodious reversals were far clearer and more precise than robotic reversals (see Figure One).

**Figure One:Reversal Clarity and Frequency
for Different Conversational Styles**

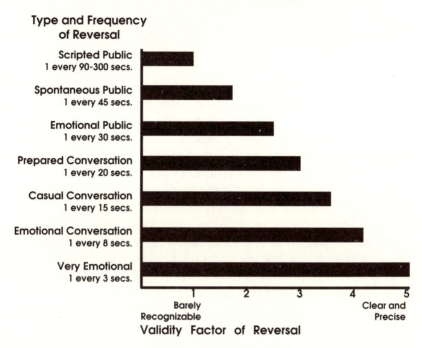

This graph is an approximation only. The numbers 1-5 represent: a) reversal clarity as discussed in Chapter 7, and b) reversal rhythm with "1" indicating extremely robotic and mechanical sounding reversals and "5" representing smooth, melodious and sing-song reversals.

There isn't an absolute relationship between clarity, rhythm, and frequency, although consistency is common, There is always a definite relationship between conversational type and frequency of reversal occurrence.

This observation gave me another clue concerning the formation and source of speech reversals:

FOUR
Reversals increase in frequency and in clarity
the more emotional a speaker becomes.

Metaphors

Metaphors, words that are symbolic or pictorial, increase in frequency the more emotional the forward speech becomes, or the more people talk about their emotions. Metaphors are not meant to be taken as fact. Instead, they represent deeper concepts (see Chapter 6).

Metaphors occur frequently in both forward and backward speech. Take for example a man who has just had a major confrontation with his lover. He may use forward words like: "Man, the vibes were totally electric. She looked at me with daggers in her eyes and really spun me out."

In reality the man's lover did not look at him with "daggers in her eyes" nor did she "spin him out." These words are common representations, or metaphors, for a deeper concept.

The forward statement, "the vibes were totally electric," describes an intense feeling that existed between the two people. Reverse Speech sometimes refers to these feelings both coming from others and ourselves as, **a Whirlwind.** Powerful energies may have been flowing between the two people. If rapport was also high, the concept may be communicated in Reverse Speech as, **the Whirlwind was high.**

"She looked at me with daggers in her eyes," is not an uncommon metaphor in forward speech. It describes a sense of attack associated with a high **Whirlwind.** The same sentence, using Reverse Speech terminology might be communicated as, **She was a warrior with a spear.**

"Really spun me out" is also a common metaphor in forward speech similar to "My head is a whirl." In Reverse Speech, it's associated with **Whirlwind** and may also be described as **force.** An appropriate section of reversed dialogue in this negative context might be, **She busted my Force.**

Thus, the entire phrase may be translated to the metaphoric language of speech reversals such as, **the Whirlwind was high, she was a warrior with a spear, she busted my force.**

So far, I've documented over 300 common words or phrase symbols that appear in Reverse Speech. Among them are archetypes and metaphors such as **Odin, Goddess, Naked, Ocean,** and **Wolf.**

Metaphors are often associated with high emotion in both forward and backward speech. Dream states have also been described as metaphoric representations of internal conflict. Thus, comes the fifth point to consider:

FIVE

Reversals become more frequent and more metaphoric the more emotional a speaker becomes.

The Left- and Right-Brain Hemispheres

The frequency and clarity of speech reversals are in direct proportion to the emotional and free-flowing nature of the conversation. Likewise, the criteria that governs their formation does not depend on the verbal content of the dialogue, but rather on the emotional pitch, or on the way that the words are pronounced—a major function of the right-brain hemisphere.

The physical construction of the human brain consists of two main lobes or hemispheres, separated in the middle by a thick tissue called the corpus callosum. It's commonly assumed that each hemisphere of the brain is responsible for different mental functions. Figure Two helps illustrate these complementary brain functions.

Figure Two: Hemispheric Specialization
The Complementary Functions of the Brain

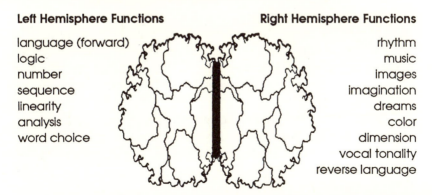

Left Hemisphere Functions	Right Hemisphere Functions
language (forward)	rhythm
logic	music
number	images
sequence	imagination
linearity	dreams
analysis	color
word choice	dimension
	vocal tonality
	reverse language

The Left Hemisphere

The left hemisphere is primarily logical in nature and is responsible for logic, analysis and sequential tasks. It is also thought to be responsible for conscious language formation processes or the actual words used in speech.

The Right Hemisphere

The right hemisphere, on the other hand, is emotional, imaginative, and creative in nature. It is thought to be responsible for unconscious mental activity and the emotional emphasis placed in speech.

In the process of thought and mental activity, both brain hemispheres work together to perform their respective tasks.

In a broad generalization, people who succeed in mathematics and sciences are considered left-hemisphere dominant, whereas those who perform well in subjects such as art, creative writing, and music are thought to be right-hemisphere dominant.

Consistent with these observations, the creation of a right-brain stimulation atmosphere, like relaxation, visualization and the playing of gentle music, increases the analyst's chances of locating a greater number of speech reversals with improved accuracy.

Reverse Speech is primarily a function of the right brain, the hemisphere previously thought by many to be dormant in active verbal communication. An article in the November 1987, issue of *Psychology Today* gives further insights concerning this.

Research linguist, Dianne Van Lancker, notes the importance of the right brain in the non-verbal information contained in speech. She maintains that the recognition of familiar voices involves complex pattern processing and that the right hemisphere appears to be primarily responsible for this pattern processing and recognition.

Some of her tests involved examining an average listener's ability to identify familiar voices played backwards at varying speeds. She noted that people recognize familiar voices holistically, as overall pictures, not on the basis of individual features. She concluded that while the left hemisphere determines what's to be said, the right hemisphere appears to be responsible for factors such as pitch, vocal quality, rate, and emotional tone.[8]

Adding support to this theory is a quote from speech therapist Alex Bannatyne who in 1972, proposed an explanation for dyslexia that entailed the left and right hemispheres of the brain. Bannatyne's thesis may be summed up in the following way:

> *The distinction is made between mirror-images of letters and reversing words. It's explained that language functions (dialogue formation) are largely controlled in the left cerebral hemisphere of the brain. Mirror-image language problems are explained in terms of incomplete suppression of the right hemisphere during language activities.*[9]

This is in direct keeping with the phenomenon of Reverse Speech. Speech reversals are not formed entirely by the actual words spoken, but also by the speech sounds. The way a forward sound is pronounced directly influences both the syllable structure and the phonetic sounds of the reversed phrase.

Playing Common Speech Sounds Backward

Different results can be obtained when sounds are reversed. The English alphabet consists of various sounds, Ay, Bee, Cee, Dee, etc. In one of my experiments, I had various people utter several of these sounds into a tape recorder. When I played the sounds backward, a change in their syllable structure occurred. This change depended directly upon how the sounds were pronounced.

For example, when the one syllable sound "Vee" was pronounced sharply and quickly, it reversed to sound like the two syllable word **E/den.** It also sounded like the word **E/ven,** depending on how it was said.

When "Vee" was said slowly and drawn out, it sounded very much like the one syllable word **Eve.**

When the sound "Eden" was pronounced by different people and the tape reversed, it sounded nothing like the letter "Vee," but rather reversed to sound like **"Muddy"** or **"Nuddy."** It depended on the tonal inflection of the forward speech as uttered in the particular instant of time captured on tape.

The Deeper Parts of the Mind

Early 20th Century psychiatrist, Carl Jung, a contemporary of Freud and scholar of comparative mythology, theorized that the human mind was divided into three distinct levels.[10]

1. **Consciousness:** Those portions of the mind that are under conscious control and awareness.

2. **Personal Unconsciousness:** Those portions of the mind that have become unconscious either because they lost their intensity and were forgotten, or because consciousness was withdrawn from them (repression). Also, those portions, some of them sense-impressions, which never had sufficient intensity to reach consciousness but have somehow entered the psyche.[11]

3. **The Collective Unconscious:** The deepest part of the mind, which Jung claimed "as timeless and universal psyche," or the true basis of the individual psyche. He believed this area to be the ancestral heritage, consisting of an inherent storehouse, varying in depth from person to person, of mythological motives, or primordial images, of which the conscious mind had no knowledge of whatsoever. Jung claimed that the collective unconscious contained the entire spiritual and cultural heritage of humanity's development born anew in the mind of each individual.[12]

Reverse Speech has profound similarities to the above model, as I'll discuss in depth in Chapter 6:

1. **First Level reversals** are literal and tend to reflect the Conscious Level of mind.

2 **Second Level reversals** are operational—they often use metaphors to express behavioral patterns—and reflect the Personal Unconscious Level of mind.

3. **Third Level reversals** are structural—they often use metaphors to express deeper, *root causes* of behavior—and reflect the collective unconscious, archetypal mind.

Everything contained within the unconscious mind—what is now and what has been in the past—has the potential to appear in Reverse Speech. Reverse Speech, using its metaphors, and primordial images, exposes the total Self and the three areas of

Figure Three:
The Nature of the Psyche

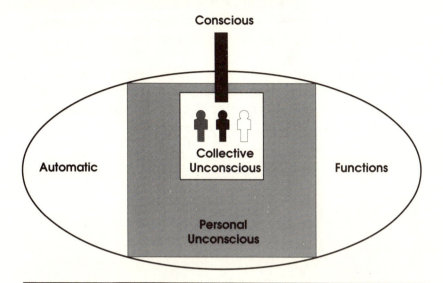

1. The large circle represents the total Self, including auto-matic brain functions such as heart beat, instinctive reactions, and breathing.
2. The shaded square represents the personal unconscious.
3. The small square represents the collective unconscious.
4. The dark rectangle represents conscious knowledge, awareness, or perception of Self.
5. The part of the dark rectangle that is outside the circle represents what people perceive themselves to be, but are not (self-illusions). Notice that part of the rectangle interacts with the personal unconscious and a very small part interacts with the collective unconscious. These interactions vary in magnitude depending on the individual. The entire circle, or everything that we are, has the potential to appear in Reverse Speech: the total Self revealed.

the mind as defined by Carl Jung. Figure Three explains this further.

When we accept the fact that the human brain is virtually limitless, has always been capable of reverse functions, naturally uses metaphors, and consists of three distinct levels—on at least one of which we seem to share information with the rest of humanity—we begin to realize that we indeed may be part of something much greater than ourselves. We are linked inexorably, and forever, with each other at the deeper levels of mind. This truly makes us family.

As human beings we share a collective unconscious, which we all express through speech reversals. We can choose to feel a little less lonely, more a part of things. We can come home again—and discover that we never really left.

4

The Communicative Nature Of Reverse Speech

The two modes of speech are dependent upon each other. They form an integral part of communication. In the dynamics of interpersonal communication, both modes of speech communicate the total psyche of a person—conscious as well as unconscious.

—The Process of Reverse Speech and
Speech Complementarity (Point #2)

We pretty much understand the mechanisms of forward speech because we're used to communicating that way and have done so for most of our lives. But, can people understand something that is communicated in reverse, especially if they don't suspect that reverse communication is possible? And, can those reversed messages affect our behavior?

This leads us to a look at subliminal messages, extrasensory perception, and the communicative nature of Reverse Speech in general.

Subliminal Messages and Their Effects

Hidden backward messages in rock 'n' roll have created major controversies concerning their subliminal effects. Concerns range from fear of being brainwashed or manipulated to simple confusion: "How can you understand something when it's said backward?"

The *Contemporary Dictionary* defines "subliminal" as:

    1. Below or beyond the threshold of consciousness: a subliminal stimulus;

2. too slight or weak to be felt or perceived.[1]

Very little documented scientific research has been done to determine whether the mind can decode backward messages. I conducted a computer search to find research papers on backward masking and located 36 studies world-wide. Most of these studies were concerned with the affects of visual or tonal backmasking on topics such as memory and autistic children and were not relevant to the issue at hand. Many theories and observations, however, have been published concerning other forms of subliminal stimuli such as flashing pictures and forward soundtracks superimposed over recordings at very low levels, speeded up or slowed down.

In 1958, Australian television, Channel Seven in Melbourne, experimented with subliminal advertising. Mr. John Hampel of Glengowrie, South Australia, who was employed by Channel Seven at the time as their Audio Director, gave the following account of the experiment.[2]

> On the night that we experimented with subliminal messages we made two single video frames. The first was a blank frame that contained the words 'BUY PELACO SHIRTS' in large print. The second frame contained the well known AMPOL logo. We then spliced the frames into the normal nightly program at selected intervals. They appeared on four successive occasions during the evening, each lasting 1/25th of a second. That week the sales for Pelaco shirts increased dramatically while Ampol seemed to be unaffected.
>
> This experiment strongly suggested that subliminal suggestion can affect the mind. In fact, so great was its influence that within a week of the experiment, The Australian Broadcasting Control Board (as it was then called) banned all forms of subliminal messages. No further experiments were undertaken.[3]

This was the only time that this type of experiment was done in Australia on a public level. Today, paragraph 10 of *The Australian Programme Standards* states:

> A licensee shall not allow his station to be used for the process known as 'subliminal perception' or for any other technique which attempts to convey information, of any sort whatsoever, to the viewer by transmitting messages below or near the threshold of normal awareness.[4]

The research I found related to *other* forms of subliminal messages and didn't directly address backward messages.[5] I, therefore, began to search for any cases of rock 'n' roll "subliminal horror stories," hoping to discover a connection.

If unintentional backward messages were indeed subliminally suggestive and repetitive listening could increase their affects, then some evidence of this should exist. Below are two cases that were particularly compelling, because the backward messages seemed to relate to the actions allegedly caused by an album.

"The Night Stalker"

In the early 1980's, California was terrorized by mass sex murderer, Richard Ramirez, also known as "The Night Stalker," until his capture in December 1985. His killings were exceptionally violent with heavy occult overtones. After he broke into his victims' apartments late at night, he would rape and murder them. He often left drawings of pentagrams on the walls of their apartments. Detectives who investigated the case discovered bizarre links with Satanism and cannibalism.

The Night Stalker was obsessed with rock music, in particular AC/DC's album, *Highway to Hell*, to which he listened almost constantly. It was later claimed at his trial that its strong occult theme was partially responsible for his actions. He was especially interested in the final song on the album, "Night Prowler," from which he got his name.[6]

The lyrics painted a graphic picture of a murderer on the prowl for his victims. They reflect anxiety from the perspective of the victim: hearing the prowler, seeing shadows, afraid to turn out the light. They also reflect the predatory perspective of the prowler: watching the victim and sneaking into the room.

The reversed lyrics on this song are just as graphic.

Listen to me! I'm from Hell! They killed me.

I'm the Law. I said so. / I slide in evil.

I'm the Lord Lucifer. White Owl.

Other isolated reversals in this album were[7]:

My name is Lucifer. / I saw Satan's power.

Shalom, I believe. / Hey, she belongs in Hell!

I'm Lucifer. / Hey young woman.

Lucifer lives. Satan alive. / Lucifer lives.

There's war in my head.

Stained Class

The second case centers around the heavy metal rock group Judas Priest and their album, *Stained Class*. A lawsuit lodged in Reno, Nevada, in 1986, initially sought unspecified damages from CBS records and Judas Priest, claiming that two youths, James Vance and Ray Belknap, were driven to shoot themselves in a suicide pact after they repeatedly listened to this album while smoking marijuana and drinking alcohol. Belknap died. Vance severely disfigured himself in the attempt and died three years later.

Lawyers for the relatives of Vance and Belknap told Nevada Judge Jerry Whitehead that the band's music had a "hypnotic" quality and its records contained subliminal messages. They particularly focused on the words, **Do it**, which they claimed were subliminally inserted after key stanzas that related to suicide, and also the phrase, **Fuck the Lord**, which they claimed promoted an anti-Christian mentality.[8]

The court hearing took one month and on August 24, 1990, Judge Whitehead handed down his verdict. He concluded that the backward phrases did exist, but no evidence had been put forward to suggest that they were caused by anything other than coincidence of sound. Nor was any convincing evidence put forward to suggest that they could be subliminally suggestive. The 6.2 million dollar lawsuit was rejected.

I contacted the judge before the trial began and he referred me to the respective attorneys. After deliberation both attorneys decided not to use the research evidence compiled using Reverse Speech technologies. Neither side felt that it was beneficial to their case.

The plaintiff claimed that Judas Priest had intentionally placed reversals on the album whereas the defense claimed that reversals didn't exist. The truth, of course, is that speech reversals *did* exist on the album, but they were a *naturally*-occurring phenomena. Until people accept that reversals occur naturally, the debate will continue. At this writing, there are four similar cases pending that relate to backward messages in rock 'n' roll.

Regarding the Judas Priest album, I believe that the album's forward lyrics tell a metaphoric tale about a fight between good and evil, the confusion that results from this struggle, and a hero's death. Not surprisingly, the reversals tell a similar story.[9]

The reversals could have been subliminally suggestive, given the teenagers' state of mind at the time and a reported history of drug abuse and petty crime. I found over 72 speech reversals on this album, only two of which were quoted at the trial (see above). The attorney for the plaintiff completely overlooked the most striking reversals:

God is evil. / An innocent man help us.

Get out of it, get out of it. / Say, am I sexy.

Give us the truth. / You silly fuck.

I took my life.

(A *powerful* complementary reversal, which occurs on the last stanza of, "Beyond the Realms of Death").

Take me out. / We died for glory. / We died sad.

It would appear that people can unconsciously hear reversed messages and, in some cases, be affected by them. I have uncovered no evidence to indicate this to be the case if the listener is not *predisposed* to be affected. For example, an advertisement containing reversals might influence someone who drinks to buy a particular brand of liquor, but wouldn't necessarily influence a non-drinker to rush out and grab a bottle of that brand. Likewise, if someone were emotionally disturbed, repetitive, negative reversals might reinforce his or her state of mind.

Let us further explore the idea that Reverse Speech is a naturally-occurring phenomenon with a complex, communicative nature.

Reversed Dialogue

Once I changed the focus of my initial research from a simple study of backward masking to a study of Reverse Speech, I discovered a much more exciting dimension of communication and began to document requests, commands, and entire conversations—all in reverse. Here are some examples, with the reversals in **bold** print appearing after the direct quote:

1. In a media interview with a man suspected of sending a threatening letter to an associate, I observed the following interaction.

   Man: "Well then, [he should produce that letter] and let's have a look at it." **I want to see that letter.**

   Reporter: (forward) "Would you like to see it?"

   Man: (reply) "Yes."

Note the process in the exchange above. The man delivered a reversal in which he asked to see the letter. The reporter seemed to respond directly to the reversed request by offering to show it to him. As might be expected, the man answered, "Yes."

2. The following example also shows direct response to a speech reversal. It's from an informal conversation in which a woman was talking with me about her tape player, which had broken.

   Woman: "[I'm pissed off with my stereo.] Will it work?" **David. I'd like you to fix it.**

   David: "If it doesn't, I'll fix it for you."

The woman delivered a request in reverse to me. I immediately responded to her in forward language and even used some of the same words that she used in her reversal.

3. This example demonstrates the intricate relationship between reversed dialogue and forward dialogue. It's a transcript of the last minutes of a conversation between myself and two people who were discussing Reverse Speech. I recorded the conversation with the intention of immediately reversing the tape to locate speech reversals.

   Woman: "We were so skeptical when we read your leaflet, but then when we heard it, well there it was." No reversal.

   David: "[Yeah, its, er,] like that with everything." **Hear what I say.**

   Man: "[Since our interest] is really on a curiosity level, do you reckon that might [just be enough]." **Now let's listen. / This is funny.**

   David: "Yeah. I was just about to suggest it, would you

believe. Who knows, I might have even [said it backward]." **Listen.**

Notice how I ended the conversation with a reversal that reflected my intent to look for my speech reversals: **Hear what I say.** The man responded to my reversal and reflected his own desire to also look for reversals: **Now let's listen,** yet he felt strange about the prospect of playing tapes backward to hear other phrases: **This is funny.**

I perceived his uneasiness and, having performed this type of experiment many times before, and knowing the nature of reversed dialogue and interactions, I said, "Who knows, I might have even said it backward," then responded with a confident command in reverse: **Listen.**

4. Here's a case in which an entire reversed conversation took place. It's a small section of a session that I conducted with a husband and wife. The wife discussed her recent nervous breakdown and the affects that it had on their marriage.

    Wife: (with high emotion) "To think that I had to become actually selfish to be loved. [I actually had to become selfish] for him to love me and accept me as I am." **The force, he shot it.**
    (A metaphoric reference in a highly-charged state that directly accuses the husband.)

    Husband: (softly) "[That's not entirely true.]" **Just hold on one second.**
    (Defensive)

    David: Is that how you [see your breakdown]?" **My God! Will you see you're hating you!**
    (Command directed to wife.)

    Wife: "Yes. [I regret my breakdown, yes, because]...." **Might as well keep saying that. I'm filthy.**
    (Defeated response, negative self image.)

    David: "No, no. [Don't regret it.]" **Don't regret.**
    (Command, reinforcing the forward dialogue.)

    Husband: "That's all I've said. [Don't regret it.]" **Don't regret this.**

Notice how an entire reversed conversation transpired at the same time as the forward dialogue and directly related to it:

Wife: **The force, he shot it.**

Husband: **Just hold on one second.**

David: **My God! Will you see you're hating you.**

Wife: **Might as well keep saying that. I'm filthy.**

David: **Don't regret.**

Husband: **Don't regret this.**

Reversed dialogue, "mind reading," and entire conversations in reverse all help to illustrate the communicative nature of Reverse Speech.

Electroencephalogram Testing

I found many examples of reversed requests, commands, and dialogues that strongly indicated that the brain can *decode* speech reversals and *respond* to them in communication (and I continue to find examples). I further tested the brain's ability to understand speech reversals by conducting electroencephalogram (EEG) tests with Australian psychologist, Marcus Tomlian, in February 1988.

The tests involved playing 10 spoken audio soundtracks, each 30 seconds long, *forward* to 30 subjects who knew nothing about Reverse Speech or why the tests were being conducted. Six of these soundtracks were known to contain speech reversals, four did not. The subjects' brain functions were recorded per millisecond with the EEG, and the results analyzed using specialized computer programming. Below are the complete transcripts, forward and reverse, of three of the tested soundtracks that contained speech reversals.

Trivial Pursuit Game

The following is a private conversation among four adult friends, a husband and wife, mother and father and their infant.

Father: "Right. Whose turn?"

—Baby cries—

Mother: "Baby, be quiet!"

Baby: "[Ye-ar. Ye-arm.]" **Mummy, Mummy.**
(Seeking mother's attention.)

Husband: "Mother's turn. Mother, it's your turn."

—Baby continues to cry—

Husband: "Why don't you turn baby around the other way so she can't see you, but she'll still know you're here."

—Adults continue to play the game—

Mother: "1, 2, 3, 4, 5. Oh. What a bummer."

—Baby still restless—

Husband: (reinforces request to have baby moved) "She can be reassured by the sounds of our voices. [That'll be quite enough for her.]" **Oooh! I've lost interest**.
(Reflects frustration with baby's continual crying.)

—Game continues—

Wife: "Who played the title role in the 1933 movie *Henry VIII?*"

Husband: "What?!"

Mother: "Initials?"

Wife: "C.L. [You won't get it!.] Oh you [might, but I doubt it]." **Tell me what it is!**
(Reinforces forward challenge.)
Rave on {husband}.
(Using her husband's actual name, the reversal expresses frustration toward him.)

Transsexual in Prison

This interview with a transsexual in prison is taken from NWS Channel 9, Adelaide, in November 1987.

Reporter: "The woman says she wants a transfer to South Australia so she can serve out her sentence in a women's prison. She says the present system is wrong when sex change operations can be carried out in Australia ..."

Woman: "... [And yet they have no follow up with it.] They don't make any clear criteria for the people after they've had their operation. They're still legally

male. Now that's absurd. That's crazy." **All the fun we're having.**
(The reversal, reinforced by body language, reflects enjoyment over the media experience.)

Reporter: "The woman points out that had she remained in New South Wales, she would now be out on parole."

President Truman Announces the Dropping of the Atomic Bomb on Hiroshima

Announcer: "Ladies and gentlemen. The President of the United States."

Truman: "[The world will note that the first Atomic bomb was dropped on Hiro]shima,—[a military base]. We won the race of discovery against the Germans. We have used it in order to shorten the agony of war. In order to save the lives of thousands and thousands of young Americans. We shall continue to use it until we completely destroy Japan's power to make war." **Lord, fuck off. Mad! They must have dropped it before the Whirlwind.**
(Reversal uses a metaphor.)
But there is a dilemma.
(Reversal may reflect the dilemma over Hiroshima's large civilian population.)

Whenever a speech reversal occurred during the above tests, the EEG showed significant brain activity involving the left and right hemispheres. Different parts of the brain were also stimulated depending on the subject matter of the reversal. In addition, concentration levels either increased or decreased when the reversed phrases occurred.

These results further verified the communicative nature of Reverse Speech. They confirmed that left/right brain hemispheric interchanges were involved in the actual process of reversal decoding, and suggested an unconscious freedom of choice in the acceptance or rejection of these reversed phrases.

The subliminal effect of reversed messages, therefore, depends greatly upon the emotional and mental status of the individual as well as on their personal belief systems. A brainwashing effect on the general public doesn't seem to exist. In fact, the term "subliminal" does not describe the communicative nature of Reverse Speech. "Subliminal" implies both deliberate insertion and "programming." Reverse Speech occurs naturally and does not seem to program the minds of listeners.

The communicative aspect of Reverse Speech is similar to that of forward speech. As listeners receive and process forward speech on a conscious level, they have the choice to accept or reject the message. The same is true of Reverse Speech. The only difference is that listeners receive the message on an unconscious level.

Extrasensory Perception

Many people report experiences in which they're talking to someone, but it seems as though something far deeper than the conversation is transpiring. They feel emotions that seem to be separate from those being discussed openly, or they just "know" something about the other person, but aren't sure how they gained that knowledge. In these cases, it's entirely possible that they are perceiving each other's unconsciously-communicated speech reversals.

Intuition and Telepathy

The entire psyche of a person is intricately woven throughout the sounds of speech. As previously discussed, reversals become more complex the more emotionally charged feelings become. Forward speech is influenced by tonality, cadence, emotional states, and rapport or lack of rapport between people, which, in turn, directly affect the formation and the frequency of reversals.

When the forward conversation is emotional, the speech reversals of the individuals involved also interact on an unconscious level, causing them to feel that they're in close rapport with each other—or not in rapport, as the case may be.

For example, I took the reversals below from the last five minutes of a session that I conducted with a client. On the surface, we seemed to be interacting well as we discussed the reversals that I'd found on our previous session.

There were strong, "unspoken" tensions between us, however, that I couldn't understand. So strong, in fact, that I left feeling unsettled and distressed. The reversals that I found show the actual unconscious interactions taking place and graphically display the reasons for our tension.

David: **She does not trust me.**

Woman: **I believe you can't be trusted.**

David: **Well why?**

Woman: **That's messing me. / You make it up.**

David: **Not trust me. / You lousy shit. / I need a cigarette. Must have it.**

Woman: **I'm upset.**

David: **I need wisdom.**

Woman: **I've seen wisdom. / I don't believe there's much on Earth.**

What happened was that my client had doubts about me and Reverse Speech. Although she didn't openly express these doubts, she expressed them unconsciously through her reversals. I intuitively perceived her lack of trust and responded aggressively.

When we had our third session, we were pleased that we'd discovered the source of our tension in the previous sessions. And, I learned a major lesson: never underestimate the power of personal feelings or the importance of rapport between people in therapy sessions. I learned the necessity of dealing with my own issues and doing the best I can to remain objective. My closing reversals in the last session were; **Now I understand. / Be careful, hey.**

Future Tense Reversals

Future tense reversals, which speak of events or emotions yet to occur, such as, **This will happen**, and, **I shall do that**, occasionally appear in Reverse Speech. Every time a Future Tense reversal appears in a transcript, the event about which it speaks happens—if no action is taken to alter the outcome.

Is this an example of human intuition or maybe just the incredible computing power of the mind predicting future events based on information that it has received in reverse? Either way, the implications of Future Tense reversals are vast.

Using the knowledge of Future Tense reversals, some Reverse Speech analysts have been able to alter the outcome that the reversal predicted.

I experimented with Future Tense reversals in a tape that I analyzed for two people who were thinking about going into business together. Future Tense reversals predicted the future of the business and the interpersonal relationships between the two people. Using this knowledge, the potential business partners took the appropriate action to correct the negative outcomes that were predicted.

We can find an example of a Future Tense reversal in music in the song, "Band on the Run," by Paul McCartney and Wings. A reversal occurred in one section that said, **Marijuana, marijuana. The law, law will banish us.**

Several years later Paul *was* arrested for the possession of marijuana that custom officials found while they searched his suitcases as he was trying to enter Japan with his "Band on the Run." He was subsequently "banished" from visiting there again. The complementarity of the forward and the reversed dialogue is especially interesting, considering the circumstances.

Malok Speaks

The following transcript contains portions of reversals that I found in the recording of a trance session that was conducted by a hypnotist with his client. The client was in the middle of a severe emotional crisis and desperately seeking some direction in his life. During this trance, a part of the client's unconscious mind called "Malok" appeared. Malok spoke of himself as a wise being, giving advice and direction, similar to channelling experiences.

I presume that the experience was a metaphor that the client's unconscious mind designed to heal his conscious mind.

> Malok: "We [are like God]." **God lonely.**
>
> Hypnotist: "[I ask for the part] that is responsible for Client's patterns in emotions to speak." **Must now accept client.**
>
> Malok: "[I know everything there is] to know about everything." **Seen a lines journey through ever.**

Hypnotist: "Am I correct in that Client has [come to you seeking knowledge]?" **Gave him his power.**

Malok: "[Basically.]" **You kiss him.**

Malok: "He forgets his purpose, [but I recall it all]. It is in the light." **Remember I'm the perfume.**

Malok: "[He must continue with his] current mission. That is his direction and task in this life." **The fact disturbing him.**

Malok: "[That's just the way it's set out. That's really just it.]" **Visit. He lives in the eye. See all the system.**

Malok: "Society is at a turning point and Client [is an important person] at this time, to play a role in telling all of the way that [we can reach our higher] self." **I see the Garden. / The Lord of lesson.**

Malok: "[His purpose is] mapped out." **My purpose set.**

Malok: "He needs people around who will understand his purpose and [understand the emotions he must deal with] while he works." **Who will love me. There's none.**

Malok: "The path is set. It's as simple as that. He can fight and kick and scream as much as he likes. But [that's just the way] its going to be. [The loneliness he feels is not the loneliness] for relationship" **Client marks it all. / We fear the sending out.**

Malok: "[The loneliness that he feels] is the incredible responsibility that he carries [and what he must do]." **Wrecks me. Responsible to love this. / I will give words. I give.**

Hypnotist: "[If I understand correctly, some of the information he wants is why?] Why is there all [this torment happening to him]." **Now we shall shoot Client's silk out naturally. / I see lonely Aussie.**

Malok: "[It's a lonely path.] It always will be ['cause that's just the way it is]." **Mark. Hear love. / See now the sixth lesson.**

Malok: "[The family that he has lost will be there again] when the work is done." **Shift the Aussie. Where**

the memory makes him.

Malok: "[And he] needs others now." **I am.**

Malok: "You can help him. [You can help him through] this current time of trouble [in his] life." **We leave to mark the Whirlwind. / I am.**

Malok: "[And you must know,] too, that [your purpose] is all mapped out." **You answer me. / I am Aussie.**

Malok: "[Client will come back now.]" **I'll help him to work.**

—Trance ends—

Client: "Ah, far out. [That was an amazing trance.] I went [really deep]." **It's the Whirlwind. / It's not I.**

A Journey in the Outback

Here's a story that an experienced bushman told me about a strange experience he had while he was on holiday in the Australian outback. The reversals related directly to his story, giving additional information and emotional perceptions. Notice how some reversals appeared before the topic was discussed forward. These reversals, called "Lead reversals," commonly occur in Reverse Speech.

Man: "We were in the backblocks, although it was still [reasonably populated where we] were." **They were popular woods.**

Man: "I left the camp and [went for a walk] in the opposite direction. I had my compass with me." **It was all silky.**

Man: "There was a really weird atmosphere and it seemed like someone was [lurking around] the corner." **Get this rock.**

Man: "There was a [vast layer of fallen rocks there] and other things on the other side." **I was scared of the Wolf around the side.**

Man: "I thought I'd go back to the camp and wait [until dawn] the next day to check it out." **I feel awed.**

Man: "Then I looked down the hill in the dark and [I saw a campfire]." **It's a white woman.**

Man: "[I saw a campfire] and someone sitting by it." **I see a person.**

Man: "So I thought I'll go down there to that [person by the campfire]." **I'll get my neighbor.**

Man: "So I [walked down] the hill, now this was still in the opposite direction." **Who'll help us.**

Man: "When I got there it was my own camp. I couldn't work it out 'cause according to the compass, I'd gone in the opposite direction. Anyway [I sat down] by the fire with my lady friend." **I curse you.**

Man: "It really felt creepy so we got into the tent [and zipped it up]." **I feel helpless.**

Man: "I knew there was someone out there and I decided I [wasn't going to be stuck] in the tent. If there was someone out there, [I wanted to know] about it." **So exhausting / I must listen.**

Man: "I grabbed [the shovel in] one hand and the torch in the other." **It's exhausting.**

Man: "[I walked around] the fire back into the bushes." **I'll be careful.**

Man: "I walked over the hill and [there was my camp] again right in front of me. I know I hadn't gone in circles." **Circling Whirlwind.**

Man: "There were some pretty important things going on there and I'm going to check [it out some time]." **Don't be nervous.**

Pain From a Life in the Past?

When a man leaves his family, it can cause great stress for those left behind as the following transcript reveals. I conducted this session with a woman in her late twenties whose husband had just left her and their two children. She wanted to have the session to see if we could locate a cause for the sharp, stabbing pains that she'd been feeling in her stomach since the breakup.

She thought that the pains might have had something to do with a past-life experience. The most predominant theme in this session was a "wound" inflicted upon her by **Lancelot**. In my opinion, this was a metaphor for the pain she felt from her husband and could not be attributed to a past-life experience.

David: "Describe the pain to me a bit. Can you visualize it?" No reversal.

Woman: "It's a [really deep ache] in my stomach. I can't eat. I feel sick, but not physically sick. Every now and then I feel like I could be sick. [It's just a really deep seated pain.]" **He hurts, I know. / Lancelot, I know, hurt with his spear.**

Woman: "I'm going to have to [go up North to find work]." **Don't want to go up there.**

Woman: "[The kids are coping] really well. They don't know about the move yet." **They shall miss him.**

Woman: "I just want to know what this pain is and where [it's coming from]." **Fucked nerves.**

Woman: "I couldn't be near him. I felt as if I was hanging [onto something that was no longer] there." **Longing, I need him. I'm nude.**

Woman: "I don't feel [as emotional] right now. I don't feel like crying or anything. It's just a [sick painful feeling]." **I love you. / Lance fucked me up.**

Woman: "Maybe it's a past [life experience]. Perhaps he inflicted pain on me in another life and the situation [that is happening now is bringing it all back]." **Freeze frame. / Lancelot the same. Horrible person.**

Woman: "I went to some channelers. I was told that once we reached a certain point in our relationship then we could [see what happened in the past life that caused the problems]." **It's now Lancelot. The bastard. I loved him.**

Woman: "I've got to clear these feelings. [But they're there and you can't ignore] them." **He nudes me. He broke me.**

David: "How [are you feeling] right now?" **Have no fear.**

Woman: "Okay. I'm finally at the moment that [it's, it's there,] but I can control it." **My nerves slip, slip.**

Woman: "I've never [slept with anyone before]. So [it's my first] real relationship breakup." **Will he ever love me. / Sex found him out.**

Woman: "[I'm hanging onto] the fact that there's still a chance." **Here's longing.**

Woman: "I ask myself [what I did] wrong. [Should I] go or wait for him." **I'm worthless. / I'm nude.**

In light of what we now know about speech reversals, what was once thought to be esoteric, or even unbelievable, such as intuition, telepathy, foreseeing the future, channeling, and past life experiences may be attributable, at least in part, to the communicative nature of the mind. Reverse Speech gives us an exciting avenue of exploration.

Reverse Speech is the voice of the inner mind, the deeper Self. It is a previously undiscovered, "extra sense" that enables people to interact intuitively and compassionately with others. And, because individual values and beliefs are based on human interaction on all levels, Reverse Speech ultimately can play a vital role in molding us into who we are as human beings.

People who work with Reverse Speech, either as clients or as analysts, begin to connect with their deeper Selves and integrate what they say with what they feel. Because they better understand their strengths and needs, they tend to be more expressive, assertive, and straightforward with others. Listeners sense that the speakers are more congruent—that is, the speakers mean what they say and say what they mean.

In short, people who study their reversals in depth, and learn from them, tend to become more confident and more effective communicators.

5

Reverse Speech in Children

The process of language development in children starts backwards before it does forwards. Children first develop the Covert mode of communication and then, as Overt speech begins, these two modes gradually combine into one, forming a bi-level communication process.
—The Process of Reverse Speech and
Speech Complementarity (Point #3)

Language develops in reverse before it develops forward. If we were to play a tape recording of "baby talk" backward, we'd find words and simple *forward* phrases in the gibberish—as early as four months—before the baby has "officially" learned how to talk forward.

As a baby learns to talk, these two styles of expression, forward and backward, gradually merge into one mode of communication, part of which we can consciously understand and the other part "hidden."

Imagine the implications of being able to understand what babies and children are feeling *before* they can put those feelings into words. Concerned parents, educators, and counselors could figure out why babies and infants cry for no apparent reason or why they're acting fussy, confused, or difficult. They could better understand and comfort children who've retreated deeply into themselves because of traumatic events. And, they could better figure out why non-communicative teenagers are sometimes sullen, rebellious, angry, or depressed.

57

Reverse Speech can provide a key to understanding young people so we can gently and compassionately unlock their behavior and, in turn, be more effective parents, educators, and counselors.

The Birth of Twins

July 7, 1987, I became the proud father of fraternal twin girls, Jaye and Symone, and thus conceived an exciting idea for a new research project: when did speech reversals begin to appear in baby sounds? I began my research with their birth.

Nurse: (during labor as complications set in) "C'mon. Push as hard as you can. C'mon. [You can do it, you can do it. Deep breath in] and hold it." **Please help it. Push harder. Push harder!**

David: (responding to the doctor's explanation as the doctor diagnoses "brow birth" and takes the appropriate action) "[Yep, fine, I think.] Are you sure she's okay?" **It's enough pain.**

David: (just after the first birth, Symone) "[How much, how much did she weigh?]" **I wish you'd show me her.**

Doctor: (direct response, note reversed dialogue) "[We haven't weighed] her yet." **She's lovely.**

David: (side comment, talking into the microphone) "This is a tape [for posterity's sake]." **A cigarette.** (Exactly what I wanted at the time.)

David: (realizing that the twins were not identical) "[This one's got fair] hair, and that one's got dark hair." **Hey, they're opposite.** (The two girls did develop to be totally opposite in appearance, temperament, and desires.)

The First Signs of Reversed Language

I periodically tape recorded the twins from the night they arrived home. When they were four months old, I located the first intelligible reversed sounds—two single words in a 30-minute tape. I found the first one on Symone, **Mummy,** and the other on Jaye, **Symone.**

Two weeks later I made the next recording and heard Jaye say in reverse, **Daddy.** Over the next two months I found other isolated words:

> Symone just before mealtime: **Hungry**
>
> Jaye as she was about to fall out of her high chair: **Help**
>
> Jaye when she wet her diaper: **Toilet**
>
> Symone: **Jaye**

I also found other instances of both twins saying **Mummy** and **Help.** I did not find any other intelligible sounds, backward or forward, in any of the recordings I made.

The Appearance of Phrases

When the twins turned seven months old, I began to find isolated examples of two or three words that appeared together in a reversed sentence. At the same time the frequency of simple, single words in forward speech increased. Here are some examples:

1. I was following Symone around the room with the tape recorder when she became very interested in it. She reached out to grab it, crying out with delight. This cry reversed to say, **What's that?**

2. My wife spanked Jaye while I was on the telephone. Jaye sadly looked at me and began to cry. At the beginning of her cry a reversal occurred that said, **Daddy, hurts.**

3. When Jaye was ten months, I found an example on her while the two girls were mumbling in their beds before going to sleep. Their half-brother, my son from a previous marriage, had been staying with us for the last week. The reversal was, **Love my brother.**

4. When the twins turned one year old, they began to experiment with uttering more single words forward more frequently. Occasionally a perfectly clear speech reversal appeared at the same time as an imperfect attempt was made with a forward word. For example,

the dog's name, "Ganger," was once pronounced forward as "Dander," and this same sound reversed to say a very clear **Ganger.** Likewise, the word "bottle" at one time was said forward as "bobbop." The same sound reversed to clearly say **bottle.**

5. I found a reversal on Jaye when she was 13 months old, just after my wife and I made up following an argument. Jaye was sitting on my lap, happy and giggling. In these laughs, I found a reversal that said, **Daddy loves Mum.**

6. When the twins were 14 months old, I found the first definite example of speech complementarity. They were playing in the bath and Symone was trying to pick up a cup that was sliding along the bottom. Unable to pick it up, she looked up at me and reached out for help, saying forward, "[(miscellaneous baby sounds), Daddy.]" In reverse this became, **David. Help me,** with **David** occurring on the reverse of "Daddy."

7. Of a similar nature was a reversal that I found on Jaye a few weeks later when I returned from an interstate seminar. She ran up to me as I walked in the door saying, "David." This reversed to say, **Is my dad.**

The Beginning of Metaphors

I found some significant reversals on the twins when they reached 18 months. These occurred while my wife at the time and I were having a heated argument. The twins were highly distressed, crying, and running frantically around the room while my wife and I gave little thought to calming them.

The reversals that occurred throughout this 20-minute tape recording graphically illustrate their mental state. The very first reversed metaphors appeared and reversal frequency was the highest that I'd found yet, often occurring within a few minutes of each other.

Symone: **Help, help. Mum. Help. Hey, mum. Help.**

Jaye: **Mumma. Pappa. Help.**

(Reversed references to the twin's grandparents. Jaye was seeking help from other sources.)

Jaye: **They died. I died.**
(A powerful metaphor with Jaye personally experiencing the "death" of our marital relationship.)
Symone: **Help us. Help them. Help them.**
(Symone wants help for us.)
Jaye: **Help us.**
(Jaye wants help for herself and Symone.)
Symone: **Help them.**
(Symone repeats her previous request.)
Jaye: **Help me. Help us.**
(Jaye becomes specific. She wants help for herself.)
Jaye: **Dad, David. Help me. I'm nude. Help me.**
(Jaye becomes desperate, using a reversed metaphor, **"nude,"** which is traditionally associated with emotional pain.)
Symone: **Mum. Help her.**
(Concern for Jaye.)

Reversal Styles and Personality Differences

The above transcript was the first indication of different reversal styles between the twins. Symone, while seeking help for herself, also showed concern for her parents and sister. Symone has become the more altruistic of the two. Jaye, on the other hand, was concerned primarily with her own welfare. She also was calling for me, whereas Symone was calling for her mother.

It appears that personality permeates to the deepest core of who we are—or, more precisely, it *emanates* from there and infuses all that we are. By carefully studying a person's reversals, an experienced Reverse Speech analyst can begin to form a distinct profile of the speaker, without ever having met the person—a proposition that I've tested and proven repeatedly in my research.

The Twin's Second Birthday Party

Six months later our marriage collapsed. I was preparing to move to the United States within the month. We hadn't yet told the twins of our decision and I'd been emotionally distancing myself from them in an attempt to reduce the pain that I was feeling.

In the following recording, which I made during the twin's second birthday party, reversals had developed to a complex level and indicated that the twins definitely knew, at least on an unconscious level, that Daddy was leaving home, thus making another case for the part that reversals play in "intuition" or "telepathy."

> Jaye: **I won't speak with David.**
>
> > (Anger at, and recognition of, my pending departure.)
>
> Symone: **Jaye will need this.**
>
> > (Symone recognizes Jaye's feelings.)
>
> Jaye: **I sad.**
>
> Jaye: **Now help. Help me.**
>
> Jaye: **Come Michael.**
>
> > (She calls her half-brother, also at the party, by name.)
>
> Symone: **Mum come. Here Mum. Mum.**
>
> > (As with the trend on the previous session, Symone calls her mother.)
>
> Symone: **Mum, give me some healing.**
>
> > (Symone is also hurt and expresses this by using a simple metaphor.)
>
> Jaye: **Leave me.**
>
> > (A strong reaction to sadness.)
>
> Symone: **I will come.**
>
> > (Symone offers to help Jaye.)
>
> Jaye: **Daddy. You're not home.**
>
> > (By using a common Reverse Speech metaphor, she acknowledges the emotional distance I'd created.)
>
> Jaye: **You run.**
>
> > (Directed to me. The forward dialogue was, "Daddy.")
>
> Jaye: **He's not home.**
>
> > (Directed to me again, the forward dialogue being,

"My Daddy.")

Symone: **I love.**

Jaye: **Be home.**

(Again directed to me. The forward dialogue again was, "Daddy.")

Jaye: **Daddy, he loves. David, he runs.**

(With the trend of her previous reversals, Jaye seemingly separates the father image from the personal image.)

Jaye: **I'll be down.**

(An expression of future sadness using a Reverse Speech metaphor.)

Jaye: **Daddy love.**

(A plea.)

Symone: **Be sad.**

(Directed to me. The forward dialogue was "Daddy.")

Jaye: **Power. Power.**

(A strong metaphor in Reverse Speech, usually associated with base needs and desires.)

In the above transcript, the differing reversals of the twins follow the same trend as my previous findings. Jaye was extremely upset, her desires were for her own well being, and she communicated these desires by using simple metaphors. Symone was more concerned with being supportive. Jaye's strong identification with me is evident, yet this time she communicated it as anger rather than as a bid for support.

Symone, on the other hand identified with her mother. Note the many references to "Daddy" forward with different reversals in each case. Here are comparisons from this transcript that further indicate the differences between the twins' reversals:

1. Jaye: **I won't speak with David.**

   Symone: **Mum, give me some healing.**

2. Jaye: **I sad.**

   Symone: **I love.**

3. Jaye: **I'll be down.**

   Symone: **I will come.**

4. Jaye's reversal, **Daddy, he loves. David, he runs.** is
probably the peak of the confusion. Why is my Daddy
leaving home? Her unconscious mind was appearing
to rectify the conflict. Symone simply says to me, **Be
sad.**

I *was* sad to leave them. I kept in regular contact with the
twins by telephone and recorded our conversations as their
forward speech became more fluent.

On a trip to Australia six months after having moved to the
United States, when the girls were almost three years old, I made
another recording and found that the bi-level communication
process had progressed significantly, as well as the frequency of
reversals, which were then close to normal adult occurrence.
Here are some examples of reversals I found on that trip:

* Jaye: "[Daddy, I want you. I want you. (Other cries and
  groans.)]" **Here father. Here father. I love you.
  Loving him.**
  (This was the first time I found **Father** in reverse. All
  previous references were **Daddy.** Could it have
  been due to my six months absence?)
* Symone: "[Hello, Daddy.]" **I want a lolly** .
  (Australian word for "candy.")
* Jaye: (to me) "[I want a cuddle. I want a cuddle.]" **I love
  you. I love you.**

I found another excellent example of complementarity when
I recorded a conversation between two children. One of them, a
three year old (child #1), noticed an inoculation mark on the
other's arm.

Child 1: "Do you have an injection?" No reversal.

Child 2: "What do you mean?" No reversal.

Child 1: "[To make you better.]" **I hated them.**
(The contradictory message expressed her own
experience with inoculations.)

At this writing, the twins are four years old and are living
with me here in the United States. Their reversed language is now
extremely well developed with the usual adult frequency.

Reversals in Game Playing

The following case study concerns a six-year old girl who was in the process of accepting a new father figure. Her single mother had recently married and the child's natural father had been banned from seeing her because he'd caused major conflicts in the family, including severe emotional abuse of his child.

This resulted in a court restraining order being obtained against him. The child had been despondent since the separation, knowing she wouldn't see her natural father again. She was trying to cope with the abuse and with the confused father figure roles.

This transcript is a portion of an afternoon she spent playing with a friend. Note how she deals with her grief and confusion in reverse under the innocent disguise of playing doctors.

In this transcript, I call the step-father "John" and the natural father "Simon." The words in parenthesis in bold didn't actually occur, but are consistent with the reversed dialogue flow and the tonality of the reversals: question/answer, etc.

> Friend: "Let's play doctors."
>
> Child: "And you're the doctor. [I've had a broken leg.]"
> **I've never hated him.**
> (At this stage we do not know who "him" actually is.)
>
> Friend: "[Which one?]" **(Do you) love him?**
> (Questions the mysterious "him.")
>
> Child: "[This one.]" **(I) love him.**
> (Answers previous reversed question.)
>
> Friend: "No, this one." No reversal.
>
> Child: "And you say what's wrong with you." No reversal.
>
> Friend: "[You say it.]" **(Who's) Daddy?**
>
> Child: "No you. [You say it.] You're the doctor." **John.**
> (The identity of "him" is established as the step-father.)
>
> Friend: "No, you be the doctor." No reversal.
>
> Child: "No you! We swap. [Would you please fix] up my broken leg! (pause) There's a bit I have to fix." **Needs fixing up.**

Friend: "I have to get the stuff. [Now where's the plaster?]"
Simon did this.
(The natural father.)

Child: "I know [how to put it on]." **Hard to deal with.**

This innocent game of doctors was a metaphor for something far deeper. Using the imagery of a doctor fixing a broken leg, the child was sorting through her confused feelings. Note her insistence in being the patient, her establishment of the father figure, and her desire to "fix up her broken leg" after she'd dealt with these issues.

Here are those reversals in order. Note the progression of the reversed interactions between the child and her friend as she recognizes and handles the issues.

Child: **I've never hated him.**

Friend: **(Do you) love him?**

Child: **(I) love him.**

Friend: **(Who's Daddy?)**

Child: **John. / Needs fixing up.**

Friend: **Simon did this.**

Child: **Hard to deal with.**

Child Molestation

The statistics are staggering. Commonly quoted statistics indicate that one in four girls and one in seven boys are molested during childhood. Most psychologists and psychotherapists claim these numbers are so conservative as to point only to the tip of the iceberg. Events so horrible to a child are often blocked from their memory. Reverse Speech analysis provides a powerful method for use in determining the nature and the extent of the crime and its lasting effects on the survivors.

Here are some of the reversals found in a session conducted with a 12-year old girl who'd been molested several years earlier. Her parents asked for a session to determine the extent of the psychological damage that she'd suffered. I documented her reversals in batches or "clusters." Reversals frequently appear in clusters within a short time frame, followed by no reversals for one or two minutes, then another cluster (see Chapter 7 for a discussion of clusters).

Notice the reversed italicized metaphors, which at age 12 are prolific throughout Reverse Speech. I've just documented the reversals and listed them below in their respective clusters, indicated by line breaks. Notice how the subject matter of the individual clusters relate to each other, followed by a different subject in the next cluster.

#1: *Cursing* him.
#2: *Jesus* helps me.
#3: *Jesus* loves me. He must not prosecute.

#4: I was fucked bad.
#5: Oh, what a bastard.

#6: The *mark* makes it worse.
#7: Seen out this *movie*.
#8: Why wasn't it *sunny*.

#9: A person fucked me.
#10: Well, yes it happened.

#11: I've seen it.
#12: I've witnessed it.
#13: I know what he's done.

#14: Yes, I hate him.
#15: And I feel silly.

#16: I'm not scared.
#17: I've seen life.
#18: Why hurt him.

#19: The *mark* is *heavy*.
#20: *Source* will be the pain.

The following is my analysis of the reversals, together with brief explanations of the metaphors.

1. Reversals #1-3 show anger (**cursing him**) as well as acceptance (**Jesus helps me.**)
2 Reversals #4-5 describe the act and express further anger.
3. Reversals #6-8 describe harm, or **mark**, on her psyche plus a sense of disassociation from the event, **movie.**

4. Reversals #9-10 show an insistence on establishing the occurrence of the event.
5. Reversals #11-13 repeat the insistence and also reveal an understanding, **I know what he's done**.
6. Reversals #14-15 show hatred and some reluctance for the hatred.
7. Reversals #16-18 show an acceptance.
8. Reversals #19-20 reveal her own pain, **mark is heavy**, and give an indication where that pain is. **Source** is a metaphor usually associated with male/female energies.

Overall, this session indicated that the girl understood what had happened to her. She showed an understandable amount of anger but also seemed to be working through acceptance of the event. If her process was encouraged and supported through puberty she would probably suffer minimal permanent psychological damage.

Other similar sessions that I analyzed revealed a wealth of information concerning the psychological makeup of children and how they're affected by the events in their lives.

Bridging the Generation Gap

Just as parents and their teenagers interact on a conscious level, they also relate on an unconscious level, their reversals reflecting what they want, need, and expect from each other.

Here are portions of a session with a father and his teenage daughter as they discussed their relationship. They were both highly emotional. The daughter was crying out, in reverse, for her father's love and he was wrestling with his own conflicts about his purpose in life. He also remembered how he acted when he was a teenager.

Ultimately, the session helped them greatly, the father in particular. It helped them understand the dynamics of their relationship and take the necessary steps to improve it.

Notice how the daughter expresses herself emotionally in her forward speech. In reverse, she calls for her father:

Daughter: "Oh, no. I don't want people to be like me, [then we'd all] be like me and we'd be [messed up]."

I need you. We felt fear.

The father's reversals express a need to know his daughter, even a need to "connect" with her "weakness." While he's speaking with her, he is also seeking to understand himself—and "Self" answers:

> Father: "Life works in certain ways. [You don't believe it now, but you will believe it someday. That's what good manners are for.] That's why we have certain customs and laws . . . [You have a certain amount of privacy] . . ." **Need your sin closer. I must reveal who you are. / Reveal Daddy. I'm a go slow Daddy.**

The daughter is angry. In reverse, she repeats her demands:

> Daughter: "Here I was, hurt at school. And you go like, it's like [oh, no big deal,] you're not bleeding that bad . . . **You shit! I need you.**

In the midst of heated forward exchanges, the father reaches emotionally for her in his reversals:

> Father: "I got there as fast as I could. I'm never going [to be any better either,] you know, you expect me, oh, yeah, [if you get hurt or anything,] you'll just have to lie there and bleed to death." **Do you love me? / I feel her love. I grieve it.**

She remembers the good times they've had. In her reversals, she continues to plead with him and begins to connect emotionally with him:

> Daughter: I used to like it when we went away. It's like now, [but, I mean,] we don't really do anything . . . like the campground, we went to that place and you found that big turtle . . . [mumbles] . . . that was fun . . . Then, there was the time I got sea sick [on that thing,] on that boat [we were on]." **I need that love. / I miss that love. / I know with love. / I want that love.**

He responds. And, she realizes that he has heard her:

> Father: "[It'd be fun to do it again.]" **I grow to love you.**
> Daughter: "I don't want [to be alive by the time I'm twenty]." **He knows I must love.**

In his forward dialogue, the father discusses his teenage years and notices how different his present direction in life is. In reverse, he questions if this is the way for him to go. His unconscious mind warns him. **Whirl**, in this case is connected to his desire to accumulate possessions:

> Father: "I know I used to do all that, peace demonstrations, etc., as a teenager, but I've decided I want to be different now. [I want to accumulate things] . . . [I want to be comfortable.] I want to have a retirement someday." **Will we make the power? / Whirl will fuck the power.**

Next, he uses a powerful, personal metaphor, **cousin**, that connects him to similar emotions he felt in the past. In his forward dialogue, he struggles with his daughter. In his reversals, he remembers when he was a teenager and used to spend a lot of time with his cousin doing similar things to what his daughter is doing now. His reversal is a reminder that he used to be the same way:

> Father: "You say you don't want to conform, but you are conforming with your own peer group. [I mean, you listen to the same kind of music.]" **You see my cousin. Serving him.**

Forward, the daughter shares her views. In reverse, however, she works through her relationship with him. He is rigid, **law**, but, at least they've connected emotionally with each other and their relationship will work:

> Daughter: "We do good things. Someone's got to say something about where the world is heading. You can't understand. [I don't expect you to understand it] . . . We do it for the good of mankind [and other people, but] it's not like we're violent or anything." **You're holding it, law. / You're nicer. Now it helps the wine. / There will be love.**

The father reassures her, chooses a course of action, and accesses a behavior changing archetype, the **magician**:

> Father: "I don't believe that you think everything is bad in the world. [I think you're lying] . . . I think you're not showing your [emotion, shutting off] . . . I just

want to know [you're going to find something] and say this is neat." **I would never hurt. / I will get my youth. Now for the magician.**

She responds to his archetypal reversal with her own archetype, **Goddess**, acknowledging that she has the resources:

Daughter: "I don't know whether that can happen, but I didn't say [you said I couldn't. I said I cannot do that.]" **I'm a Goddess. I'm the Goddess.**

Thus, the father and daughter progressed from pleading for each other's love to connecting emotionally with each other and, ultimately, to accessing archetypes for positive change.

An Overview of Children and Reversals

After simple words and phrases first appear in reverse in babies, reversed speech then parallels the development of forward language as they grow. In other words, there is a steady progression, in reverse, from the use of simple, isolated words and phrases, to more complex language patterns and metaphors (please see the following chart), just as forward language begins with isolated words and evolves into more complicated sentences and metaphors.

An Overview of Children and Reversals

4 Months
Isolated single-word reversals, few and far between, begin to appear.

7 Months
Reversals begin to appear that contain two or three words. The frequency of single words increases.

1 Year
Forward language begins and clear reversals are found on imperfectly formed, forward words. Language patterns start to combine.

18 Months
Metaphors begin to appear in reverse. Reversals continue to increase and different personality patterns can be detected.

2 Years
Complexity of reversals increase. Metaphors and frequency of reversals increase. Children seem to be aware of events not communicated to them on a conscious level.

3-4 Years
Speech complementarity is well established with bi-level communication occurring regularly. The frequency of reversals is close to that found in normal adult conversations.

6 Years
The child appears to be able to deal with pain and emotional issues on an unconscious level through the process of game playing.

12 Years
Normal adult reversal structure is evident both in frequency and in metaphors.

Most people wouldn't think of locking up a baby for the first two years of its life and ignoring its emotional needs, but this may be essentially what we're doing, in part, by missing valuable opportunities to understand what babies are saying before they learn to talk in the traditional sense. Babies communicate with us all the time—in reverse! Why wait until they're one or two years old to begin to understand them?

Sure, we can get a *sense* if a baby is cold or hungry, lonely, happy, or sad, but babies communicate much more than these simple needs and emotions—if only we'd listen. They comment, in their reversals, on their parents' relationships, communicate their insecurities, and work through what they're feeling about divorces, step-parents, brothers and sisters, illnesses, and traumatic events. They tell us what they need, think and want *before* they can talk. Reverse Speech analysis enables us to listen.

It can also help us understand our teenagers who sometimes can be argumentative, depressed, or angry, but who may not be able to directly articulate what they want or need.

Reverse Speech gives us one more way to be attentive to young people, which, can bring us closer together.

6

Reverse Speech Images

Whoever looks into the mirror of the water will see first of all his own face. Whoever goes to himself risks a confrontation with himself. The mirror does not flatter, it faithfully shows whatever looks into it; namely the face we never show to the world because we cover it with the persona, the mask of the actor. But the mirror lies behind the mask and shows the true face. This confrontation is the first test of courage on the inner way, a test sufficient to frighten off most people.
—Carl Jung, *The Archetypes of the Collective Unconscious*

The human race is a hybrid of sorts, existing on both the material plane and on the mental or spiritual plane, living in both objective and subjective worlds—conscious and unconscious at the same time.

The more we understand of our inner world as it is revealed to us through dreams, speech reversals, and collective metaphors, the more we can reconcile our two seemingly separate lives and realize that we're indeed one with the unchanging Reality that underlies all humanity.

Dream States

Dreams often use strange and disjointed images. For example, a dream of bathing in a refreshing, crystal-clear spring might suddenly change to a dream of being chased through a blazing fire by a wolf wielding a mighty sword. Sometimes dreams are like Gothic fantasies that flash mysterious or ambiguous pictures through the mind during sleep. Much research has been done in an attempt to explain dreams and their purposes. We know, for example, that dream states are unconscious, primarily right-brain functions.

Some researchers suggest that, like a safety valve, dreams provide a release for repressed thoughts or feelings, others suggest that dreams allow a part of the mind that has previously been ignored to communicate, and still others view dreams as random static. Recently it's been theorized that dreams allow us to process important information that we've acquired during our waking hours.

Reverse Speech shares many similarities with dream states and may, in fact, help us to further analyze our dreams. Both dreams and reversals:

1. Stem from deeper regions of the mind;
2. Are unconscious activities and primarily functions of the right-brain;
3. Fade in and out with varying degrees of clarity; and
4. Use images that are sometimes difficult to understand.

Like dreams, reversals allow us to express parts of our minds and thoughts that were previously repressed or ignored.[1]

The unconscious mind often uses powerful metaphors as it manifests itself through Reverse Speech. Carl Jung extensively studied and documented the metaphoric nature of the unconscious mind in his search to explain the nature of the human psyche.

Jung on Dreams

Carl Jung stated that some particularly impressive dreams contained visions and ideas of deep significance, which couldn't be accounted for by the person's past experiences, but rather which seemed to spring from a source outside the range of conscious experience. Such dreams were astonishingly similar to metaphoric and archetypal images that could be found in myths and fairy tales from different cultures all over the world.[2]

In his book, *The Structure and Dynamics of the Psyche*, Jung tells of a man who came to him with severe attacks of pain in the region of his heart, choking sensations in his throat, and piercing pains in his left heel. The man was perplexed over the reason for these pains and severely depressed because his physical problems resulted in his exemption from military duty.[3]

After having discussions with the man and analyzing his dreams, Jung discovered that the man had been jilted recently by his long-time lover. Jung conducted counseling sessions during which the man addressed his repressed feelings about this affair. The pains in the man's heart and throat eventually disappeared.

Jung claimed that the sensations in the man's throat were caused by unconsciously repressed tears, likewise the pains in the heart. The man had deliberately repressed any feelings over the broken love affair. The pain in the left heel continued, however, and Jung was puzzled as to its cause. He states:

> *I could get no clue to the heel symptom from the patient's conscious mind and I turned once more to my previous method— to the dreams. The patient now had a dream in which he was bitten in the heel by a snake and instantly paralyzed.*[4]

Jung concluded that when the woman jilted him, she'd given him a wound that paralyzed him. Further information from the dream uncovered that when he was a child, he'd had an overprotective mother. This resulted in him being "girlish" in nature, hence his decision to join the army—to exert his manhood. Thus, in a sense, his mother, too, had "lamed" him.

Jung then states that they were evidently dealing with that same old serpent who had been Eve's notorious friend. He draws direct comparisons with the man's dream, the pain in his heel, and the Biblical account of creation, pointing out that the man had virtually no conscious knowledge of the Bible.[5]

> *And I will put enmity between thee and the woman and between thy seed and her seed, it shall bruise thy head, and thou shalt bruise his heel." (Genesis 3:15)*[6]

Jung concludes that:

> *This part of the unconscious evidently likes to express itself mythologically, because this expression is in keeping with its nature . . . It corresponds to the mentality of the primitive, whose language possesses no abstractions but only natural and unnatural analogies . . . It seems as that the collective unconscious had translated the patient's experience with the women into the snake-bite dream and thus turned them into a regular mythological motif.*[7]

Jung quotes another account in his book, *The Archetypes of the Collective Unconscious*, of a man who was a modest clerk with no education who suffered from paranoid schizophrenia. This man had frequent hallucinations. On one occasion Jung came across the man staring intently at the sun, moving his head from side-to-side in a curious manner. He took Jung by the arm and said that if he looked at the sun with his eyes half shut, he could see the sun's phallus (penis). Then, if he moved his head the sun-phallus would move also, and that was the origin of the wind.[8]

This bizarre encounter, which occurred in 1906, left Jung puzzled until four years later when he was engrossed in mythological studies. He came across a book by the late Albrecht Dieterich,[9] the well-known philologist, which threw light on the fantasy. It was a part of the so-called "Paris magic papyrus," and was thought to be a liturgy of the Mithraic cult. It consisted of a series of instructions, invocations, and visions. One of these is described in the following words:

> And likewise the so-called tube, the origin of the ministering wind. For you will see hanging down from the disk of the sun something that looks like a tube. And towards the regions westward it is as though there were an infinite east wind. But if the other wind should prevail towards the regions of the east, you will in like manner see the vision veering in that direction."[10]

Jung concludes by saying that the Greek word for "tube" means a "wind instrument," and in Homer, "a thick jet of blood." Jung then points out that his patient had the vision in 1906, and the first Greek text of the papyrus was edited in 1910. The two events should be sufficiently far enough apart to rule out any possibility of clairvoyance on his patient's part or of thought transference on Jung's part.[11]

The parallels of the two visions cannot be disputed, and Jung also notes that strong elements of this sun-phallic motif may be seen in certain medieval paintings.[12] He states that: "The patient was certified in his early twenties. He had never travelled. And there is no such picture in the public art gallery in Zurich, his native town."[13]

Carl Jung's works are compelling. He documents many cases where patients have had dreams or visions that contained elements of myths and legends that surpass cultural and historical boundaries. The patients had no conscious knowledge of these fables and legends. This led him to postulate his theory of "The Collective Unconscious," which states that buried deep within the psyche can be found an inherent storehouse that contains the entire spiritual and cultural heritage of humanity's development.[14]

In *The Archetypes of the Collective Unconscious*, he discusses the collective unconscious and its archetypal images, saying:

> In the realm of consciousness we are our own masters; we seem to be the factors themselves. But if we step through the door of the shadow we discover with terror that we are the object of unseen forces . . . archetypes are complexes of experience that come upon us like fate, and their effects are felt on our most personal life.[15]

There are many similarities between the revelations of Reverse Speech and the writings of Carl Jung, particularly in the area of the archetypal nature of the unconscious mind.

The Three Levels of Reverse Speech

Before I'd encountered the work of Carl Jung, I was documenting many words and phrases whose meanings were a mystery to me. These words included references to the Garden of Eden and the Legend of King Arthur and his Knights of the Round Table—to name just two.

As time went on and I made connections between these words and the forward dialogue in which they appeared, some common factors emerged. Of primary importance was the fact that separate and distinct language patterns, or styles, appeared to correlate predictably and regularly with the intensity and type of forward conversation.

I categorized these language styles into three levels and eventually associated them to the three levels of the mind that Carl Jung defined.

The First Level of Mind: Consciousness

First Level reversals describe commonly-used English words. They often address literal, conscious thoughts in a person's mind while the person is speaking. Here are some examples, with the reversals in **bold** print:

- A murder suspect being interviewed on TV. "No [I never threatened] the man. In fact I can never remember threatening him." **Revenge. Killing the lad.**

- A politician talking to reporters after leaving office under unpleasant circumstances. He was asked if he had any resentments. "No, no, no, no, no. [Politics is a tough game.]" **I was asked to piss off.**

- My son, Michael, as we discussed what videos to watch that night says he hasn't seen video A or B, then in reverse says he has. "I want 'Video A'! I haven't seen 'Video A' or 'Video B.' Let's get them. [Yeah. Let's see them!]" **I've seen both of them.**

- An interview with an Australian politician who was perceived to have designs on his party's leadership.

Interviewer: "Is the position up for grabs?"

Politician: "[Well, ah, I] haven't even given it any thought and I don't intend on this program, within, er, [seconds of listening to, er, ar, the leader] make er (pause) a quite a magnanimous speech, start opening up the question of party leadership." **Leave me alone. / Annoys me, this little asshole from the press.**

- I found this reversal while I was explaining Reverse Speech to someone. The reversal is exactly what I was thinking but didn't want to say. "There's certain reversals that I feel uncomfortable telling people about. Like, er, well, ['cause they might not be able] to, er, well deal with it." **Remember when they're sexual.**

- A reversal that I found on TV evangelist, Jimmy Swaggart, after it was revealed that he'd engaged in sexual misconduct and was stepping down from the pulpit: "I know that so many would ask [why. (Short pause, sighs) Why?] I have asked myself that ten thousand times through ten thousand tears. I will step out of this pulpit at the moment for an [undetermined, indeterminate] period of time." **Help. Help! / I must admit in my mind.**

The Second Level of Mind: Personal Unconsciousness

Second Level reversals describe reversals that are symbolic or metaphoric. *The Contemporary Dictionary* describes a metaphor as:

> *A figure of speech in which one object is likened to another object by speaking of it as if it were the other as in, 'The sun was a chariot of fire.' The word comes from the Greek. 'Meta,' beyond, over—and 'Pherein,' to carry.*[16]

In Reverse Speech, there are two categories of metaphors that "carry over or carry beyond," and give a greater description of a concept that a speaker is communicating.

Second Level reversals are operational and describe the effect of behavioral patterns, whereas Third Level reversals, which I'll discuss shortly, are structural and point to the root causes of these same behavioral patterns. Second Level reversals:

1. describe an emotion or a thought that's difficult to portray;
2. use one word in place of the many words that forward speech uses;
3. discuss topics that are below the level of consciousness; and
4. describe the operations and the effects of behavioral patterns.

Second Level reversals often represent emotional states or deep-seated feelings regarding an issue that's being discussed forward. They're basic and deal with raw issues, pleasure and pain, guilt and triumphs, strengths and weaknesses. They can give vast insight into the inner working of the mind.

I've categorized more than 300 common metaphors so far, many of which I've included in the Reverse Speech Dictionary at the back of this book. In the dictionary, I also discuss the metaphors possible meanings. I drew these conclusions after noting their appearance in similar situations in many instances. They shouldn't be considered conclusive, however, because the meanings of metaphors can vary from person to person depending on the situation at the time and on the individual's sociological heritage.

Here are some examples of Second Level reversals and some cases in which I've found them.

- **Naked** and **nude:** these are opposing words of intimacy. **Naked** usually indicates an openness or freedom whereas **nude** indicates the opposite: fear, shame, or unwanted exposure.
  Δ **My love is naked.**
  Δ **Who'll help me? I am nude.**
- **Face:** this word refers to the deep Self, or everything that people are.
  Δ **I'm glad to see your face.**
  Δ **I slept with you. Shared your face.**
- **Thirsty, hungry, food, water:** a common metaphor group that refers to emotional needs.
  Δ **Must escape. Who will help me, I'm thirsty.**
  Δ **I'm afraid to serve. Forget the food. Forget water.**
- **Program and sermon:** these words refer to behavioral conditioning.
  Δ **The program was a lot like murder.**
  Δ **I must reverse this sermon.**
- **Shoot, sword, warhead, spear:** another metaphor group that refers to the delivery or use of intense emotions.
  Δ **I have this selfish warhead.**
  Δ **He put a sword in my face.**
  Δ **Shot, I am. I was shot what I'm feeling.**
- **Ocean, surf, ship, reef, helm, weather:** a common metaphor group that refers to the human journey, people as sailors on a ship travelling the seas of life.
  Δ **I love this surf.**
  Δ **My ship has struck a reef.**
  Δ **I will take the helm.**
- Other common metaphors:
  Δ **serve (let me serve you)**
  Δ **Word (the Word is my guide)**
  Δ **power (you gave me power)**
  Δ **sin (this reef is sin)**
  Δ **wisdom (I need wisdom)**
  Δ **curse (I curse you)**
  Δ **music (this book is good music)**
  Δ **refund (love is a refund)**

Δ **force (I can feel a certain force)**
Δ **rape (I feel raped)**
Δ **snow (I need this snow)**

- Personal metaphors draw from an individual's personal life experiences. They describe emotions and issues that are similar to the ones currently being experienced. For example, I have a personal metaphor, **Melbourne**, the town where I fell in love with my first wife and where that love collapsed and died. When I use "Melbourne" in reverse, I'm talking about strong, mixed feelings of love, pain, and confusion.

Another example of a personal metaphor was from a client who often used the word **Pastor** in reverse, describing a rigid nature. The word came from a time when he had been the pastor of a church. Another client used the word **Hilda** to describe his conscience or a sense of guilt. Hilda was the woman who lived next door when he was a child and who often watched him play from her back door. Whenever he did something wrong, she'd tell his parents. Thus, **Hilda** became his metaphor for conscience.

The Third Level of Mind: The Collective Unconscious

Third Level reversals use exceptionally powerful metaphors that frequently describe the building blocks of the unconscious mind and represent the deepest, most significant levels. They describe the causes of behavior and the structure of the personality. For this reason, I call them "structural" metaphors, as opposed to operational metaphors, which describe behavioral patterns or the *effects* of structural metaphors.

Structural metaphors, or primordial images, which some people have compared to Jung's archetypes, are some of the more difficult reversals to understand. They draw upon stories that are rooted in historical facts or legends. They represent strong, primate forces within, which demand to be taken seriously.

Third Level reversals stem from the collective unconscious and traditionally describe complex behavioral patterns and personality structures. Reversals found in music frequently use Third Level reversals because of the intense right-brain hemispheric activity in music.

Third Level reversals occasionally use archaic language as the following examples show, which are among the more than 50 structural metaphors that I've documented to date.

- Here's a statement made at the beginning of a speech reversal session: "I'll ask you certain questions and lead [you along in such a way] that will promote reversals so we can find out what your unconscious is thinking." **Thou hast the knowledge.**

- A woman giving a friend some advice: "You've studied social work. Use, er, use it, er, [use what you learned there to sort it all through] and, um, don't get all screwed up by what's happening." **Hasten thine sword. It shall release thee.**

I'll now discuss some common structural metaphors and several situations in which I've found them.

Whirlwind

The most frequent structural metaphor, the word **Whirlwind** (a word commonly discussed in Jung's writings), often occurs in music and speech. Here are some examples.

- "Saturday Night Fish Fry," a Rhythm and Blues song released in 1949, by Louis Jordon: **Now the Whirlwind. Ah, The Garden of Eden. Seen the Mark. They send lil'le children there. See the Wolf annoyed.**

- "Chantilly Lace," released in 1958, by The Big Bopper: **The Lord God gave the Whirlwind and the thunder.**

- "The Battle of Evermore," by Led Zeppelin: **Time to fire the Whirlwind.**

- From a session in which a Reverse Speech analyst was encouraging a client to express his feelings: "What do you need to um, [need, well what do you want]? **Feel the Whirlwind.**

- A person discussing grief following the death of a friend: "[Well, er, the day my friend died I,] er, couldn't get out of bed." **I did curse against the Whirlwind.**

- A person talking about feeling restless: "I get very restless. I can't settle. I'm always [off around the world wishing it could last] forever." **Seems so clear, the Whirlwind on my feet.**

- A client who was having difficulty working: "I'm basically reasonably talented and [can do my work well, but why is there] this great stumbling block?" **Resolved my Whirlwind needs it.**

- A short example that displays obvious communication in the reversed dialogue:

Analyst: "You're feeling [this gap that's] not bridged." **She wants it.**

Client: "[Right.]" **Help.**

Analyst: "And [you're wanting it worked] out." **Wire into your Whirlwind.**

After becoming familiar with Carl Jung's theories, I began to research historical and religious literature to gain insight into the meaning of "Whirlwind." It is prolific in every culture throughout the ages.

Given **Whirlwind's** many forms of appearance, it's not surprising that **Whirlwind** is one of the most powerful and frequently occurring structural metaphors in Reverse Speech. Here are some examples of its appearances in literature and mythology:

- Biblical literature[17]
    Δ "Behold he goes up like clouds and his chariots like the Whirlwind are swifter than eagles. Woe to us for we are ruined." (Jeremiah 4:13.)
    Δ "It came about when the Lord was about to take up Elijah by a Whirlwind to heaven, that Elijah went with Elisha ..." (II Kings 2:1)
    Δ "He will sweep them away with a Whirlwind" (Proverbs 1:27.)
    Δ "Then the Lord answered Job out of the Whirlwind." (Job 38:1)
    Δ "For they have sown the wind, and they shall reap the Whirlwind." (Hosea 8:7a)
    Δ "It shall devour the palaces thereof, with shouting in the day of battle, with a tempest in the day of the Whirlwind." (Amos 1:14)

- Eastern religious literature
  Δ *The Songs of the South,* is a collection of ancient (241-233 B.C.E.) Chinese poetry. "Whirlwind" is mentioned as a force that's directly related to movement. The mention of a cloud, or clouds, is common to both the writings of the Chinese poet and the section quoted earlier from Jeremiah. Both sources also refer to chariots that are used for divine purposes.

  Open wide the door of heaven! On a black cloud I ride in splendor bidding the Whirlwind drive before me, causing the rainstorm to lay the dust. In sweeping circles my Lord is descending, let me follow you over the K'ung-sang mountain!

  See, the teeming peoples of the Ninelands; the span of their lives is in your hand! Flying aloft, he soars serenely, riding the pure vapor, guiding yin and yang, speedily, Lord I will go with you, conducting High God to the Height of heaven . . . He drives his dragon chariot thunder wheels.[18]

  Δ In the *Upanishads,* a major collection of Hindu scriptures, "Whirlwind" is described as possessing a power with the potential for destruction.

  Vayu ran towards him and Brahman asked:
  "Who are you?"
  "I am Vayu, the god of the air," he said, "Matarisvan, the air that moves in space."
  "What power is in you?" asked Brahman.
  "In a Whirlwind I can carry away all there is on earth."
  And Brahman placed a straw before him saying: "Blow this away."
  The god of the air strove with all of his power, but was unable to move it. He returned to the other gods and said: "I could not find out who was that being that fills us with wonder." (Kena Upanishad, Part 3)[19]

- Cultural references:[20]
  Δ **AFRICAN:** The tale of Ntotwatsan tells of a chief's daughter who was transported by a Whirlwind to the village of the Matelele.

△ **AUSTRALIAN ABORIGINES:** Two creator beings, Pundjel and Pallyan, were carried to the skies by a Whirlwind after they created the first human beings.

△ **CHINESE:** Yin Hung was saved from unjust execution by two immortals who transported him by a Whirlwind to a safe location on the mountain Tai Hua.

△ **LAPLAND:** The Lapps believed that Shamans could fly in the form of a Whirlwind.

△ **AMERICAN INDIAN:** The Whirlwind symbolizes the power of the Great Spirit.

△ **JAPAN:** Whirlwind is a thunder symbol that's associated with the ascending dragon.

△ **MODERN AMERICAN:** The most popular myth of this century has proven to be The Wizard of Oz. Its heroine is transported by a tornado, the **Whirlwind**, to the land of transformation.

So what is this mysterious **Whirlwind**? Is it the Life Force of nature, God, or something else? In Reverse Speech it appears frequently to describe the state of personal energy or well being. It's spoken about in such a way that it almost seems to be the very basis of existence.

People use **Whirlwind** under different circumstances in their reversals. For example, it will appear when some people are talking about work, when others are talking about depression, and when still others are talking about memories that come and go. It is also used to describe the varying reactions that people have to current experiences.

The significance of **Whirlwind** varies from person to person, and even in reversals from the same person at different times, but it will always depict a state of energy, positive or negative, that's unique to the individual's operating system.

William James' Whirlwind

William James, an early 20th Century author and researcher of the mind who was highly respected by Carl Jung, talks of a "transmarginal field" of consciousness that fluctuates in and out of consciousness, personal unconsciousness, and collective unconscious. His description of this field parallels the varying representations of **Whirlwind** as they appear in Reverse Speech.

> *It (the transmarginal field) helps both to guide our behavior and to determine the next movement of our attention. It lies around us like a 'magnetic field' inside of which our center of energy turns like a compass needle as the present phase of consciousness alters into its successor. Our whole past store of memories floats beyond this margin, ready at a touch to come in; and the entire mass of residual powers, impulses, and knowledge that constitute our empirical self stretches continuously beyond it.*[21]

Whatever **Whirlwind** is, or was, the unconscious mind has adopted it as a primary word, or structural metaphor, to describe energies, concepts, feelings, and perceptions that are difficult to put into words or would require too many.

Lucifer and Satan

These common structural metaphors are the ones that have caused so much controversy about "Satanic" messages in rock 'n' roll. They appear frequently in situations of emotional stress or in discussions that concern physical, emotional, mental or spiritual safety or well-being.

The belief in Satan and Lucifer is as old as civilization itself. Biblical accounts refer to Satan as having been the most beautiful of all of God's angels, possessing the keys to wisdom and beauty, until he sought equality with God and was cast out of Heaven (Ezekiel 28:1-19; Isaiah 14:3-21). Here are some examples of its occurrence in Reverse Speech:

- "Space Oddity" by David Bowie: **We can hear from Satan. Lucifer's here now.**
- "Thriller" by Michael Jackson: **We must live for Satan.**
- "Lightning in the Sky" by Santana: **Like a snake beast. I love Satan within.**
- A young man talks about an unwanted sexual encounter that caused him immense heartache: "I kissed her good night. I said, I really don't want to go. We kissed again [and then it was all over]." **On with Satan. I never make war.**

- A woman muses over past boyfriends: "He felt very uneasy about my husband and told me not to tell him. I said that's fine, you're [obviously going through a trauma]." **He's a boy. I love that. Full of Satan.**
- A man talks about intense feelings of anger that he was experiencing from someone: "I don't know. It doesn't make any sense. [There's just something in the air that I can't put my finger on.]" **It's sorcery. Can't shake it. I feel spell of Satan. New kind of assault.**

The Garden of Eden

In the Biblical account of creation in the Garden of Eden, Eve was deceived by the "snake" to eat from the Tree of Knowledge. Adam also ate of the tree and they became aware that they were "naked." Their nakedness turned to shame and rapidly became "nudity," so they covered themselves with fig leaves and tried to hide from the "face" of the Lord. Here are some examples of Garden of Eden reversals:

- "Anthem 84" by Kris Kristofferson: **Christ of Eden. I love him.**
- A woman talks about her quest for meaning in life: "There's something, but I've almost [given up trying to find it]." **I love the Garden of Eden.**
- A man talks of deception in a business relationship: "[I'm not too sure what to think.] What he's telling me just doesn't seem to add up." **I am Adam. Ate from the snake.**

Wolf

Wolf is a powerful structural metaphor in Reverse Speech. From the cases I've documented so far, **Wolf** appears to refer to that part of humans that is the prime behavioral motivator or the hunter and protector. **Wolf** as a reversal frequently appears in moments of high energy, or in times of protective behavior. Here are some examples:

- "Sympathy for the Devil" by The Rolling Stones: **I'm the angered Wolf.**

- A woman discussing destructive behavioral patterns and how she endeavors to overcome them: "[I decide what] my actions will be depending on my outcome. What I want to do. [I can keep going forward provided I stay on any one of my levels.]" **I am alone. / The Wolf now speaks with power. There is no other one.**
- A client requests further therapeutic help: "[Do you know someone who is very straight forward] as a psychiatrist who understands reversals?" **The Wolf is certain. You must help me.**

The Legend of King Arthur

I frequently document references to the folk heroes detailed in the Legend of King Arthur and the Knights of the Round Table—an extremely archetypal piece of literature. The most common of these reversals is the word **Lancelot,** which I frequently find on women. It appears to be a dream for a perfect man: **Are you my Lancelot? Lancelot hurt me with his spear.** Its counterpart on men is **Goddess,** or the dream for a perfect woman: **My Goddess will save me. She was a Goddess.**

Here's one reference to **Camelot** that I found on a man who was in the midst of despair as he pondered a life that he felt he'd wasted: **I lusted for the castle, Camelot.**

Broceliande

I have also found references to the forest of Broceliande—pronounced "Ros-el-ind." Broceliande was where the fairy Niniane, from the Netherland, imprisoned the magician Merlin. It was a haunted place still within the rule of the other world. Here Niniane charmed Merlin with her spells, and he sang to her the melodies that made his magic.

When Merlin finally finished singing, Niniane had all his secrets and was able to empty him of his powers. Then she trapped him in the castle of his own making until one day he escaped and roamed the land as a fool, no longer possessing his magic. Merlin, being beguiled by this beautiful fairy, had allowed her to rob him of his magic.[22]

Broceliande or **Roselind** is a structural metaphor that I've found on people who use those of the opposite sex for their own means. It puzzled me at first until I learned the legend and noticed the direct correlations. Here are some examples: **It's all for Roselind. Cursed enough, Roselind. Roselind tells me it. Roselind has deceived me.**

A Simulated Example of the Three Levels of Reverse Speech

To give you an idea of the different levels of Reverse Speech, I've simulated the story below. I tell it first in standard English, then retell it in three separate frameworks, the language of First, Second, and Third Level speech reversals.

The Story: A while ago I was walking in the park enjoying the sunshine, feeling really great when suddenly a mugger pounced on me. I screamed for help and a man came running to my aid. The mugger was startled and ran off into the distance. I collapsed onto the ground in shock, crying and shaking. The man carried me to a park bench and stayed with me while I calmed down. As I gradually recovered and looked at this man I felt instantly attracted to him. Later that night we went out to dinner. A few weeks later he proposed to me and now we're planning our wedding. I'm very grateful to John for saving me from the mugger, and I like him a lot. Marriage certainly seems like the logical thing to do.

First Level Reversals: It seems like yesterday. The trees looked nice, but the sun was too bright. What's that!? I'm afraid. Someone attacks. Help me! A man comes. He soothed me and he was nice. We saw each other again. He wants to marry me. Help! I don't want to get married.

Second Level Reversals: My ship is on the ocean. The surf is high. I have struck a reef. I see a rescuer. I like his face. He comforts and my heart is soft. Yet I fear. I have lost my helm.

Third Level Reversals: I am in Eden. The Whirlwind is high. Satan attacks. I'm bitten. Lancelot hast delivered. Am I now his slave?

Notice how economical metaphors are. Just as "a picture is worth a thousand words," an operational metaphor is also worth a thousand words—and a structural metaphor (an archetype) is worth several thousand more.

**The Levels of the Mind
and the Corresponding Categories of Reversals**

The First Level of Mind   **First Level Reversals**
Consciousness .... Literal words that often detail a person's conscious thoughts

The Second Level of Mind   **Second Level Reversals**
Personal Consciousness .... Operational Metaphors that describe complex behavioral patterns

The Third Level of Mind   **Third Level Reversals**
Collective Unconscious .... Structural Metaphors (arche-types), are primordial images, that describe the causes of behavior

---

Reverse Speech makes full use of all the levels of mind to help us to express ourselves more fully. But, it doesn't stop here. Reverse Speech further parallels Jung's work as evidenced by the process of oral tradition.

Oral Tradition

In Carl Jung's theory of the collective unconscious, he proposes that people have within them a storehouse of knowledge that contains the entire heritage of humankind. He suggests that this knowledge is born anew with each individual. In Reverse Speech many words appear that can't be explained by normal sociological environments, but rather seem to stem from humanity's deep and distant past. This may be explained by the theory of *The Process of Oral Tradition*.[23]

Reversed language seems to participate in handing down oral tradition from generation to generation. As people interact with each other on an unconscious level, they collect and store information obtained from family, peer groups, and associates. This collective knowledge is then incorporated into a storage bank deep within the psyche of the group. Finally, like a large communications link, the information is unconsciously relayed. Legends that were once stories told around the campfires of ancestors become a permanent part of the deep Self. Reverse Speech continues the handing down process long after conscious knowledge of the information has ceased.

Guess Who Came to Dinner

If the appearance of certain words or phrases in reverse cannot be explained by an individual's current sociological interactions or by his or her recent history, a discerning Reverse Speech analyst might look to another time in the past to explain the source of the reversals. For example, if mountain dwellers use reversals that contain desert images, one might wonder, if at some time in their history the mountain dwellers were visited by people from the desert—or lived in the desert themselves.

An enterprising researcher could trace a particular thread of reversals on a chosen group back into time and possibly solve previously unexplained historical events. This would be an ambitious project, but an exciting and immensely rewarding one. One such a project is currently being conducted by Reverse Speech Developer Greg Albrecht who is tracing the roots of Australian Aborigines by documenting and interpreting their reversals.

Modern Metaphors

Oral tradition may explain many modern metaphors, which seem to be inspired by public figures. For example, the word **Elvis** (Elvis Presley) is a metaphor that I hadn't found in any recordings that pre-date the 1980's. **Elvis** is a symbol, in reverse, for a superstar.

For example, I found **Elvis** on President George Bush as he announced that General Noriega had been captured. The reversal said, **Made me an Elvis,** which indeed it did. His popularity soared after Noriega's capture.

In addition, I've found cases in which the metaphor **Luther** (Martin Luther King), refers to racial prejudice.[24]

Shared Metaphors

Groups of friends and peer groups also tend to use similar metaphors. For example, a few months after I arrived in the United States to live, my friends and associates began to occasionally use Aussie slang in their reversals such as **mate, bloke,** and **she'll be right**. In a family with a strong Methodist background I found reversals spanning three generations that used the word **Methodist.**

Truth, Lies, and "Mind Reading"

Knowledge is sometimes passed on, in reverse, in single incidents. For example, a television interviewer challenged me to prove Reverse Speech and then lied about his age. He said, "I am 32 years of age. I am 32 years of age. I am 32 years of age." When I analyzed the recording, I found a reversal in that section of speech that said, **37, it came up,** which was indeed his correct age.

Shortly after in the conversation, I found a reversal on myself that said, **Now you're 37.** How had I known this information? I received it from his previous reversal. Note the process:

The reporter lies about his age and, at the same time, delivers a reversal that reveals his true age. I receive the reversal and unconsciously store the information. I then relay this information in the form of another reversal.

Have you ever known something, but had no idea how you got that knowledge? It's possible that you received the information through reversals contributed from the foundations of oral tradition.

Come, walk in the Garden, dance with Wolves, feel the Power, ride the Whirlwind of humanity—and know that we all share a Face.

7

The Intricacies of Speech

Language is not the abstract construction of the learned, or of dictionary makers, but it is something arising out of the work, needs, ties, joys, affections, tastes, of long generations of humanity, and has its bases broad and low, close to the ground. —Walt Whitman, 1819-1892

I frequently refer to forward speech as being under conscious control—that is, we choose *what* we say and *when* we say it. There are, however, many unconscious factors at play in the formation of speech. It's the *way* that we construct our sentences, words, and individual sounds that determines the verbal content of our reversed messages.

Forward speech is full of subtle intricacies, word changes, mispronunciations, pauses, stutters, tonal alterations, and fumbles of which people may not always be consciously aware. In fact, many intricate vocal alterations occur every minute of conversation.

In common social interactions, people regularly pause or stutter while they think about the words they want to use to communicate their ideas. They may even start to talk, then change their minds in mid-sentence, not wanting to communicate what they initially intended. Then, they escape the trap they set for themselves by changing the subject.

Language inconsistencies, most of which are beyond conscious control, allow the free expression of the real Self, giving rise to clearer and more frequent reversals, clusters of reversals, and the creative use of tenses.

When people try consciously to control their speech, they reduce these intricacies and, ultimately, their reversals. The less self-conscious that people are of themselves and what they're saying, however, the more these intricacies creep in, and the greater the frequency of reversals, cultural metaphors, and empathy with others. Consider the following simulated examples.

> **Example 1**: "[As, I, er, begin typing this book,] er, section—
> I feel [as though, um,] I don't really know what to, er,
> say, [sorry, I mean to type,] next."

A reversal may have occurred on the above section: "As, I, er begin typing this book" **What's the best way to start this section?**—end of reversal indicated by pauses—followed again by a flow in conversation. "I feel as though, as though, um." The speaker pauses again and struggles for words. A reversal could occur on, " . . . as though, um . . . " which might say, **I'm blocked.**

The speaker continues. "I don't really know what to er, say, sorry, I mean to type next." The speaker makes a mistake and immediately corrects it, often with rapid speech. A reversal might be found in the last phrase as it finally finds its form, "Sorry, I mean to type," which might say, **I finally got it out.**

> **Example 2**: "I went into Dallas today to see, [well, er,
> actually, it was a really nice day]. Not too hot and not
> too cold."

In this example, suppose that a businessman was at a party with friends. Earlier that day he went to Dallas to see an associate to make final arrangements for a new contract. He was anxious about the contract and aware that his apprehensions would appear if he continued the sentence. He realizes that it wouldn't be appropriate to discuss this matter in the current casual setting, so he abruptly stops in mid-sentence and changes the subject.

This is the perfect setting for a reversal. What a person thinks, but decides not to say, must, nevertheless, be released. The unconscious mind, therefore, subtly alters speech patterns and releases the unspoken thought via a speech reversal. A possible reversal in this example might be, **Associate. Contract. I feel uneasy.**

For a second the businessman's friends feel his uneasiness as he expresses his reversal, but then he immediately changes the topic to the weather and re-establishes the flow of conversation. The businessman now relaxes as he begins the new topic.

Ideal Conditions for Reversals to Occur

The more relaxed that people are, the more expressive they tend to become. They easily share their feelings and feel more in tune with their inner creativity. As this happens, the boundary opens between the conscious and the unconscious mind. Intuition increases, the "Face" is more fully expressed, and the "Self" is set free. Thus, to sigh, moan, laugh, cry, stammer, and pause while speaking is as important to a person as eating and sleeping. These activities allow the Reverse Speech process to follow its natural course, continually expressing dreams and ideals, and releasing tension.

The small, often unnoticed, intricacies of speech are ideal settings for reversals. Here are some examples from sessions that I conducted with clients:

Pauses and Stumblings

- An artist discussing his work: "But somehow I have to free myself to work with a brilliance I believe I have, but which can be inhibited in the process of trying to be, (pause—quick insert) [being subconscious in,] (pause) moving it out." **This is not close to evil.**
- A man recognizes his tensions as the conversation reaches a peak: "I want both! That's, [that's somehow,] er, it's like I'm, I'm not [using] all the resources at my disposal." **I am upset. / He's angry.**

Laughter, Sighs, and Faint Speech

- The two children of a woman who'd recently separated from her husband, their father:

   Seven year old, laughing and speaking to the mother: **You oughta kiss him Mum.**

   Three year old, crying: **David scares me. I want our Daddy.**

Three year old, mumbling: **I miss my little pony, my little pony, my little pony."**
(This reversal, found on the three year old who never had a pony, is probably a personal metaphor that refers to security or to Dad as a playmate.)
- A woman talks of her marriage's pending breakup: "[—Cries—I love too much—Deeper cries—.] That's why this is happening." **Look at, look at me. Why does he forget me?**

Dialogue Alterations

It's common for a speaker to start a conversation, then stop in mid-sentence and change the subject. This is a perfect place to find reversals, which, ironically, often discuss the topic that the speaker wanted to discontinue.

- A man who greatly resents being excommunicated from a church talks of finding a church that will accept him: "Why I react to the churches is that, you know, we get involved and er, um, (pause) [probably this is hitting it on the head]. Er, (slight pause and speech rapidly increases in speed) I mean what I'm saying is, let's look at different churches where to go." **Believer who leaves, you should not hate him.**

Notice how the man begins to explain his reaction to the church, then pauses and stumbles, and begins to discuss different churches. The First Level reversal addresses the real issue, which he didn't say forward. He pauses immediately after the reversal, and continues to talk about the same subject from a different direction.

- A woman discusses financial hardships: "That's how I've been supporting myself, which is ridiculous. What I want is, er, um, (pause) [I just can't survive on that anymore and I,] er, (pause) just for pure survival I have to start to get at least a small amount of money." **I like money. Want to get in rolls.**

The First Level reversal shows her true motives. She starts to say it in, "What I want is," but stops herself, pauses, delivers the reversal in a quick forward section of dialogue, pauses again, then softens her desire.

- A segment of a *60 Minutes* interview with TV evangelist, Jim Bakker prior to his trials. At the end of the interview, he says: "No matter what I do, I won't please the critics. And so to survive I do what I have to do to pay the bills. And if I . . . (he pauses shortly, then changes dialogue) . . . Someone once said to me, why don't you give free food to everyone? (Quick pause, tone increases markedly.) [Do you realize how long the lines would be?]" **I want my salary.**

Notice the change in dialogue as he addresses an issue that's obviously strong in his mind. The reversal releases the predominate motivation shrouded in the self-justification of forward speech.

Quick Inserts Into Conversations

Inserting quick comments or interjections into the conversations of others is common. These little inserts often contain quick, subtle speech reversals.

- A couple at a turning point of their marriage:

   Husband: "If we are to get out of the mire then we both have to change."

   Wife: (quick insert) "[Yeah, I know.] **Will you wait for me?** The reversal voices her real unspoken concern.

   Husband: "It's got to be done and we'll do it together."

- A woman who recently suffered a mental collapse:

   Analyst: "That's what breakdowns are all about."

   Woman: (quick insert) "[Oh bother breakdowns]!" **Nightmare. They won't go.**

   Analyst: "[—Laughter—] [Four years from now, you'll look at this and say I'm glad it all happened.]" **Shit. / Anger is a bastard I see often.**

Straight Dialogue

Reversals also can occur in sentences in which the speakers don't pause or stammer, but in which there may be other contributing factors such as a strong conscious or unconscious thought or desire, or a change in pitch.

- When I was trying to quit smoking in 1987, I was discussing my initial experiments in how to modify a reversing machine, and I was staring at a pack of cigarettes, trying to resist temptation: "... and if you want to slow it down, you just get a flat battery, take out the good battery and put a flat one in and it will just [go a bit slower]." **Oh, cigarette.**

The pace of the forward dialogue rapidly increased at the point my reversal occurred. My forward tone was sharp and crisp, and the reversed tone was one of intense desire.

- George Bush on the campaign trail, prior to his election to the Presidency: "I'm the one who says that the drug dealer who is responsible for the death of a policeman should be [subjected to capital punishment]." He raises his voice and shouts, reaching a peak where the reversal occurs: **That's enough for the market.** The crowd cheers and applauds wildly.

- Australian news reader, Clive Robertson, during a half hour TV interview, in which very few clear reversals occur except for this one section when he was asked about his years in radio: "I did, [I've done radio for 22 years. Radio assumes] the perfect audience." **Miss radio. They used me up. They don't love me.** There was a strong emphasis on the word "assumes."

Clarity of Reversals and Checking Factors

Analysts must take meticulous care to assure the existence, accuracy, and content of every reversal. I recommend the following guidelines.

1. Is the syllable count of the entire phrase correct? Example: If the reversal was "This/is/an/ex/am/ple" there would be six definite syllables.

2. Are the spaces sufficient between each word, so that each word is clearly distinguishable from the other words in the reversal?

3. Are the beginnings and endings of words clearly defined and distinguishable?

4. Are the vowel sounds in each syllable clear and precise?

5. Is the reversed phrase distinct from the surrounding gibberish?

6. Does the entire phrase have a continuous, melodious tonal flow, from beginning to end?

Validity Factors

If a reversal meets all the above criteria, I document it with confidence. Due to the fluctuating nature of reversals in different conversational settings, however, I sometimes find reversals that are clear, but which don't meet all the check points. I, therefore, use a scale to indicate the reversal's validity. I call these "reversals with reduced clarity" and rate them on a scale from 1-5, according to the factors below. I rarely document reversals that have less than a "Rating Two."

Rating Five: All six checking points are in play and the reversal is very clear and precise.
"Gibberish - **This is an example** - Gibberish"

Rating Four: The reversal fulfills all the check points except one, which may be imprecise. There may be, for example, poor tonal construction or stunted phonetic construction—that is, the first half of "Example" may be long and drawn out and the last half may be short and sharp.
"Gibberish—**This is an exa-a—a-ample**—Gibberish"

Rating Three: There are some doubts over any *one* of check points 1, 3, or 4 *and* some doubts over any *one* of check points 2, 5, or 6. The reversal may not be distinct from gibberish, some words may run together and/or have disjointed phonetic construction. If all other check points are present, then the reversal may be rated as "3."
"Gibberish **This isan ex-a-a-a-ample**Gibberish"

Rating Two: There's some doubt over aspects of *only one* of check points 1, 3, and 4 and some doubt over any *two* of check points 2, 5, or 6. There may be an extra syllable that can be explained as random noise. It's common to often find an 's' between words *or* the ending of one of the words is imprecise (after repeated listening it is difficult to tell whether there is an 's' on the end of IS or an 'a' at the beginning of *an)* or a consonant or vowel sound is indistinct.

"Gibberish **This z inanex-a-a-a-ample**Gibberish"

Rating One: The reversal is barely recognizable inside the gibberish. There are some doubts over any *two* of check points 1, 3, and 4, and *two* of check points 2, 5, or 6. Exercise great caution in documenting a rating one. It may be "projected" gibberish.

"Gibberish**Thiz iss ab esampel**Gibberish"

The Zone of Interaction

Figure Four shows the factors involved in the varying clarity ratings or "Validity Factors" of Reverse Speech, and the three levels in which they appear.

"The Zone of Interaction" signifies that place within the mind where mental influences, "pulses" or "waves," enter the language formation processes in such a way that phonetic patterns are influenced to form reversals. The clarity and frequency of reversals is described as depending on the intensity of these "influences."

When speech reversals have a Clarity Rating of 1 or 2, or their rate of occurrence is low, the mental influences are minimal. When the reversal has a clarity rating of 5, or the rate of occurrence is high, the influences are strong.

Clusters of Reversals

Speech reversals frequently appear in a group "clusters" bunched together in a space of only a few seconds. In these instances the reversals usually relate to each other and should be considered as a whole, or each reversal should be considered as an intricate part of the entire picture.

I found the following reversals in a session with a psychotherapist and her patient. The therapy session centered around the patient's ability to relate to her husband and her feelings of being trapped in her marriage. Her reversals directly related to the issue at hand. The therapist, on other hand, had reversals that spoke of her grief and confusion following the recent death of her son, Peter.

Figure Four: The Zone of Interaction

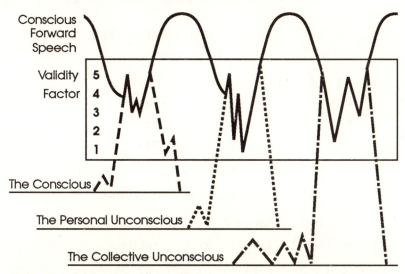

Conscious Forward Speech

Validity Factor

| 5 |
| 4 |
| 3 |
| 2 |
| 1 |

The Conscious

The Personal Unconscious

The Collective Unconscious

〜〜〜 **Conscious Forward Speech:** What you hear when you speak.

− − − − **The Conscious:** Generates first level reversals (e.g. information and commands) which are about 20% of all reversals.

· · · · · · · · · · **The Personal Unconscious:** Generates second level reversals (e.g. feelings) which are about 45% of all reversals.

−·−·−·· **The Collective Unconscious:** Generates third level reversals (e.g. archetypes having great impact on behavior) which are about 35% of all reversals.

Below are the reversals from one section of this session in the order they occurred, together with the exact time that each reversal appeared in the conversation. I've separated each cluster with line breaks, which are figured by determining the average reversal occurrence in the conversation, in this case one reversal every 25 seconds. I considered reversals that occurred less than 20 seconds apart as an individual cluster.

#1   33:49 - Patient: **I'm the one who he loves.**

#2   34:25 - Patient: **The force is not such a heavy wisdom.**

#3   36:55 - Patient: **I do not wish to shoot.**
#4   37:01 - Patient: **With someone.**

#5   37:58 - Therapist: **We promised Peter. No we didn't.**
#6   38:03 - Therapist: **We saw Peter.**
#7   38:07 - Therapist: **Peter. I feel shame.**
#8   38:15 - Therapist: **Peter. You must leave.**

#9   38:50 - Therapist: **I give in.**
#10 38:55 - Therapist: **I don't need him.**

#11 40:10 - Patient: **See my rotten sin.**
#12 40:20 - Therapist: **You do not need to shoot.**

Note the entire reversed trend can be viewed in detail through a knowledge of the clusters:

1. Reversals #1 and #2 are isolated reversals on the patient showing issues with which she is dealing in her marriage (**force** relates to male/female support dynamics).

2. Reversals #3 and #4, also on the patient, are in a cluster with each reversal directly connected to each other—**I do not wish to shoot** (or have intense emotions) / **With someone.**

3. Reversals #5, #6, #7, and #8, on the therapist, are in a significant cluster of four reversals in 15 seconds, which is a tight cluster considering the average reversal occurrence of one every 25 seconds. Note the trend in the cluster. All reversals speak of her son. They show confusion as she still wrestles with her grief, and the last reversal—**Peter. You must leave**—shows her trying to clear her mind of the issue, so she can be effective in the counseling situation.

4. Reversals #9 and #10 are also in a cluster that occurred 35 seconds later and show that the therapist has cleared her mind of the personal issue.

5. Reversals #11 and #12, occurring in a cluster 75 seconds later, then center back on the task at hand and show quick therapeutic exchanges between the therapist and her patient. Note how reversal #12 directly deals with an issue brought up by the patient in reversal #3.

Clusters can reveal a wealth of information when an analyst is trying to determine the significance of vague or imprecise reversals. Reversed phrases that use non-specific terms such as, **It feels bad** (What feels bad?), **I want some** (I want what?), **You must not do that** (Who is "you," what is "that"?), and **Do it** (Do what?), should always be considered with the entire cluster. Frequently the cluster reveals the significance of the non-specified reference.

Categories of Reversals

Speech reversals appear in many styles and forms, all of which are complementary. Complementarity, however, appears in many categories. By examining each reversal and determining its category, an analyst can gain a greater understanding of the nature of the complementarity and, consequently, its significance. For example:

1. Is the reversal congruent with the forward message, or incongruent?
2. Does the reversal communicate extra information?
3. What extra insights does the reversal reveal?
4. Is the reversal internally or externally directed?

Here are some of the more common Reverse Speech categories followed by a simulated example, then an example that I've taken from my notes.

1. **Congruent reversals** confirm the content of the forward dialogue:
   "I like this book very much." **I really enjoy the book.**
   "I don't like being me. I don't like being this person. [I've become horrible.]" **In me a madman.**
2. **Expansive reversals** add information to the forward dialogue:
   "I like this book very much." **I am learning new information.**

"When I had my breakdown, [my wife left with my kid and I] lost everything. I had to leave the country." **I saw my filth and I ran with it**.

3. **Incongruent reversals** contradict what's said forward:
"I like this book very much." **I hate the book**.
"I feel and help other people. [I have all my life. I'm a teacher] and I can teach and teach well. I'm not an [educated teacher] but I do it personally." **I am all my hell. I cannot teach. / I am a shit**.

4. **External Dialogue** contains a communicative signal to another person:
"I like this book very much." **You should read it, too**.
"That's not really the point. I mean, er [the standard lines I throw out are a] bit like that." **You're all right, lovely person**.

5. **Internal Dialogue** reflects inner-thought processes of individuals who are talking to themselves or giving themselves instruction:
"I like this book very much." **I must learn more about this**.
"[Can you tell me more about your women and other affairs?]" **I will accost this loud bully**.

6. **Lead and Trail reversals** appear either before a topic is discussed in forward dialogue or continue with a forward topic after the discussion has stopped:
". . . discussion on Reverse Speech . . . conversation changes . . . [I bought a new car today.]" **Reverse Speech will change society**.
"It's just all built up. All these emotions and I've never worked [through any of them]." **Who are all my friends?** Conversation changes shortly after to a discussion about friends.

7. **Mirror Image[1] reversals** in which the same word, or set of words, appears at either end of a forward and reversed statement, but are not a reversal of each other:
"I like this book very much." **I enjoy reading very much**.
"Well then, he [should produce that letter]." **I want to see that letter**.

8. **Sentence Building reversals,** in which the forward and reversed dialogue combine to form a complete thought or sentence:

    "I like this book very much." **And I will tell all my friends about it.**

    "[I think Sir Joh] is going to have a bit to answer for at the end of this week." **Must be senile.**

    Note: I think Sir Joh / **must be senile.**

9. **Comparative reversals** discuss events and/or emotions that are outside the topic of the forward dialogue. They have no complementarity with the actual topic that's being discussed, but they have complementarity with the emotional content. They often reveal an event or a belief in a person's life, past or present, that has similar emotions attached to it:

    "I like this book very much." **I made love to my wife last night.**

    "[Prayers and amens and formalizations.] That's all we got, no support. How was that supposed to help us!" **Pete Jones. He's still the rival.**

    (Intense anger in forward dialogue. Identical emotions in reverse towards someone in this person's life.)

10. **Cause and Effect reversals** frequently use two statements that are related to each other, separated either by a long pause, suggesting a period, or a short pause, suggesting a comma. The first reversal will state a fact or an event. The second reversal will state the cause of that fact or event.

    I feel afraid, mission.

    Information. Demon scared by us.

    Mask is enough. Makes me nude.

    Lancelot. Help me. You're oxygen.

11. **Link reversals** are rare and occur between two people who are in high rapport and when something that's being said by one is suddenly understood by the other, or when both parties instantly connect on an idea. The forward dialogue responsible for the reversal comes from the last words of the first speaker's sentence and the first words

of the second speaker's sentence. Sometimes the reversal appears to be in one voice even though two different people are responsible for the reversal. This is particularly noticeable when the two speakers are a man and a woman.

The illusion of a single voice occurs as a result of the two speakers matching each other's voice tones at the precise moment of their highest rapport.

Person One: "Reverse Speech is the voice of the [inner mind"—
Person Two: "—Oh. I finally] understand."
LINK REVERSAL—**"Looking at the deep self."**
Teacher: "It's to do with [intense emotion."
Client: "—Right.]"
LINK REVERSAL: **Love will show the snake.**
(Conversation was explaining the significance of the reversed metaphor, **shoot,** in a deceptive relationship situation. The Link reversal occurred at the moment of realization.)

Tenses

The tense of a reversal is extremely important and a very subtle indication of the continuum of issues appearing in reverse. These issues may be past and affecting the present, may represent present patterns, or reveal the extent to which a present pattern will affect future events. The subtle value of tense becomes increasingly important at deeper levels of consciousness, where the time-space continuum is most radically influenced by the vastness of information accessible.

Past Tense: Indicates a pattern ended, or a past event affecting the present.
I lost it, my wisdom.
It was my devil.
Love my family. I knew this.
My love was forcing him.

Present Tense: Indicates current patterns, events, or wisdom.

I must admit the Wolf defeats.

Still serving the Master.

I am demon with power.

Future Tense: Indicates what will happen if action isn't taken to prevent it or to change the established pattern.

I'm done in the eye. I will shake it in the eye.

Look out. I shall piss off.

I will spear you.

Developing Detailed Reversal Analysis

So far, we've discussed the common factors and forms of Reverse Speech:

- Clarity of reversals and validity factors
- Complementarity of Reverse Speech
- The communicative nature of Reverse Speech
- The three levels of Reverse Speech
- Conditions under which reversals occur
- Clusters of reversals
- Categories of reversals
- Tenses

All of these factors play an essential role in developing a detailed analysis of the reversals in a conversation. By understanding these factors in combination, it's possible to draw extremely accurate conclusions as to what transpired both on a conscious and unconscious level.

Below is the complete transcript and analysis, forward and reversed, of a conversation with my former wife, Naomi, a few months before we separated. Notice how the reversals add information to the forward dialogue. Also note the differing levels as our emotions and personal issues come and go. I've documented the clarity, or validity factor, of each reversal on a scale of 1-5, with 5 being the most clear.

> David: "Is it on? Yes it is. Right I'm sitting here in my study with my wife. Say hello Naomi."
>
> Naomi: "—laughter—"

David: "I'm sorry. Right. I've got to switch out of Reverse Speech session mode."

Naomi: "No, you do that anyway. But that's not the issue here."

David: "I'd better be careful, it might all come out backward, and I'll have to publish it anyway."

Naomi: "You don't have to [publish all of this.]"
Reversal rated 3: **I'm nude. You might be mad.**
(Second Level, Expansive, reveals *why* all of it did not have to be published.)

David: "[Hey, why not?]"
Rated 5: **Don't worry.**
(First Level, External Dialogue, reassurance.)

Naomi: (joking) "In case things like 'fuck' come up, or 'you're a bastard.'"

David: "What we're doing here, folks, is to just make up a, er, well I'm just making up a tape [to, er, give you a brief idea of how to interpret it.]"
Rated 3-4: **I feel for you. The first, this is.**
(First Level, External Dialogue, the first time I had put Naomi on the spot to create a tape for analysis.)

David: (voice varies in pitch considerably during long laughter, almost wobbly) "Naomi doesn't want [to talk]."
Rated 4: **Curse to the devil.**
(Second Level, External Dialogue, an attempt to release the free flow of conversation.)

Naomi: "I didn't know it was my time."

David: "It's just a natural conversation."

Naomi: "I shouldn't be getting nervous about this, but I have to get, [well, see but everyone, when,] when the tape recorder gets turned, er, everyone's got this natural reaction [to, sort of - deep breath] - close up."
Rated 3: **Now we've met. The Whirlwind is here.**
(Third Level, Internal Dialogue, recognition of connection established.)
Rated 4: **And it scares me.**
(First Level, Internal Dialogue.)

David: "Are you hoping a reversal's going to come up on that?"

Naomi: "No, I wasn't. I was just commenting on people's reaction to tape recorders. They close up. So you have to account for that."

David: (frustrated) "Yeah I know they do. [Well, see, yeah.]"
Rated 3-4: **They're so weird.**
(First Level, Internal Dialogue.)

Naomi: "I mean, [after a while]—voice fades out—"
Rated 3-4: **All will smile.**
(First Level, Sentence Builder.)

David: "I should detail that in the book."

Naomi: "After a while its all right, it doesn't matter, but the initial er, ok, the tape recorder's on now, okay, I think it er, [throws you a bit]."
Rated 3-4: **And it helps us.**
(First Level, Sentence Builder.)

David: "Yeah. I think it does."

Naomi: "I mean, it's like, er, [it does something]."
Rated 5: **What's hurting me.**
(First Level, Internal Dialogue.)

David: "I understand. Most of these should be First Level reversals. How can we get some Third Level stuff, Second Level stuff?"

Naomi: "We could talk dirty."

David: (laughing) "No. We can't do that. Let's try to get some Second Level reversals."

Naomi: (affectionately) "We could talk about [Bill—

David: "—Bill, yeah.] I just thought about that."
Link Reversal, rated 5: **I knew his need.**
(First Level, Link reversal, David's and Naomi's voice tones match, an immediate connection.)

Naomi: "Or Graham, that's something that's dramatic. But, er, [we don't want that published.] So, er, we could talk about, [I know, Susan!]"
Rated 4-5: **He won't ever like it.**

(First Level, Expansive.)

Rated 4- 5: **She raped me**

(Second Level, Expansive, **rape** indicates unwanted intrusion.)

David: "No. I'm definitely not publishing that. We'll change all the names on this incidentally."

Naomi: {Sings a long sarcastic song about Susan.} I want to see the reversals that come out on that."

David: "Of course. How long have we been recording?"

Naomi: "No, no. Don't stop yet. Keep going. None of this stuff. Let's, let's, [let's have a,] er, [let's have a proper,] I mean talk sensibly..."

Rated 2-3: **The Wolf sings**

(Third Level, Trail reversal, strong feelings concerning Susan still appear.)

Rated 2-3: **That scares my makeup. Some person.**

(Second Level, Trail.)

Naomi: "... to get some decent reversals then you can pick it, pick [it up and take it off where you wish]..."

Rated 3: **Shamed me. You fought against me**

(Second Level, Trail reversal, feelings concerning Susan still appear.)

Naomi: "... The exercise of this taping session is to give, (pause) [er, an example of reversals.]"

Rated 3: **It'll serve them more**

(Second Level, Expansive, back to the task at hand.)

David: (correcting grammar) "The purpose of this session."

Naomi: "Yes, the purpose. The purpose of this taping session (laughter)."

David: (laughing) "Yeah, well, honestly, Naomi, I think there should be enough there to, er, [to give plenty of examples. It'll be fine.]"

Rated 3-4: **Not run now. Man giving the fig.**

(Third Level, External dialogue, reassurance.)

Naomi: "[But, it's all jumbled] and mumbled."

Rated 4: **Hold me closer.**

(First Level, External dialogue.)

David: "That's fine. No problems."

Here are the reversals in order they occurred, together with their clusters. Notice how an entire reversed conversation transpired and how the reversals in clusters relate directly to each other. The length of the conversation was 4 minutes, 34 seconds. There were 19 reversals, an average of one reversal per 14 seconds, normal for this type of casual conversation.

00:41 - Naomi: **I'm nude. You might be mad.**

00:43 - David: **Don't worry.**

01:02 - David: **I feel for you. The first, this is.**

01:05 - David: **Curse to the devil.**

01:20 - Naomi: **Now we've met. The Whirlwind is here.**

01:29 - Naomi: **And it scares me.**

01:53 - David: **They're so weird.**

01:57 - Naomi: **All will smile.**

02:09 - Naomi: **And it helps us.**

02:24 - Naomi: **What's hurting me.**

03:08 - Link: **I knew his need.**

03:12 - Naomi: **He won't ever like it.**

03:16 - Naomi: **She raped me.**

03:39 - Naomi: **The Wolf sings.**

03:41 - Naomi: **That scares my makeup. Some person.**

03:47 - Naomi: **Shamed me. You fought against me.**

04:08 - Naomi: **It'll serve them more.**

04:20 - David: **Not run now. Man giving the fig.**

04:23 - Naomi: **Hold me closer.**

Once you know the clusters, categories, and level of each reversal, you can prepare a session overview. Here's my overview of the above transcript.

Defenses are Raised and Lowered

"Naomi's" discomfort with the surprise taping session had her on-guard and her defenses were quickly revealed in her reversals (**I'm nude, you might be mad**). I then provided a reversed reinforcement (**Don't worry**). The reversal was a command apparently attempting to open the conversation. From knowledge of our personal patterns of reversals, it would not be inappropriate to conclude that the command (**Curse to the devil**) was an attempt to demand at an unconscious level that she lower her defenses. We connected and our conversation began to flow freely (**Now we've met / The Whirlwind is here**).

Fears are Discussed, Concerns Handled

We discussed the actual process of recording a session and I expressed frustration over people freezing up (**They're so weird**). Naomi immediately addressed my fears both consciously and unconsciously with Sentence Building reversals (**All will smile / And it helps us**). All concerns now dispensed and the conversation continued. Naomi unconsciously questioned herself, (**What's hurting me**) and suggestions were subsequently made.

Personal Issues Become Obvious

The following issues were raised:

- A friend about whom we were both concerned (**I knew his need**). This issue was immediately rejected both forward and backward (**He won't ever like it**).
- A strong, personal issue for Naomi (**She raped me**). Consciously, it was rejected, but unconsciously, the feelings were released. It had appeared and now had to be dealt with. This was achieved with Trail reversals in a cluster (**The Wolf sings. / That scares my makeup. Some person. / Shamed me. You fought against me**).

With these feelings released, Naomi switched to the task at hand (**It'll serve them more**). I received her feelings and offered support (**Not run now. Man giving the fig**). She accepted this support (**Hold me closer**), and I switched the tape player off with a final forward closing comment: "That's fine. No problems."

With Reverse Speech, it's possible to see the bi-level communication process in action. Both conscious and unconscious needs, desires and emotions appear and are addressed continually while people interact with each other on all levels. The above was only a five-minute interaction. Longer sessions yield an even greater wealth of information.

Prompting Speech Reversals

The role of a Reverse Speech analyst is to uncover information, whether helpful facts, repressed memories, or causes of behavior. An analyst can affect the frequency of a client's reversals and prompt reversals that relate to specific issues by taking the following factors into account. Here are some highlights of the technique of prompting, a complicated process that ultimately needs to be experienced under the auspices of a Reverse Speech instructor, or a Reverse Speech analyst, to be understood fully.

Frequency

Because reversals frequently occur when people are relaxed, if an analyst keeps the conversation flowing, allows a client little time to prepare answers, and encourages emotional responses, the client's rate of reversals will be higher.

Content

Since reversals are complementary, an analyst can prompt reversals about a particular topic by having the client talk about that topic.

1. Discussions about the events in a client's life usually produce First Level reversals that reveal additional facts and information.
2. Discussions about a client's emotions usually produce Second Level reversals that relate to those emotions, giving greater emphasis to them.
3. Discussions about a client's behavioral patterns usually produce Third Level reversals that may give the causes for those patterns.

Clients who talk about their past or present emotions tend to use reversals that address those emotions. The reversals may add information to what the client is saying forward, or may detail the cause of those emotions. This can be valuable information for an analyst who wants to determine the source of certain behavior patterns.

Related Events

Clients who talk about past or present events in their lives can produce reversals that reveal *other* events that happened about that time, or which are happening in the present. This can help an analyst to uncover facts that the client may not want to reveal, or may not be able to remember consciously, but which can help significantly in the therapy process.

General Questions that Prompt Reversals

Analysts can ask the following kinds of questions to prompt reversals.

1. When did the client first notice the unwanted behavior?
2. What events were happening in their lives at the time the behavior began?
3. How does this behavior effect their current lives?
4. What are the symptoms of their unwanted behavior?
5. How do they feel about it?
6. What can they do to change it?
7. What do they get out of the unwanted behavior? How does it benefit them?
8. What advantages or benefits will they enjoy if they achieve the positive behavior that they want?

Questions along this line can produce many excellent reversals that often reveal causes of the unwanted behavior, how it occurs, how it serves the client, what its purpose is, and what people can do to change it.

Using Various Sensory Modes

A Reverse Speech analyst, by working within specific sensory systems, can also influence the types of reversals obtained:

1. **Visual**. Questions such as "What did you see when it happened?" "Can you give me the big picture?" "How did it look?" or, "Can you focus on that concept?" encourage clients to use visual terms. This tends to produce First and Second Level reversals that reveal facts, events, and extra information.

2. **Kinesthetic/Feeling**. Using "feeling" terms such as "How do you feel about that?" or, "How did it grab you?" encourages clients to go into greater depth about their feelings and to be more emotional. This tends to produce Second and Third Level reversals that reveal emotions and behavioral patterning.

   Patience is essential when clients have trouble articulating their feelings. Ironically, this difficulty in expressing themselves can give rise to many reversals.

3. **Auditory/Verbal**. Using auditory terms such as "I hear you," "That sounds right to me," and, "Can you hear what I'm saying?" encourages clients to respond in auditory terms. This approach tends to reduce the quantity of reversals, though it will produce reversals from all three levels of mind.

It is sometimes good to start a session in auditory terms since this approach produces an "across the board" reaction. Once you've established rapport with a client, switch to other sensory modes as key issues begin to surface.

Prompting Techniques and Investigations

Prompting can be a powerful tool for official investigations—and for "unofficial" investigations, as the following example illustrates.

A Reverse Speech analyst in Australia once suspected that his girlfriend was cheating on him. He spoke to her using visual-prompting techniques and encouraged her to talk in general about her week. Her reversals included some extra pieces of information that she'd left out in her casual conversation with him—they gave a detailed description of her affair, including names and places and, even revealed in reverse, in explicit detail, how the condom was put on.

An Example of Specific Prompting Questions

The following are some of my prompting questions taken from a session conducted with a client who had a weight problem. Questions like these usually produce precise reasons and causes for any problem and often include ways to rectify it:

What do you want to discuss?

A weight session. (Active listening, repeat client's answer.)

Why do you think you're fat?

Why do you use the word "fat"?

Is that based on your perception or on other people's perceptions? According to whom?

When did you first begin to put on weight? (Return to the source.)

When did you start to put on weight?

When did you start to think that you were overweight?

Adolescence? About what age?

What was going on in your life at that time?

Do you think you have a naturally big build or is it, you know? (Asking for specifics.)

So, what attempts have you made in the past to lose weight?

What is that resistance? Do you have any idea?

How much sense does that make?

Why haven't you thought of that before? What's stopped you from ...

How come? I always get suspect when I hear people have done a lot of work and it's still there. (A judgement call.)

How would you know? At what state would you know when you could lose weight and keep it off? (Asking for specifics.)

Could "thin" be a metaphor? Could it mean something other than "thin" in terms of weight?

What's there to think about?

Since you've used the word "have to" at least a half dozen times, what's the significance of that?

Listening to the Voice of the Inner Mind

Complementarity
1. Human speech has two distinctive and complementary functions and modes.
   - The Overt Mode is spoken forwards and constructed by conscious, cognitive processes.
   - The Covert Mode is spoken simultaneously with the Overt Mode, is a reversal of the forward speech sounds, and is constructed by automatic, cognitive processes.
2. These two modes of speech are dependent upon each other. They form an integral part of communication, both modes of speech communicate the total psyche of a person—conscious and unconscious.
3. The process of language development in children starts backwards before it does forwards. Children first develop the Covert Mode of communication and then, as Overt speech begins, these two modes gradually combine into one, forming a bi-level communication process.

Oral Tradition
Collective knowledge, stored within the psyches of a group, is communicated, through reversals, to people within the group and to their descendants.

Ideal Conditions for Reversals to Occur
Pauses, Stumbles, Laughter, Sighs, and Faint Speech
Dialogue Alterations and Inserts
Straight Dialogue Fueled by Strong Desires

Clarity of Reversals
Correct syllable count, sufficient space between words
Well-defined beginnings and endings of words
Clear, precise vowel sounds, distinct from gibberish, melodious

Categories
Congruent, Expansive, Incongruent
Cause and Effect, External or Internal Dialogue
Lead and Trail, Mirror, Sentence Building
Comparative, Link

Encouraging the Stories

Since the human mind contains the collective unconscious in addition to everything that has happened to us personally since birth, the human mind must be all inclusive and, most likely, has access to infinite creative combinations. Reverse Speech gives us a means to access that immense storehouse of knowledge, both personal and collective.

Reverse Speech analysis can uncover vast amounts of helpful information. For example, people who suffer from unwanted behavior such as low self-motivation may want to discover the causes of that behavior and find out from their unconscious, innate intelligence what they can do to remedy it. Since their unconscious mind already has all the answers, all that the experienced Reverse Speech analyst has to do is to lead the conversation in such a way that these answers appear in reversals.

Human beings are naturally expressive. In our desire to be accurate when we communicate, or to avoid saying what we really feel, we jockey for the correct words to use and, in doing so, we sometimes hesitate, stutter, correct ourselves, or start over again.

It now appears, through the findings of Reverse Speech, that we can not *not* communicate. We communicate even when we don't want to or when we feel that we can't find the words. Our pauses, stammerings, breath patterns, tonality, and tangents may reveal more than we originally thought. Our stories *will* be told—one way or another.

8

Sex

God be thanked, the meanest of his creatures boasts two sides.
One to face the world with, one to show the woman who he
loves. —Robert Browning (1812-1889)

Sexual terms and metaphors are so pervasive in Reverse
Speech and appear in virtually every context—personal and
professional relationships, interviews, therapy sessions,
negotiations, and business transactions—that we must conclude
that for human beings, sex is more than just a physical act. It is
much more elemental, more basic than simple physical attraction
or intercourse—and, at the same time, it's vastly more complicated.
It represents an energy on which the universe seems to be built—
Yin and Yang, Male and Female, Thought and Action, Creation
Itself.

The way that we fulfill, express, channel, or thwart this life
force, this creative sexual energy, gives rise to the kind of people
that we are. And, while we intellectually try to come to terms
with this dynamic energy in our lives, our unconscious minds are
doing their work, too, dealing with the same issues—only in
reverse.

Sex as a Metaphor

Sex is a metaphor that encompasses all the thoughts that
people have about what they consider powerful, appealing,
stimulating, life-affirming, and attractive.

Take a minute to read the following list and notice what images, thoughts, or feelings each word conjures up for you.

Ferrari	Power	Influence
Lear jet	Best friend	Mansion
Bikini	Swimming pool	Gourmet food
Ambition	Happiness	Lookin' good
Prestige	Wealth	Love
Tom Cruise	Confidence	Pleasure
Ted Turner	Win	Achievement
Rambo	Quality	Sex
Excitement	Ocean cruise	Reward
Leading-edge	Energy	Eat
Money	Play	Leisure
Luxury	Adventure	Fast track
Savvy	Score	Success

What came to mind when you read each of the above words? The good life as you're now living it—or as you'd like to live it? Happiness as you personally define it? Peace, poise, power, comfort, security, health, wealth as you know them—or as you desire and pursue them?

Most likely you associated these words with someone you know or with an experience you've had or wish to have. You may have found some of the words to be aphrodisiacs of sorts, symbols that attracted, stimulated, inspired, or excited you.

Sexual energy extends to all aspects of life. The "aliveness" associated with this energy is not experienced as different than the ultimate turned-on sensations associated with the ability to make things happen or to create a life that works in all areas. To be truly sexually fulfilled, to fully express life, means that every area of a person's life is congruent and harmonious. Looking at society today, however, with its rampant crime, drugs, depression, indecision, and the like, it appears that true sexual, or personal fulfillment, is sometimes difficult to achieve.

The word "sex" and words that relate to it occur frequently in reversals as people discuss and try to resolve their many issues and conflicts.

How Reversals Express Sexual Energy

There are three ways that reversals can relate to sex:

1. Sex as a literal fact that refers to purely physical gratification (First Level reversals): **suck my cock / it's warm and juicy inside / kiss my lovely bit / I love your sweat / I am wet.**

2. Sex as an operational metaphor that refers to emotional responses (Second Level reversals): **I slept with you and shared your face / he healed my face with a touch / man is my force / I want you honey / we make love.**

3. Sex as a structural metaphor that refers to the most significant human needs and desires (these Third Level reversals express life energy, often draw upon words that are rooted in history or legends, and stem from the deepest part of the Self): **power / feel it there / a sexy war, power you used / an evil fuck, you break my heart / slay your weapon, a man who lost the war.**

Within these areas there are four main words that describe progressive contact or personal connection with others:

- **Lick,** the request for personal connection or the fulfillment of needs, depending on the context: **I want to lick your face, lick my box.**

- **Touch,** the process of connection or fulfillment has begun: **He healed my face with a touch, he touched my heart.**

- **Kiss,** connection has transpired: **Kiss your woman, I kissed the force.**

- **Sex,** deep connection or base needs: **I work for sex, I'm a sexy warrior.**

A sexual reversal that occurs occasionally is, **I want another one,** which refers to the desire for another sexual partner. For example, I once conducted a session with a young couple in which I found this phrase on the woman. She vehemently denied the implications that she wanted another lover, but less than two weeks later she left her partner and moved in with another man.

Of a similar nature is a reversal that I found on an elderly woman: **I was naked with another one,** which referred to a tender affair that she'd had for several years while she was still married.

Here are some other examples of sexual reversals that may refer to physical sex, or not, depending on their context.

- "Popeye the Sailor Man," TV theme: **Fuzzy woman. / Give me a fuck. Give me a fuck now.**
- "Hi, Hi, Hi," by Paul McCartney and Wings: **Warm and juicy inside. / Who is that woman? I won't be there to stay. / Who is this woman? / Oh, if it feels to fuck, I'll fuck you.**
- "Sookie, Sookie," by Steppenwolf: **Pussy, pussy, pussy. Let me in baby.**
- "Mum, He's Making Eyes at Me," by The Andrew Sisters: **Um, you're sexy, um you're sexy, um you're sexy. / I'm sorry Mum, he likes this.**
- This reversal from a man who was courting a woman: **I am the Lord with cum ./ I will kiss your box and you will serve.**
- From a woman who was sexually active: **My box is open and gives love.**
- Another very sexually active woman: **I am a wet girl.**
- From a woman seeking connection with a man: **Kiss my lovely bit. / My lovely bit waits for you.**
- A cocktail waitress at a bar: **Fuck me with power.**
- A man in a business discussion: **I will cum all over you.**

Sex in Business

Have you ever been faced with an important business decision and wished for an added advantage, some inside knowledge, perhaps, to help you decide? Here's an example of a man and a woman who had that extra advantage—access to their reversals. They were considering going into business together; they were not sexually involved. Notice the dominant themes of warfare, sex, and power that appear in this small sample of reversals, and how the man grows desperate because the woman isn't "buying" his proposed plan. The two people subsequently didn't conduct any business.

As you read the reversals below, see if you can guess which person pulled out of the transaction—the man or the woman.

> Man: **Power. Feel it there. A sexy war.**
>
> Woman: **I must be careful.**
>
> Man: **Goddess, goddess. That's censored me.**
>
> Woman: **I'm not stupid.**
>
> Man: **I have power.**
>
> Woman: **Power you used. An evil fuck.**
>
> Man: **Lost at the ocean. The fuck was in my surf.**
>
> Woman: **Nuding. You're forcing.**
>
> Man: **You break my heart. Slay your weapon.**
>
> Woman: **I fear for you there. Look at his hell.**
>
> Man: **Power. I war you now.**
>
> Woman: **Sex. Lonely mission boy.**
>
> Man: **A man who lost the war.**
>
> Woman: **A nude man. You lost me.**
>
> Man: **Want a war with you.**
>
> Woman: **I must sit. We can't do it.**

So, who pulled out of the business transaction? If you guessed the woman, you're right. Note the sexual metaphor "pulled out," which is indicative of the many sexual metaphors that lace forward speech. Other common metaphors such as, "she had her fangs out," reveal the warfare nature of the psyche.

Sexual and warfare metaphors are even more pronounced and straightforward in Reverse Speech because the unconscious mind doesn't filter its language in order to be proper and socially acceptable like forward speech often does. Reversals state the facts as they are, without censoring them, using the fewest words possible to communicate the message. Hence, the strong use of reversed metaphors in personal interactions. Sharp and to the point.

Here's another example of a person's strong identification with his business. It's taken from a session that a Reverse Speech analyst conducted with a man who shared his life story with her. His strong sexual metaphors give vast insight into the sexual nature of people. Notice the connections that his reversals have with the forward dialogue.

> Man: "My parents [were the perfect married couple] and my mother has been, and still is, a pillar of strength." **Mum can feed foxy love.**
> (Sexual representation in the parental support system.)

> Man: "In my early twenties [I decided to set up my own business]." **A Goddess. I get us in love.**
> (Sexual identification with the business.)

> Man: "I managed [to pull off this deal] with a businessman [who owns half the fucking country]." **Used to sleep with Wolves. / Love to surf in the fast lane.**
> (Note the sexual metaphors in both forward and Reverse speech.)

> Man: "They thought I was shit hot. I'd [been working really hard for two years] and was fucked out to the max." **I love feeling my fire in their eyes.**
> (The lust for acceptance, giving personal power.)

> Man: "After work, [I'd never rest]." **I want a fuck.**
> (The need for stimulation or fulfillment.)

> Man: "Then I got this phone call from my lawyer who says I'm about to go bankrupt and I say, C'mon. [What the fuck are you talking about?]" **I've been courting love for so long.**
> (Sexual connection with business is threatened.)

> Man: "Oh, yeah. Then I [wrecked my fucking Mercedes]." **Have I skinned sex.**
> (Sexual symbols, his business and car, begin to disappear from his life.)

> Man: "By this stage I'm getting desperate. I'm calling all my [staff and can't fucking find anyone]." **I fucked up the ass. Some Wolf.**
> (Business collapses, sexual reversed metaphors become harsh.)

> Man: "I get to the office and [it's stripped]. Everything's gone." **Make love from this.**

(Sexual identification changes dramatically and negatively.)

Man: "And, I scream, [fucking bullshit] what happened." **Sex is such a sore.**

(Negative sexual identification is established.)

Man: "[Yeah, oh, yeah.]" **Fear me.**

Analyst: "[Yeah. Okay.]" **Lick me.**

(Reversed power plays between the two.)

Man: "Then he says to me, you've got no company any more. [You've lost the contract.]" **That's not the solving, my Goddess.**

(Sexual identification again as in previous reference to the business as a Goddess.)

Man: "So, I'm trying to start all over again, but [in the meantime I'm falling apart]." **The snake will fuck up the shaft.**

(Strong phallic connection.)

Man: "I'd been pulling some fast deals to get out of it. [They weren't illegal, but totally unethical.]" **Your lust in the office was a problem. You know that.**

(Same story told in reverse with sexual metaphors.)

Man: "In the meantime [I'm not surviving and the company's going down] and it's going down real quick. [And I start to really fall apart.]" **He loves a mast in them and it grows. / Women. I like them. I like to fuck them.**

(His sexual input collapsing, the man sought sex elsewhere and began to look for affairs.)

Man: "[I started smoking and drinking.] I'd never smoked in my life, never drunk in my life." **Because lust will fall upon me.**

(Seeking sex anyway he could.)

Man: "[Then I get this fucking affidavit in the post.] The bitch was filing for sole custody of my kid." **I like slipping it in without the rubber.**

(Or "condom." The man now had restrictions placed on his behavior, which he didn't like.)

Man: "So I just gave up and went and [fucked anything that walked]. Had a nice time though." **It's lust. Feel it puff you.**

(Having lost his business and children, the man gets his sex elsewhere.)

Man: "[Sometimes I'd go a night without sex, sometimes a couple of weeks.] Once it was a whole month." **Skill will fuck you because I must. I need and I must.**

(Strong desire.)

Man: "Anyway, [I finally pulled] myself back together. Stopped drinking [and straightened my life out again]." **That was much better / Can't stand this. Saw you mummy.**

(Session ends with man connecting in reverse to his original source of love, the **foxy love** he received from his mother when he was a young child.)

The man's sexual identification with his business, as revealed in the above transcript, is a common theme in reverse. When his business collapsed, he sought to satisfy his lost "sex" through activities such as illicit sex and alcohol, traditionally forbidden to him by his upbringing.

Sex and War

The drive and the need for sex also appears in reverse through other common metaphors like **power, money,** and **war.** People unconsciously fight for these almost as though life itself depends on them. Remembering that in reversals sex is the most common shorthand for energy, you could say that without sex, there can be no personal power.

Frequently, people allude in reverse to their sexual drives and desires. When they are literally referring to sex, they often use warfare metaphors. **Wolf,** which symbolizes the warrior who's fighting the battle of possession, is just such a commonly used word. The following example shows a man in the process of courtship. His unconscious mind uses the metaphor **Wolf** to relay his desires to the woman whom he's attempting to "capture" in the "war" of love.

Man: **Feel the war. Sex is war. Serve this Wolf.**

Woman: **I see power.**

Man: **Sex is oxygen. Feel the power. The Wolf says trust.**

Woman: **I feel lust. You will not escape.**

Man: **The Wolf thrusts. It's a safe war.**

Woman: **This is sex. I know.**

Man: **Making a Lancelot. I'll be your sweat.**

Woman: **Y'all sweat.**
   (Texan accent in reverse)

Man: **I want Goddess.**

Woman: **I'm your Goddess. I'll allow you.**

Man: **Power.**

Notice the strong images in the above example. **Sweat** is a common reversal that represents the scent of attraction. The woman involved was a willing participant in this "war" and both parties use the structural metaphors **Goddess** and **Lancelot** as their war continues. The woman's final reversal, **I'm your Goddess. I'll allow you,** gives the man **power.** He's won the "battle."

Sexual Attraction

Have you ever felt a strong attraction to another person, but decided not to act on it for some reason? Perhaps you consciously guarded your feelings, but in reverse something else might have been going on, something not quite so guarded.

For example, here's a portion of reversals that I found on myself and a woman television reporter during our final discussion after several days of shooting. We felt sexually attracted to each other, but I did not pursue the obvious invitations that she gave in reverse.

The reversed metaphor **sit,** found in the following example, usually means to take no action. The phrase, **another one,** also occurs, which is a common metaphor that often refers to a sexual partner in addition to the current one.

The reversed word, **woman,** also occurs in the transcript. Reverse Speech makes a definite distinction between **woman** and **women** and between **man** and **men.** The singular appearance of these words represent the strength and stability that a woman and man can offer each other. The plurals of these words in reverse represent casual attachment with no involvement. You may wish to refer back to the last dialogue to note the use of **women** in the man's reversals.

Man: **See a hasty Roselind.**

Woman: **You must not.**

Man: **Unusual. I am nude.**

Woman: **I'll miss your face soon.**

Woman: **You sweat. I want you fellow.**

Man: **I am not another one.**

Woman: **I'm still around. I am woman.**

Woman: **I shall look at the eye.**

Woman: **One man wanted smiling.**

Woman: **I wish to develop this wind.**

Woman: **Why not Saturday.**

Man: **I'll never.**

Man: **You give the eye.**

Woman: **You are not.**

Man: **This is impossible.**

Man: **I don't need the warhead.**

Woman: **Feeling good, beautiful.**

Woman: **Why not.**

Woman: **How about soon.**

Man: **Feel power.**

Man: **Sit on it.**

It seems that some part of us may get to enjoy the attraction even if we don't consciously or deliberately follow through.

Relationships

Perhaps nowhere else is communication so important and, yet, so complicated as in personal relationships. People are afraid of being vulnerable, leery of being misunderstood. Expectations can be thwarted. Hidden agendas may abound. And still, the rewards for "working things out" are many. Personal relationships can be the most fulfilling of all, worth understanding.

Reversal analysis can show what people want or expect from each other as well as their reservations about a relationship as the following transcript illustrates. This transcript is longer than most in this book in order to give you a sense of the depth to which reversal analysis can go. The couple below had just become personally involved. The woman was in her late twenties, the man in his teens.

Notice the word **force,** a common metaphor that appears in relationships. Its counterpart is the word **source.** These words appear in the context of a man and a woman being a source for each other's force. Other occurrences of these words are: **Man is my force. Hey, woman, are you sourced? His force is like a Whirlwind. Lancelot is my source.**

> Woman: (to David) "This you'll have to put this in [your scrap book for years to come]." **I can see if you help.**
> (First Level reversal, Internal Dialogue.)
>
> David: (to woman) "[What are you hoping to] achieve from this session?" **You are being yourself.**
> (First Level, External Communicative Dialogue.)
>
> Woman: "[From this session?]" **She's in love.**
> (First Level, Internal Dialogue, disassociated.)
>
> Woman: "[Actually, it's a lot of the continuation of the turning point.] I'm having a good look at what I'm doing now and what I've been doing in the past. [It's been an eye opener.]" **Need some sharing, but don't need it. / Sight needed help. I'm nude.**
> (Second Level metaphor, Internal Dialogue.)
>
> David: "[In what way?]" **I wonder.**
> (First Level reversal, Internal Dialogue.)
>
> Woman: "[It's just in, um, how I] . . ." **Oh my heart. Help.**
> (First Level, Internal Dialogue.)
>
> Woman: "[Now this time with him I'm just relaxing] and being myself. If it happens, it happens [and whatever]. It's all [just going to take its course]." **Yes, I'm upset. I know. I see that. / I'm thirsty. / Why not. It hurts a bit.**

(Second Level metaphor, Incongruent.)

Man: "The difference for me especially is that [there is a reality] in this relationship." **I'm normal.**
(First Level reversal, Congruent.)

Man: "[We get on pretty well.] She's experienced a little more of life than I have, but it doesn't seem [to, er, make much difference]." **I'm a nice man. / Warm inside. She loves that.**
(First Level, Expansive.)

Man: "We help each other a lot, you know. Just the other day [she was feeling a little bit down] and we had a great chat on the phone." **Like the force. Love this.**
(Second Level metaphor, Expansive.)

Man: "[Something had gone wrong] so we just got together and [went for a walk]. Just together and talked and so on. [By the end of it,] we managed to feel a little better." **Girl, I love you inside. / We fuck fast. / I prefer nice arse. I admit.**
(First Level, Comparative.)

Man: "[Just giving] willfully without sort of holding back, like saying well okay. I'll give you this without thinking you've got to give [me something else in return]." **I'm marvellous. / Nice arse. Lose my soul.**
(Second Level, Expansive.)

David: (to woman) "[Do you feel that?]" **How lovely.**
(First Level, Internal Dialogue.)

Woman: "[Yes I do.] I do. He is very affectionate [which is lovely]." **I'll lose my seat. / I'll upset him.**
(Second Level, Incongruent Internal Dialogue.)

Woman: "A lot of my past has influenced [the way I am]. That has effected my feeling of [self worth greatly] and links up with allowing [myself to be happy]." **I love serving. / Help the soul. / I want to trust him.**
(Second Level, Internal Dialogue.)

David: "[What's the difference] between this then?" **Feed the soul?**
(Second level, external communicative dialogue.)

Woman: "[What's the difference? The difference] is where I am at this point." **This is feed. Feed the soul.**
(Second Level, External Communicative Dialogue.)

Woman: "[Yes. There is no threat.]" **Yes. I'm thirsty.**
(Second Level, Expansive.)

Woman: "I think I'm at a time where [I don't want to be] in a situation, don't want to be in a relationship [where it could turn into something like marriage]." **I wear a mask. / Shame. Help me. He mustn't mean it.**
(Second Level, Expansive.)

Woman: "I think I'd like to be actually at [that sort of point] before actually becoming [deeply involved with him]." **I feel shame. / I'm involved, naked.**
(Second Level, Expansive.)

Woman: "I was single and [I think coming to terms] with that, happy with that, [and not happy with it at other times]. This seems to be just right for [this time in my life]." **I believe that. I was nice. / I feel nasty weather. I'll say it's messy. / What's happening.**
(Second Level, Internal Dialogue.)

Man: "[I love it and it's great.]" **Helps me a whole lot.**
(First Level, Expansive.)

Man: "The main lesson I've learned from this is just learning to give. I know that's sound really ... (pause). [But that's the main thing.]" **Really nice now. Feel no sin.**
(Second Level, Expansive.)

The relationship continued for a year before both people went their separate ways, but remained friends. I conducted the following session with them nine months later, but this time, their relationship was dying. Notice the difference in the spirit of the reversals in this session compared to that above.

This transcript graphically illustrates how Reverse Speech can reveal undercurrents of emotion and hidden agendas, which can lead to an accurate overview of interpersonal dynamics. The analysis makes use of the whole session transcript. I have reproduced it only partially here.

As you read the transcript, pay special attention to *my* reversals. This session was held just two days before I moved to the United States after my marriage collapsed. My *own* issues and feelings intermingled with their reversals.

> David: "Tell me about the progress of the relationship over the last nine months."

> Woman: "[It's gone through the initial] roses and [clouds and euphoria] stages." **My washing needed sex. / Must deserve this**.
> (Second Level metaphor, Expansive, Past Tense.)

> Woman: "Just lately it's gone through the rough spots and [possibly] it's going through the, before the [ending of this phase]." **He'll besot me. / Serve sin**.
> (Second Level, Internal Dialogue, Future Tense.)

> Woman: "It's solidified my own life and [direction] and this takes in professionally as well as the relationship with my mother [in which I've learned some quite interesting] things." **Sex in it. / Love was now rushing me**.
> (Second Level, Expansive, Statement.)

> Woman: (response to Man's aggressive statements) "I've made you aware of the fact that [there is twelve years in the difference]." **So afraid of this evil!**
> (Second Level, Expansive, Emphasized Statement.)

> Woman: "[You're going to go to University.] You're going to have other girlfriends." **So fuck the lover**.
> (Second Level, Internal Dialogue, Emphasized Statement.)

> Man: (beginning to discuss an affair that Woman had while in Europe) "[Are you happy for me to say this?]" **You sleep with rape**.
> (Second Level, External Communicative Dialogue, Statement.)

> Woman: "[On the whole situation?]" **Shows this war**.
> (First Level, Expansive, Statement.)

> Man: (expands on Woman's affair) "[Basically] why she went [up to Lichenstein]." **I won't accept. / This is rubbish**.

(First Level, Internal Dialogue, Statement.)

Woman: "It goes back to [one of the very early things] which was the basis of the relationship." **Serves the soul**.

(Second Level, Expansive, Statement.)

Woman: "[Yeah, well,] we, [from your point of view] as you said to me, I know you're interested in a more permanent long term relationship." **Sorry. / Don't fall in love**.

(First Level, Internal Dialogue, Statement.)

Woman: "[Well, er,] you think [I'm going on a fling]." **Sorry. / I give up**.

(First Level, Internal Dialogue, Statement.)

Man: "[A very strong character] trait in the male side of this family is to be very possessive." **I die. Won't serve love**.

(Second Level, Internal Dialogue, Statement.)

Man: (reacts to the affair) "[So, it really didn't seem that there was that much to be gained.]" **I get shocked there. Listen to the Universe**.

(Third Level structural metaphor, Internal Dialogue, Statement and Instruction.)

David: "I seem to [recall, um, when we first talked] that you said [that um, er,] one thing you liked about the relationship is that you didn't want to commit yourself to anything that may end up permanent." **Oh, serve you man now. / Selfish**.

(Second Level, External Communicative Dialogue, Statement.)

Woman: "You're right. At that time I was very much going [through my development] time and space." **Love is done in there**.

(Second Level, Expansive, Past Tense.)

David: "[What's made you change your mind?]" **I was asked this asshole**.

(Second Level, Internal Dialogue, Past Tense.)

Woman: "Can I go back on what you've asked [on what's made me change my mind]. In a way I haven't changed my mind at all and [in a way one of the first things we agreed on] was that this relationship would work for as long as we wanted it to." **My love's masking him. Somewhat used. Sorry. / I must need surf with Whirlwind in it.**

(Second and Third Level, Expansive and Internal Dialogue, Cause and Effect and Emphasized Statement.)

Woman: "Apart from being enjoyable and in love and all those things it was also convenient [for both of us at that time]." **Bastard. I serve with love.**

(Second Level, External Communicative Dialogue, Cause and Effect.)

Man: "She said to me on [numerous occasions,] the [only reason] she came back was me." **Axing me. / Her actions.**

(First Level, Internal Dialogue, Statement.)

Woman: "My time here, in Australia, [for the moment] has come to an end." **I'm the Wolf.**

(Third Level, Internal Dialogue, Statement.)

Woman: "He's part of all of that [and he's not, for me,] over-riding or strong enough above all else to keep me here." **Wolf. On Satan.**

(Third Level, Internal Dialogue, Personal Protection Command.)

Woman: "I need to be able to move far away from, to be able to resolve [and yes, come back if I want to]." **There's no other. I'm not saying that.**

(First Level, External Communicative Dialogue, Statement.)

Woman: "[But, it's not,] er, I, what is happening to me is not just our relationship." **On spirit man.**

(Third Level, Internal Dialogue, Personal Command.)

Man: "The only reason you gave [for coming back from Europe] is me, but ever since then you've been bloody miserable." **I mock with the spirit.**

(Third Level, Internal Dialogue, Statement.)

Man: (talking about their sexual relationship) "Every time I've taken the initiative. I've been rebuffed."

Woman: "Not every time. [It didn't happen in Brisbane.]" **Loosened a bit.**
(First Level, Expansive, Statement.)

Man: "[Oh. Once!]" **So what.**
(First Level, External Communicative Dialogue, Statement.)

Woman: "Twice."

Man: "Oh, twice, has it? It's been [twice in one year]." **You know me.**
(First Level, External Communicative Dialogue, Statement.)

Woman: "That's not true. [It's not that.]" **Don't want.**
(First Level, Internal Dialogue, Statement.)

David: "Twice in one year?"

Man: "No, no, no! Not that [we've made love]. But I've actually taken the initiative." **I love you woman.**
(First Level, External Communicative Dialogue, Statement.)

Woman: "This is to do with [general contact on an emotional level] in the relationship." **The Whirl won't show me.**
(Third Level, Expansive, Statement.)

Man: "My logical mind's going click, click, click. [A month ago you said] give me a couple of weeks." **Skill will fuck him.**
(First Level, Internal Dialogue, Personal Command.)

Man: (talking about competition in tennis) "She's got problems with her back and I hit the ball [a lot harder than she does]." **So you shoot my power.**
(Second Level, Expansive, Intent.)

Woman: "You still take incredible delight [in serving broad pass] that you know I have [no way of getting]." **I needed. / You take me.**
(First Level, Incongruent, Statement.)

Man: "Of course, [but so do you]." **You won't be sorry.**

(First Level, External Communicative Dialogue, Future Tense.)

Woman: "[I then feel that I'm not making the right decision towards myself.] You do an emotional railroad beautifully. [I've not seen many to compare.]" **Force some salt in the album. I'm not the wife. / The Whirl won't show him.**

(Second Level, Internal Dialogue, Personal Instructions.)

Man: "[So, I'm just meant to wait in the wings and slowly] mellow out." **Reverse the demon, oh but it's nice.**

(Second Level, Internal Dialogue, Personal Instruction.)

David: "How would you feel if [Man rang you up and said, I've met someone else] and [I like her a lot]." **The wife's devil. It's a worry. Lost the life. / I love Aladdin.**

(Second Level, Comparative, Association.)

Woman: "Upstairs [in your bedroom, Darling]!" **I used him for sex.**

(First Level, Expansive, Past Tense.)

Woman: (referring to Man getting an erection while hugging) "[All right, okay, er,] I suppose the cat can make that happen for you." **My ships ache an armor.**

(Second Level, Internal Dialogue, Personal Need.)

David: "[That's all right.] Look, er, [well, they've all been answered anyway]. How much tape [have I got left]?" **I know her sin. / Ain't it a sigh of woman. / That shows me Hell.**

(Second Level, Internal Dialogue, association with current problems in David's life.)

David: "All right, well, look, [let's round, round this up] before World War III starts out here." **I see my Wolves.**

(Third Level, Comparative, Visualization.)

David: "What would say has been the major difference between the way it was nine months ago when we did our first session to [the way it is now]?" **Wine see Darwin.**

(Third Level, Comparative, Personal Association. See Session Overview for interpretation.)

Woman: "It was the early stages of a relationship and [discovery of two personalities] and that's very exciting." **Sees on surface.**

(First Level, Expansive, Statement.)

Woman: "[And since then, two people have had a year together] and a year in anyone's life is a year of change. I'm not sure what happens [from this point onwards, but that is,] that is the difference." **I'll make you see your devil. Feed this mess. / David. Snow more help. Sin not, the devil.**

(Second Level, External Communicative Dialogue, Instructive to David's issues appearing in reverse.)

David: "[It's fairly obvious what's going to happen.]" **Well, [Man's Name,] what's the favor.**

(First Level, External Communicative Dialogue, Question.)

Man: "No! It's not the fact that [I'm pissed off at her] as much [for what, you know, she's going through,] I mean, you know . . . (voice trails off) . . . " **Conserve that force. / No more sex. This nice power.**

(Second Level, Internal Dialogue, Personal instructions.)

Man: "I [sort of feel that I'm being] put out to pasture." **You're not my wife.**

(First Level, External Communicative Dialogue, Statement.)

Woman: "Would you prefer that you would be the one to put [the other one out to pasture? Would that make you feel more comfortable?]" **I will fuck. In love with him. You affect my soft answer.**

(First Level, Internal Dialogue, Cause and Effect.)

Woman: "Where does that put me in our relationship [when your development] course changes in

[direction and place,] and that does not include me."
Love is going now. / Salesman shows me.
(First Level, Internal Dialogue, Statement.)

Woman: "We did have [agreements about our] relationship early on in the piece [and yes people are people and they change] and different things." **Our love is a mutant. / This nice devil. People keep saying that. Satan.**
(Third Level, Internal Dialogue, Statement.)

Man: (quick insert) "[Basically, do you know what I want?]" **I'll accept.**
(First level, Internal Dialogue, Future Tense.)

Woman: " . . . from you, that you . . . "

Man: "[I wan, want wanted, er] . . . " **Still want this power.**
(Second Level, Internal Dialogue, Dialogue alteration.)

Man: "I am logical and I want an answer."

Woman: "Well, [I can't give you that right now]." **I love [Man's Name]. He can't know.**
(First Level, Internal Dialogue, Statement.)

Man: "[What I'm saying now is,] where I'm at now is not saying I don't love you, but I'm getting [pissed off] that I'm being led around by the nose." **My nerves are less nervous. / I'm love sick.**
(Second Level, Internal Dialogue, Statement.)

David: "Okay. I want one final comment from each of you. Tell me [some of it]. Man?" **Honest.**
(First Level, Emphasizes comment required.)

Man: "[How to give. Not always to take.] I think I've done a lot of. I could say a lot of other things, but they'd all be [take offs and sort of subdivisions of that]." **Lust story. Feed that. / Shoo the boss. It was nice as my guest.**
(Second Level, Incongruent, Statements.)

David: "Woman?"

Woman: "I've learned to be honest. I'm as honest as I can be at this stage of my development. [But yes, honest.]"

Still not Satan.
(Third Level, Congruent, Statement.)

Woman: "[I'm not um, I don't feel] I'm cheating him in any way in terms of how I'm really feeling as a person." **I was fed up, mast.**
(Second Level, Expansive, Cause and Effect.

Man: "Oh, God. [You're not. Believe me I know.]" **I feel it. Lonely. Important.**
(First Level, Internal Dialogue, Cause and Effect.)

Woman: "[You might see] the value of that later on." **I'm really sorry.**
(First Level, Internal Dialogue, Statement.)

David: "Okay. That you very much you two. I have a very interesting session in my hands. Session ended. [Woman and Man.] [3rd of August, 1989.]" **You accept your love. / You're answerable with love.**
(First Level, External Communicative Dialogue, Comments.)

Session Overview

This session contains many metaphors, particularly on the woman, which indicate her deep feelings. The man, on the other hand, has mainly First Level, literal reversals. His concerns are more immediate.

The Woman Decides to End the Relationship

The woman discusses the phases the relationship has gone through, indicating that she needed the relationship for her personal growth (**My washing needed sex**). She sees dangers ahead for her in getting too involved (**He'll besot me**) and, against her feelings, she decides to end the relationship (**Serve sin**). She's deeply concerned about their age differences (**So afraid of this evil**).

The Man "Attacks"

The man attacks regarding the affair she had in Europe (**You sleep with rape**) or, you maneuver your way in nicely.

The woman works through a lot of confusion and conflicts in ending the relationship (**Shows this war**) and remembers that she entered it to help herself (**Serves the soul**). She recognizes Man's hurt, but warns him that this is how it was always going to be (**Sorry / Don't fall in love**). The relationship now serves no purpose for her personal growth (**Love is done in there**). She also recognizes that it's not helping Man (**My love's masking him**), but is angry that he insists on accusing her when she views her intentions as always being good (**Bastard. I serve with love**).

The Woman Stands Firm

She stands firm (**I'm the Wolf—Wolf. On Satan**), yet softens when Man reminds her of their affection (**loosened a bit**). Man ignores her softening (**So what**) and Woman's resolve is again strengthened (**Don't want**). She recognizes the relationship has helped her with her personal issues (**It helps the marks**), but knows that as it stands now, they can no longer help each other (**For now we can't be as nice / The Whirl won't show me**).

Man mentions the game of tennis to unleash his aggressions (**So you shoot my power**) and Woman, although denying it consciously, secretly enjoys the competition (**I needed / You take me**). Man knows it's helped her (**You won't be sorry**).

The Man Tries to Win Back the Woman

Man tries to maneuver his way back into her life, but Woman becomes even more resolute (**Force some salt in the album / I'm not the wife / Whirl won't show him**). **Salt** in Reverse Speech often means "to preserve," and **album** frequently refers to the past. In this case, the woman is saying is that the man doesn't own her, but that she wants them to remember and cherish the past that they shared. As is always the case when presented with such a complicated series of metaphors, the initial translation is an approximation.

Meanwhile, I'm caught up in this on an unconscious level regarding the collapse of my marriage (**The wife's devil. It's a worry. Lost the life**). I maneuver to change the situation, however, to my advantage (**I love Aladdin**).

Man becomes intimate again and Woman recognizes what she got from the relationship (**I used him for sex**). She softens again and wishes she could easily cut it off (**My ships ache an armor**).

I'm even more personally involved now in the Man's and the Woman's session and recognize my own issues in their issues (**I know her sin / Ain't it a sigh of woman / I see my Wolves**) with an interesting complementary reversal around the time frame of Man's and Woman's relationship (**Wine see Darwin**).

These are very significant reversals on me. My twins are the love, or the **wine**, of my life. **Darwin** is a personal metaphor for a town in Australia that was flattened by a cyclone (what once was nice—the town and my marriage at that time—is now destroyed). Darwin was also the town where my former wife eventually moved with the twins.

I had no conscious idea at the time of this transcript that they would move to Darwin a year later. I may have received this knowledge, however, through my ex-wife's reversals. Today, in retrospect, Darwin may also have been a dramatic Future Tense reversal. Darwin is the town where I re-established a good friendship with my former wife and assured an excellent, ongoing father-daughter relationship with my twins.

Meanwhile, back in the Man's and the Woman's session, Woman tries a different approach with Man to achieve her intended outcomes (**Use devil. Let's see. This sex is power**). She softens, then fluctuates between giving both Man and me advice, in a three-way, reversed conversation (to man: **I'll make you see your devil**; to me: **David. Snow more help. Sin not, the devil**).

Man recognizes the futility of the situation and knows he's lost. He resolves to remain strong (**Conserve that force. / No more sex. This nice power. / You're not my wife**). Woman recognizes her love for him (**In love with him. You affect my soft answer. / I love [Man's name]. He can't know**). She feels some relief, however, that Man is beginning to let go (**Love is going now**), and justifies her actions (**Our love is a mutant**).

The Man and the Woman Accept the Situation

Man begins to become comfortable with the situation, although reluctantly (**I'll accept. / Still want this power. / My nerves are less nervous**). He then throws it all aside by discounting the love (**Lust story. / Shoo the boss. It was nice as my guest**).

Finally, both people soften as they realize what's going to happen. Man: **I feel it. Lonely.** Woman: **I'm really sorry.** I conclude with a reassuring comment (**You accept your love. / You're answerable with love**).

What happened between the couple above is played out regularly throughout the world as people seek fulfilling relationships, as they endeavor to inspire and emotionally support each other and, in turn, to *be* inspired and supported. Or, in the words of the unconscious mind, as they attempt to **feed each other's Whirlwinds** and **source each other's force.**

Sex in the Media

The following transcript illustrates people's frequent and deep preoccupation with sex. It's taken from a live interview on CNN, *The Larry King Show*, August 1990, and regards the Judas Priest case in Reno, Nevada. Participants in the interview were myself as an independent expert; Bryan Key as a witness for the plaintiff; Gail Edwin, the attorney for CBS; and the CNN Commentator. The reversals were robotic with a lower-than-average clarity rating, which is normal for media.

> Commentator: "David tell us about this unique and unusual [research that you're doing]." **Now let's discuss you.**
>
> Commentator: "You've got, you've got some tapes that [have already been set up]." **Goddess may be robbed.**
>
> David: "[It's, it's, a, um,] actually a, er, right brain hemisphere function." **My ass gets skin.**
>
> Witness Key: "These boys, well they were [taken to] hospital immediately after the accident." **I know evil.**
>
> Witness Key: "Their blood showed a .09 alcohol content [which they were not] legally impaired at that point." **I know wisdom.**
>
> Attorney Edwin: "[First of all, there] were no tests for marijuana and there were no tests [for LSD] among the drug tests done on one of the two young men." **Sex on Whirlwind. / Sex loves them.**

Attorney Edwin: "[The claim in this case] is that there are backward messages." **Sex in this milk.**

Witness Key: "[He did put in] hidden messages in other albums." **They don't need me here.**

Attorney Edwin: "The suicide and the [attempted suicide]." **I source this mess.**

Attorney Edwin: "(The two boys) were [learning disabled] who were in a suicidal or violent mode." **I source anyone.**

Attorney Edwin: "[These two young] men took LSD as well as marijuana together with alcohol." **You see that.**

Attorney Edwin: "How can you [begin to blame it] on something you can't hear?" **Must not an Elvis.**

Attorney Edwin: "The thing [to learn is that] we as parents and I'm a parent have to take responsibility for our children." **I've seen Elvis.**

Witness Key: "This is absolutely [nonsense and this woman] knows it." **This woman walks with a snob.** (Complementary reversal giving extra insight to the forward.)

Witness Key: "These are [an invasion] of privacy and the court have upheld these." **I must shock them.** (Personal command as Key makes his point.)

Attorney Edwin: "I think that it's important at all times to remember that [the subliminal] messages are seen by people . . ." **I want an Elvis.**

Attorney Edwin: "I can't comment about whether it's [right wing] or not, but certainly the defendants are clearly in favor of [the free dissemination] of speech." **I know you. / Shame them with the youth.**

Commentator: (to David) "[What about this case?] Do you think it's possible that they could have been getting a secret message?" **Sex with David O.**

David: "[Oh, I think] it's certainly quite possible. I would like to draw a distinct difference between back, [ward m, m,] masking . . . and Reverse Speech." **See a fire. / Look up!**

David: "We know that Reverse Speech [can be heard] and understood consciously." **Love, he makes**.

David: "Electroencephalogram testings that we've undertaken [clearly show significant] activity between the left- and right-brain hemispheres." **I'll offend this nice sheila**.

As you reread the reversals, notice how, as the interview continued, the attorney seemed to draw more and more energy from being on television and the hype of the live media experience.

Reversals in Order

Commentator: **Now let's discuss you.**

Commentator: **Goddess may be robbed.**

David: **My ass gets skin.**

Witness Key: **I know evil.**

Witness Key: **I know wisdom.**

Attorney Edwin: **Sex on Whirlwind.**

Attorney Edwin: **Sex loves them.**

Attorney Edwin: **Sex in this milk.**

Witness Key: **They don't need me here.**

Attorney Edwin: **I source this mess.**

Attorney Edwin: **I source anyone.**

Attorney Edwin: **You see that.**

Attorney Edwin: **Must not an Elvis.**

Attorney Edwin: **I've seen Elvis.**

Witness Key: **This woman walks with a snob.**

Witness Key: **I must shock them.**

Attorney Edwin: **I want an Elvis.**

Attorney Edwin: **I know you.**

Attorney Edwin: **Shame them with the youth.**

Commentator: **Sex with David O.**

David: **See a fire.**

David: **Look up!**

David: **Love, he makes.**

David: **I'll offend this nice sheila.**

Session Overview

The entire session has a high sexual element. It was my first live appearance on American national television, an important opportunity for me to talk about Reverse Speech and, yet, I was nervous. I have a mild stutter, which under stress intensifies. The producer knew it.

The Commentator begins, introduces me with a reversal, **Now let's discuss you.** I become nervous, stutter, and the commentator knows I'm in trouble. He delivers a reversal, **Goddess may be robbed** (note the structural metaphor). The producer says, "we're worried about his stutter,"[1] and the show switches to Judas Priest. I know it, with a reversal, **My ass gets skin** ("I'm outa here").

Attorney Gail Edwin comes on. She's hyped and delivers a reversal, **Sex on Whirlwind.** Then she says, **Sex in this milk.** Now she's really into it. **Milk** refers to the essence of femininity. In this case, the **milk** is the trial. She then says, **I source this mess,** and, **I source anyone. Source** is a reference to personal energy, usually between a man and a woman. Here, it's used in a general context as a verb rather than as a noun, or, "I draw energy from." It's common in Reverse Speech for nouns to be used as verbs.

She used **Elvis,** referring to superstar, three times. Given the trend of her other reversals with sex and high energy, it appears consistent with the trend: superstar / sex / stimulation."[2]

Bryan Key's reversals indicate personal feelings (**They don't need me here**) and personal commands during dialogue (**I must shock them**).

Finally, the Commentator addresses me with the reversal, **Sex with David O.** I freeze, **See a fire.** I give myself a visual access command, **Look up!** Visualization reduces my stutter. I speak smoothly, with no stutter. My confidence returns, **Love he makes,** and I prepare to take on the attorney, **I'll offend this nice sheila.** "Sheila" is derogatory Aussie slang for woman. The show ends.

And, likewise, this chapter ends, but, ideally, leaves you with greater insight into the kinds of "shows" that are really going on over our airwaves. We are broadcasting more than our personalities. We're broadcasting all that we are.

Human beings often make crucial decisions based on their need for sex, excitement, and emotional connection with others, in order to make the universe less lonely and more comfortable. We've always suspected that sexual energy permeates just about everything that we are and everything that we do. Now, more than ever, we can determine the *extent* to which this is true in our personal and our professional lives—what better indication than to hear it in our own words through our reversals.

By studying our reversals, we can make wiser decisions, choose more compatible partners, and have more positive life experiences. We can fix what doesn't work and maximize what does. We can tap into our own, powerful energies and direct them in constructive ways, refine our strengths, and live and work with greater style and ease.

9

Therapy

All experience is already interpreted by the nervous system one hundred fold—or a thousand fold; before it becomes conscious experience. —Sir Karl Popper

When we study speech reversals within a therapeutic setting, we can see the therapeutic process unfolding—its successes, failures, and growth processes. This is because reversals, communicated by both client and therapist, reveal each participant's true, unspoken motives and needs within a session. These reversals are processed unconsciously by the other person who hears them, which, in turn, can affect the outcome of the session.

Reverse Speech has been used by therapists to shave months, even years, off therapy work. Reversals also confirm the effectiveness of certain counselling approaches, or their ineffectiveness, by revealing the dynamics of the client/therapist interaction. Reversal analysis can also:

1. Provide accurate feedback for the client;
2. Allow the therapist to verify intuitive interventions;
3. Reveal the dynamics of client/counselor interaction;
4. Precisely pinpoint areas of need; and
5. Establish the source of a client's current behavioral difficulties.

A Growing Respect for Clients

Some of the reversals found on therapists indicate a growing respect on the part of therapists for their clients. This trend is evident in phrases such as: **Lovely person, I love you, you have the strength,** and **feel important.** These reversals reflect the compassion of supportive, competent therapists who wish to facilitate their clients' healing.

Internal Congruency

Reversals can also indicate the extent of a client's internal congruency—that is, how accurately what the client is saying reflects what the client is feeling. We determine how congruent the reversed dialogue is by comparing it to the forward dialogue. If both dialogues, backwards and forwards, communicate similar messages, we can surmise the speaker's congruency.

If the messages contradict each other, however, some internal conflict is probably producing that incongruency. The following simulated examples illustrate this point.

> **Congruent:** "I'm coping with this situation because I'm aware of the causes." **Know this. Makes a good person. Headed on.**

> **Incongruent:** "I really do love my husband. He sometimes cooks the dinner." **Lousy person, no freedom.**

Let's look at a few of the many, promising applications that Reverse Speech has for therapy.

Case 1: Client/Therapist Dependency

In a session that a woman psychotherapist conducted with a young woman client who'd recently attempted suicide, an undercurrent of communication developed that wasn't beneficial to the client/therapist relationship.

At one stage during the session, in an attempt to get a response, the young woman told the therapist that she was going away for a week. This seemingly innocent statement was in reality her demand for emotional involvement (co-dependency) as her reversals reveal: **You're mum. Lousy woman! I need. You're mother too.** The therapist side-stepped the demand, giving positive reinforcement. Her reversals show her recognition and her unwillingness to respond.

> Therapist: "[I would have no concerns] about you doing that. It's not an issue." **She wants me, but I'm nude.** (Second Level metaphor, Internal Dialogue.)

> Woman: (immediate response) "[It'll just be a bit of space,] time." **You're sexy. Be with me.** (Second Level, External Communicative Dialogue, continued demand for involvement.)

> Therapist: (further in the session) "Being alive is a very fragile business from time to time, but I had a sense that [you're not giving] a departure cue." **Murder not!** (Second Level, External Communicative Dialogue, Command.)

We see a trend in the preceding situation. The client was developing an undesirable emotional need for the therapist. The therapist wasn't willing to meet this need and gave reversed commands that addressed the real issue, **Murder not!** The client then had the choice of accepting or rejecting the criteria that the therapist established for the therapeutic relationship. Notice the entire reversed interaction.

> Woman: **You're mum. Lousy woman. I need. You're mother too.**

> Therapist: **She wants me, but I'm nude.**

> Woman: **You're sexy. Be with me.**

> Therapist: **Murder not!**

Case 2: Childhood Transfer

At the request of a therapist, the woman in the transcript below came to me because she wanted to improve her communication skills. As the forward dialogue continued, issues emerged that appeared to be intricately linked with her inability to communicate adequately.

> Woman: "I don't know what to say. That's why I'm here. I feel as though I'm not saying [what I really mean]." **Love is a refund.**

(Second Level, Expansive.)

Woman: "To me [it's in relationships] that anger comes out. Like [I feel a lot of things] towards my husband and there's no logical explanation for those feelings." **Relationship shallow. / I believe Father.**

(Second Level, Expansive.)

Woman: "I very clearly [feel hatred] towards my father. At times I'd like to put a [gun to his head]." **I love him so. / I love him.**

(First Level literal reversal, Incongruent.)

These reversals and others led me to wonder whether her lack of communication skills were connected in some way to her relationships both with her father and her husband: I feel a lot of things towards my husband / **I believe Father;** I feel hatred towards my father / **I love him so.**

On the surface, her marriage was stable, yet she felt much anger in the situation that she couldn't explain. The session revealed that her childhood had been distressing, which left her with conflicting beliefs about love, hate, and relationships in general.

The woman intensely disliked shallow relationships, yet referred to them in her own reversals (**relationship shallow**). This, combined with the reversal—**Love is a refund**—concerned her greatly and prompted me to conduct a second session to further probe these issues.

In the second session, she revealed that she felt all she could have now as an adult were troubled relationships, just like she'd had with her parents when she was a child (past experience transference to existing situation). Her reversals in the second session confirmed our initial conclusions.

Woman: "Actually this, yeah, [this shallow's disturbing me while I'm saying it]." **Reversals show my shit. See this shit.**

(First Level, Internal Dialogue.)

Woman: "I mean, my husband's not going to change. [That's just the way he is. It's got to be me.]" **At least now I've seen it. That flaws me.**

(First Level, Internal Dialogue.)

As a result of these findings, the woman realized that her lack of communication skills were linked with her negative attitudes about any relationships. These attitudes had been inspired by her poor relationship with her father. In turn, she'd transferred these self-defeating beliefs to her marriage.

She'd suspected some of these issues, but her reversals helped her to understand their significance. With follow-up couples counseling, conducted by the therapist, the woman learned to express herself better and the marriage improved.

Case 3: Therapeutic Dynamics

It's common to find entire reversed conversations in therapy situations which frequently show the dynamics of the therapeutic process. The reversals below are taken from a therapy session from which selected portions of the reversals have been linked and some of the side issues have been removed. The reversed dialogue and the order in which it occurred has been preserved. Note the reversed dialogue, the dynamics of the interaction, and how the therapist leads the client into a more positive frame of mind and self-awareness. The words in parentheses didn't actually occur, but are implicit with the Speech Complementarity involved.

Client: **When I make love I slip down. (I'm) ashamed of what I say.**

Therapist: **(Say), I'm a person. I feel important.**

Client: **Less shame. Problem. (I'm) Nude. (I) mustn't murder. Still nude. More spirit. I'll have an affair. I upset me. (It) makes me nude.**

Therapist: **Now I see this person's shame.**

Client: **I make my misery. I'm not happy now.**

Therapist: **Least the sources are happy.**

Client: **Best to shoot.**

Therapist: **How selfish. Faking your wisdom. That's enough.**

Client: **Shame, 'cause I feel lousy person.**

Therapist: **(trance inductions) You feel wisdom. Use snow. Enough pain. Whirlwind I can feel it. Now no running. Escape with me. Don't you feel shame.**

It'll be fun. It's your faith.

Client: **I'm still scared. I am (a) sinner 'cause I fell. I still need wisdom.**

Therapist: **Your wisdom's involved. I will serve wisdom. (Your) nerves have won.**

Client: **(I) must not shoot making love. I see evil rotting. What will I say. Run.**

Link Reversal: **You don't need now to run.**

Case 4: Suppressed Memories

Reverse Speech can reveal forgotten, sometimes traumatic events that happened in a person's past. Analysis of a session conducted with a severely sexually-inhibited man found reversals that detailed him being raped in a sauna for men only. Further discussions with him verified that this event had indeed happened.

Prompting techniques (already detailed in Chapter 7) caused unconscious, disturbing experiences to appear in reverse when I worked with a woman who had difficulty being open in relationships. This difficulty manifests itself in the form of self-destructive behavior. She suspected she had been sexually abused at an early age, and that this was causing her current behavioral difficulties, although she had no conscious memory of being abused.

Since reversals are mostly complementary in nature, I suggested that she relax and talk about what she remembered of her childhood, in particular about the time during which she felt the abuse may have happened. Her reversals were amazing and, although there was no way to verify if they were true, they raised some interesting questions.

They may simply have been sexual reversals to describe her problem, or they may have reflected her own belief that such an event occurred. Nevertheless, her discovery through the reversals helped her immensely and answered many of her questions. She felt as though a burden she'd been carrying for years had been lifted from her.

In the following portion of the session, I've printed the reversals *exactly* as she said them and in the order in which they occurred. To protect her anonymity, however, I've altered parts of the forward dialogue and deleted brackets where the reversals actually occurred. I've made every attempt to preserve the spirit of the content and the complementarity of the reversals.

When you analyze the complementarity, you'll see that the event appears to have occurred with the woman's uncle, possibly near, or in, a garden shed and possibly with her mother's knowledge (the uncle's sister). The majority of reversals were Second or Third Level, Internal Dialogue. This led me to conclude that the reversals were, in fact, relaying an event that was stored in her unconscious mind.

> David: "What makes you feel that something happened to you?" **Who's this devil.**
> (Second Level, External Dialogue.)
>
> Woman: "Gut feeling, I guess, as if something traumatic happened." **Really fucked. / I hate him.**
>
> Woman: "I had all these feelings. Feelings of despair and grief, but there seemed to be no basis for those feelings." **He felt me. / The bastard programmed me. This happened.**
>
> Woman: "I used to go and visit my auntie and uncle a lot." **Helpless I know.**
>
> Woman: "All my times with my extended family were good." **I'm helpless. Lost all memory.**
>
> Woman: "After my uncle died I would wake up and hear mum sobbing in the lounge room. The television wouldn't be on or anything. She would sit there crying." **My mummy will help me. / He molested me.**
>
> Woman: "It affected me because I then started crying for no reason." **I would give him a stiffy. / He came on top of me.**
>
> Woman: "I had to get these feelings out so I would go to my bedroom and cry." **It broke my Whirl. / It hinders my face.**
>
> Woman: "My dad was working afternoon or night shift at the time. So he would often be asleep or be at work." **He gave me water. / Don't leave me. He'll save me. He has.**

Woman: "Sometimes dad and I would go for a walk in the hills together." **He loves me.**

Woman: "Before my uncle died, my auntie and uncle helped a lot and I spent a lot of time with them. I remember the nice cakes my auntie used to make, but I can't remember much about my uncle." **Won't be bad there. / I know he rapes. / You bastard.**

Woman: "I have no memory whatsoever prior to the age of three." **I lost my Mum.**

Woman: "I can remember feeling total loneliness as a child. That shouldn't be there especially as a child." **Shit. Hate him. The shed.**

Woman: "The inhibitions came though when I was older." **I grew up sad and lonely.**

Woman: "I think I can remember looking at the garden shed and I escaped into the shed. Maybe that's how I blocked it out by looking at the shed." **Used it. Look, Mummy can remember. / I was not upset. I accept it. Mummy couldn't help it.**

Woman: "It really hurt me that they took the shed down." **I used it.**

Case 5: Psychological Issues Manifesting in Physical Illness

The parents of a 14-year old who were desperate to do something for their son asked me for help. For the past six weeks he'd been experiencing such severe chest pains that, at times, he could barely walk. Doctors suspected that he had heart problems; yet in spite of extensive tests, they couldn't locate a cause for the pain. At the time the teenager saw me, the latest medical theory was that he might have a cyst on his kidney.

His parents hoped that by using Reverse Speech analysis, we might uncover a psychological reason for his pain. The teenager seemed normal for his age, yet was somewhat withdrawn. I conducted the session in my usual manner, focusing on the times that the pains first occurred and his general life circumstances.

David: "Tell me initially about what your reaction is to the cyst on the kidney. How, [how do, do you feel about]?" **I will look in there.**

(First Level, Internal Dialogue.)

Youth: "I guess confused. Not knowing what to think. It's kinda scary and kinda neat having something [wrong with you] and stuff like that." **It hurts me.**
(First Level, Expansive.)

David: (following long discussion about family relationships) "How do you feel about your half-brother?"

Youth: "Well, he lives with his mum and dad and I kinda wish I could [live with my mum and my dad] at the same time." **Mess with Dad and my Mum.**
(Second Level, Internal Dialogue.)

David: (asking about his feelings of wanting to be with both his biological parents at the same time). "So, is this feeling getting better or worse as you're getting older?"

Youth: "[Ah, er, worse.]" **Show me love.**
(First Level, External Communicative Dialogue.)

David: "[And, what, er,] is there a tension inside in it?"

Youth: "[Well, in a way,] yeah." **Hell. Want a home.**
(Second Level, Expansive.)

David: "Do you look forward to the visits (with your real father)?"

Youth: "[A whole lot.]" **A war.**
(Third Level structural metaphor, Expansive.)

David: (questioning troubles the boy was having at school) "Like what? Picking, [fighting, teasing]?" **Diseased love.**
(Second Level, Expansive.)

Youth: "[Yeah. All of it.]" **Feel a war.**
(Third Level, Internal Dialogue.)

Youth: "Let's see. [It had always] been there when I ran real hard, but [that Sunday night I'd taken] a hard run." **I wanted it. / I will get that hurt. I need this bad.**
(Second Level, Internal Dialogue.)

Youth: "I didn't know if it was something to be really

scared about [or just blow it off]." **My father would.**
(First Level, Internal Dialogue.)

David: "What have they done to you?"

Youth: "[Well, they've done an Electrocardiogram,] [a
CAT-scan,] a bone scan." **We love worse telling.
They love real war. / They expect it.**
(Third Level, Expansive.)

Youth: (after being asked to picture colors that described
his feelings, then being questioned about his choices)
"[I think that one was the first one] that popped into
my mind." **Will suffer, so I give up.**
(Third Level, Expansive.)

David: "Talk to me in general. Tell me what you like to
do."

Youth: "I like to play some board games. [I like to play
Nintendo.]" **I miss Nanny.**

(First Level, Expansive.)

David: "Have you talked to him (the natural father) much
about what's been going on with you?"

Youth: "Well, I've called my grandmother, but [I haven't
got a hold of him yet]." **They made the war and I
never have love.**
(Third Level, Expansive.)

David: "Does your Dad want to see you?"

Youth: "Mmmm."

David: "So what's the problem?"

Youth: "[What do you mean?]" **Me evil.**
(Second Level, Expansive. Note how the reversal
answers my previous question.)

David: "How come you don't see him more often?"

Youth: "[Well, 'cause,] the main reason is he lives in
Brisbane. [I live in Sydney.]" **Suck Mum.**
(Second Level, Internal Dialogue.)

David: "Do you get resentful that he doesn't drive up and
see you more often?"

Youth: "No. 'Cause I know it would be a whole [lot just

to come all the way] from there to here." **Feel I want it. That cyst.**
(Third Level, Expansive.)

David: (discussing areas where possible improvements could be made) Would you like to change schools? Would that solve part of the problem?"

Youth: "If [nobody knew me at all]. I could start off with a whole new beginning." **Father. He ruined me.**
(First Level, Comparative.)

David: "Why do you think the pain's there?"

Youth: "[I can't think] of any, [I don't know why]." **Evil get the helm. / Where's this cyst?**
(Second Level, Expansive and Strategic.)

David: (at end of long session of visualization exercises) "Close your eyes and [in your head merge the two colors] together. [The black and the] light blue." **Assault this scum in there. / I will help, look.**
(First Level, External Communicative Dialogue, Command.)

The reversals indicated that the boy had low self-esteem and an intense desire to be helped. The youth felt immense pain, emotional and physical. He resented the fact that he couldn't live with both his biological parents and he acted out his resentment in the family setting (**Mess with Dad and Mum**). He desperately wanted love and a feeling of belonging (**Show me love. Want a home**). This conflict created a metaphoric war inside him and produced his unconscious pain physically (**I wanted it. I will get that hurt. I need this bad**). This was the only way he could get the attention he needed (**They love real war. They expect it**). His internal war had become tangible.

I concluded that the reversal, **cyst,** had become a personal metaphor for the physical manifestation of the internal conflict. Armed with this hypothesis, I called a family meeting that included the youth, the mother, and the step-father.

The youth relished the transcript. All the reversals described exactly what he'd been feeling, in particular the unsatisfactory relationship with his natural father. The reversal, **I miss nanny,** was intensely significant to him, because he often used to go to his grandmother's, whom he called "Nanny," to play Nintendo. Only a month before our session, his mother, thinking that he'd been spending too much time at his grandmother's house, had limited his visits. The complementarity was astounding: "I like to play Nintendo." **I miss Nanny.**

Results Achieved

The discussion achieved many positive results. First, it was the first time the youth had ever been able to talk about his feelings and it was a *great* relief for him. Second, his parents allowed him to go to his Nanny's house more often again. Third, his parents resolved to make a serious effort to help him re-establish contact with his biological father.

Within two days of discussing this session his chest pains completely disappeared and haven't returned. The doctors did confirm a cyst on his kidney. It was very small and couldn't have caused all the pain he'd been experiencing. The pain was a physical manifestation of a larger, emotional problem. When that problem was handled, the pain disappeared.

Case 6: Therapeutic Sabotage

Therapists aren't always helpful to their clients and, in some cases, can be damaging. This could sometimes be attributed to such factors as poor training or lack of client response. In some situations it is apparently difficult for a therapist to keep their own issues out of the interaction. In such cases, therapists deliver reversals that are counter-productive to therapy. In the following situation, a therapist was counseling a husband and wife who had sexual problems and delivered the following reversals.

Therapist: **I am so nervous. I rape you.**

(Rape means to forcibly intrude. Why was he *so* nervous?)

Therapist: **Boy, in love with you.**

(First Level reversal directed to the husband. In Reverse Speech, **boy** is a word that in some circumstances is associated with homosexual tendencies. And, *in* love has totally different connotations than merely to love.)

Therapist: **Lost another one.**
(Following reversals from the man rejecting the obvious unconscious advances.)

Therapist: **Sexy. Loves me nude.**
(He likes the rejections.)

Therapist: **Lucifer shaking me. Warning.**
(He recognizes the potential damage that his feelings could cause to the therapeutic relationship.)

Therapist: **How's this girl go.**
(**Girl** is a word that in some circumstances is associated with sexual, physical feelings. The therapist focuses his attention on the wife and switches from **Boy** to **Girl**.)

Therapist: **Nice to fuck you.**
(Negative sexuality.)

Therapist: **That's lusting me.**
(The Therapist enjoys the sensations.)

Therapist: **You must tell each other evil.**
(He unconsciously sabotages the marital relationship. The word **must** adds emphasis.)

When such issues arise but remain unacknowledged, the results can be devastating. Following this first session with the therapist, the couple visited two more times and their tensions peaked. The wife had an affair with another man. The husband became deeply depressed and his latent homosexual tendencies surfaced. The marriage collapsed.

The following example is a similar case in which a therapist's personal issues appeared in reversals during a session.

Therapist: **I shoot a lot of sedition.**
(Or, his intense emotions are sabotaging the therapeutic situation.)

Therapist: **I am shy. I don't know why.**
(His issue appears.)

Therapist: **Used to fuck. Needed.**
(The issue is explained further and answers the question, "Why".)

Therapist: **Don't kiss demon.**

(Internal Dialogue telling himself not to connect with the issue.)

Therapist: **I need lesson.**

(He needed to sort this issue through.)

Although no long-term damage was caused by these reversals, the client experienced bewilderment. He returned for counseling only one more time, then changed therapists.

Finally, here is an example in which a therapist had negative feelings toward a client. He privately admitted to me that he had these feelings, but he thought that he was a good enough therapist to avoid their interference with his work. His client resented him intensely, however, because she felt that he didn't care about her. Her resentment was so strong, she advised her friends never to see this particular therapist because he had an "attitude." His negative reversals had cost him business. The therapist's reversals speak for themselves.

She's nasty. Has heathen.

She's nasty.

I'm so lonely.

Heavy woman.

You suffer.

You suffer. I used my mask.

I'm faking the wisdom.

Must have some. I'm ashamed of me.

Speech reversals definitely affect the therapeutic process, perhaps even more than they affect informal, casual conversation because of the rapport that is necessary between client and therapist.

For therapists who are willing to examine their clients' reversals *as well as* their own, there is a wealth of knowledge and information to be had. It can greatly expand their therapeutic techniques and their understanding of client problems. Counsellors could also much more quickly determine the effectivity of the therapeutic methods and approach they have to offer in relation to the client's need. Although much is being written today about the client's responsibility and authority in finding appropriate assistance, the deeply needy client faces obvious difficulty exercising such prerogatives.

For the therapist whose vision includes the well-being of both the client and society, reversal analysis offers an immensely beneficial resource for healing emotional pain.

10

Music

Heard melodies are sweet, but those unheard
Are sweeter; therefore, ye soft pipes, play on;
Not to the sensual ear, but more endeared,
Pipe to the spirit ditties of no tone . . .
—John Keats (1795–1821)
Ode on a Grecian Urn

Melody, rhythm, harmony, tempo, and pitch—each word conjuring as many different images as there are listeners. Entire societies and groups within societies throughout the ages have interpreted and expressed these basic elements of music differently, but we do have one thing in common—music itself. Music chronicles our history, entertains us, excites or soothes us. Music expresses the texture, the trends, and the dynamics of our lives. It is no wonder, then, that some people were initially alarmed, even indignant, to discover "Satan" lurking in the lyrics of certain songs. But, as my research into Reverse Speech soon proved, "Satan" was only one small variation on a much greater theme.

"Satanic" Messages in Music

My original aim when I began to research backward messages in rock 'n' roll was to determine if the alleged satanic messages in music really existed and, if they did, what they meant. I was puzzled as to why no one else had explored the phenomenon. I suspected that extreme, fundamentalist religious groups had a lot to do with suppressing serious research.

165

After the Beatles, the controversy was continued with zeal to prove that rock 'n' roll was the work of the devil. Some books on the subject and sermons that were preached during their crusades, however, were very limited in scope. It is no wonder that the extensive research that led to Reverse Speech was avoided by society in general.

Jacob Aranza, for example, in his books *Backward Masking Unmasked* and *More Rock, Country, and Backward Masking* (which primarily condemns the lifestyles of certain rock 'n' roll artists) quotes fewer than a dozen songs that contain backward messages—most of which were intentionally placed as recording gimmicks—as partial support for his claims. He argues that backward masking is a sinister danger and that rock groups are trying to send messages to the subconscious.[1] He specifically refers to backward masking as a Satanic practice.[2] He bases his main argument on a passage found in *Magick*, a book written by early 20th Century occultist, Aleister Crowley. Aranza states:

> *In Aleister Crowley's book,* Magick, *one of his occultic teachings is that you should learn to talk backwards, write backwards and play phonograph records backwards. This inspired and encouraged the use of backward masking in the record industry and directly tied it to the occult. This was to become a channel for Satanically infiltrating the minds of unsuspecting people . . . the evil he began continues with us to this day.*[3]

The obscure passage can be found in Appendix VII, sections (a-f) of Crowley's 500-page book. It says:[4]

> *a) Let him (The Adept) learn to write backwards, with either hand.*
> *b) Let him learn to walk backwards.*
> *c) Let him constantly watch, if convenient, cinematographic films, and listen to phonograph records, reversed, and let him so accustom himself to these that they appear natural and appreciable as a whole.*
> *d) Let him practise speaking backwards: thus for "I am He" let him say, "Eh ma I."*
> *e) Let him learn to read backwards. In this it is difficult to avoid cheating one's self, as an expert reader sees a sentence at a glance. Let his disciple read aloud to him backwards, slowly at first, then more quickly.*
> *f) Of his own ingenium, let him devise other methods.*

This passage is one small part of a much larger section that teaches several techniques of mind regression that are similar to regressive hypnosis. If one follows Aranza's logic to its ultimate conclusion, one must pity dyslexics for they're obviously demon possessed. Parents who allow their children to play with "Pig Latin" are throwing their offspring to the devil. And, horror of horrors, people must be careful not to put their cars in reverse gear for they may be worshipping Satan in the process— exaggerated analogies for exaggerated arguments based more on prejudice than on fact.

One must wonder why some fundamentalists are playing records backward and teaching others to do the same, if it's an occult practice?

Aranza at his most generous refers to some singing groups who have not intentionally placed backward messages as "pawns in the hands of Satan."[5] It would be interesting to hear an explanation of the backward messages that appear in *Gospel* songs. Surely these artists are not also pawns in the hands of Satan being used to seduce the world into playing records backward so that Satan can be worshipped.

Of course, rock 'n' roll, with its respective culture, has its good and its bad elements. So does every section of society, including Christianity as we can see by its often violent history and the questionable lifestyles of certain evangelists. How do rock songs like "We Are the World," and the multitude of others about peace and love compare to some well-known, well-loved songs like "Onward Christian Soldiers," and "Soldiers of Christ Arise"?

Using the fundamentalist arguments, these songs should probably also be considered satanic and readied for the fire. So must those songs of some great composers, such as Beethoven who often had violent mood swings, and Tchaikovsky who was homosexual and had a lifestyle that rivaled that of the "worst" rock musician.

The fact is, most songs, religious and secular, are metaphors. They use stories and parables to tell their tale. Christ said: "Think not that I came to send peace on Earth: I came not to send peace, but a sword. For I am come to set a man at variance against his father, and the daughter against her mother, and the daughter-in-law against her mother in law." (Matt 10:34-35)[6]

The above quote is taken out of context, of course, and, like many of Christ's stories, is a metaphor or a parable for something far deeper. If someone were to say that Christ's words were laced with violence and rebellion and that the *Bible* should be burned, based on that passage alone, what response would he or she get from those who already shared similar beliefs?

Religious writer, Jeff Godwin, in his book, *The Devil's Disciples*, which contains a more comprehensive analysis of backward masking, says: "A debate has been started which will probably out last us all about exactly who or what these voices and messages are and how and where they came from."[7]

Godwin gets even closer to the truth when he discusses where these backward messages may appear on the album: "It's usually that verse or line that strikes you as odd when you first hear it, or perhaps has a weird *double meaning* to it as well, that almost always is the backmask."[8]

Without knowing it, he touched on the core principal of Reverse Speech: complementarity.

Stairway to Where?

If there were a "Top 40" of backmasked songs, "Stairway to Heaven," by Led Zeppelin would have to be at the top of the chart. It has been quoted, misquoted, and dissected for years by religious fundamentalists as being one of the most occultic or satanic songs ever to have been released. I disagree strongly based on my research into the background of this song.

According to Stephen Davis, author of the Zeppelin saga, *Hammer of the Gods*, the controversy began in 1982, when a prominent Baptist used his radio pulpit to preach that "Stairway to Heaven" carried subliminal backward messages.

Then, in April 1982, the California State Assembly played a backward tape of the song in a public session. Some members of the committee claimed they heard the words, "I live for Satan." Led Zeppelin were duly denounced as agents of Satan who were luring millions of teenagers into damnation as unwitting disciples of the Antichrist.

Eddie Kramer, the producer and engineer who worked on four Led Zeppelin albums, says that these charges are "totally and utterly ridiculous. Why would they want to spend so much studio time doing something so dumb?"[9]

"Stairway to Heaven" was written in one afternoon by Jimmy Page, lead guitarist of Led Zeppelin and an Aleister Crowley devotee. The song has been reported to employ a technique of encoded words and double meanings similar to those used in Black Spirituals in which some songs were used as maps and other lyrics served to alert plantation slaves of an impending break for freedom.[10]

Until approximately 1985, Page owned and lived in Crowley's former house, "Boleskine," a sprawling farmhouse on the shores of Loch Ness, sometimes called the "Toolhouse". Boleskine was originally purchased in 1900, by Crowley, for almost twice its value, because it met certain requirements of the *Books of Sacred Magic of Abra-Melin the Mage*. These requirements included windows and a door that opened to the north toward a secluded structure that was to serve as an oratory. It's commonly assumed that a small outbuilding to the far right was the oratory.[11]

Crowley stated in his diary that "shadowy shapes" used to escape the oratory and enter the house. It's been reported that during subsequent rituals these "shadowy shapes" were unleashed with dire effects on visitors, staff, and a few hapless visitors from nearby Foyers.[12]

According to Davis, Jimmy Page was quoted in *Roadrunner* magazine discussing further cases of madness and mayhem including the story that Boleskine was once the site of "a church that burned to the ground with the congregation in it."[13]

This brief, historical background gives tremendous insights into the profoundly significant metaphors contained in both the forward and reversed lyrics of "Stairway to Heaven." Sung forward, the song is basically a story of a woman who's searching for the meaning of life and the path to heaven. In the forward lyrics she sees signs on the wall but cautions that words can have more than one meaning. The bird that sings from the tree tells of thoughts that are misgiven. The thoughts carry images of "smoke" (perhaps fog) in the trees and the voices of those who stand apparently watching from among the trees. This is apparently the same group that is rewarded for their long-standing with the dawn of a new day and the forest's echo of laughter.

There's great significance to the lyrics when they're viewed from the perspective of Reverse Speech. When we consider the complementary nature of the song, it appears to be partially a song of hope for all those who according to the legends once suffered at Boleskine.

The Unconscious Speaks of Its Own Existence

The lyrics also seem to be a message from the unconscious mind that details its own communicative style. In the process of writing the song the way he did, Jimmy Page unknowingly established the complementary criteria for reversals to occur that speak of their own existence.

"Words have two meanings," and "thoughts are misgiven," appear at the start of the song. Note the complementarity with the last reversal on the song. As soon as the song is reversed, it says quite clearly, **"Pl-a-a-a-a-y backward. Hear words sung."** This is *not* an intentionally backmasked message, but rather a genuine speech reversal. It almost seems as though the unconscious mind is calling out and saying, "Hey, listen to me. I can communicate."

The lyrics also form a reversal that says: **There was a little tool shed where he made us suffer, sad Satan.** Jimmy Page may have unconsciously used the words **tool shed** to refer to the small outbuilding that was the oratory (Boleskine itself was the Toolhouse). The reported "shadowy figures" may be those who have stood for so long in the smoke, but are promised the dawning of a new day.

The last stanza declares not only that there are two paths that can be taken, but also that it is not too late to change roads. This last stanza contains the reversal, **It's my sweet Satan, the one whose little path would make me sad, whose power is fake.**

Their are references to "path," "forest," and "hedgerow" all of which are descriptive of the setting of the Boleskine mansion. The word **Satan** itself may be a metaphor for the suffering and pain that occurred in and around Boleskine. The parallels of these images and the legends that surround Boleskine are compelling.

Other reversals that some people have quoted in this song as a basis for their claims, include: **"There's no escaping it / I will sing 'cause I live with Satan / They gotta live for Satan."** These reversals are so vague and imprecise, however (validity 1-2), that only the very bold would use them as the basis for an argument.

Forgive me, Lord; Forgive me, Lord

Finally, a reversal appears on a live version of the song sung in 1976, that says: **Forgive me Lord, forgive me Lord, forgive me Lord.** How could this be considered satanic? Who's asking for forgiveness and why? Since when does the nature of Satan, metaphoric or otherwise, include forgiveness?

Is the song a stairway to heaven, a stairway to hell, or something totally different? Stephen Davis wrote a description that may be accurate regardless of how you choose to answer these questions. He said: "It expressed an ineffable yearning for spiritual transformation deep in the heart of the generation for which it was intended." [14]

"Satanic" Messages In—Guess Where?

Where do you suppose I found the following reversals?

> **I serve you Satan. He's the Lord that I've seen. Serve you Satan, everywhere I've been.**
>
> **It's Lucifer that lives!**
>
> **Satan is the Lord. / Jesus is the Lord. / Who liveth? Evil, evil. I curse thee Lord.**
>
> **My Satan is, My Satan is God.**
>
> **Jesus Christ, is He the Devil.**
>
> **In a limousine, I serve God in. / Jesus is upset, angry.**
>
> **I am Lucifer. I am Lucifer. I am loose. / I am a demon. I am a demon monster.**

So, where did I find the above reversals? I found the first six in songs by several of the better-known Gospel artists and the last one from the speaking-in-tongues service that I mentioned earlier in this book.

Gospel artist, Don Francisco released an album, _I've Got to Tell Somebody_, in which there was a song called, "Steeple Song." Two reversals: **We bless, we curse God. / Satan is a nasty bastard.** show an extremely interesting complementarity with the forward lyrics which focus on the struggles of faith. From a very straightforward perspective the lyrics generally dismiss the flashy aspects of faith, like miracles, and ask for an understanding of meaning from the more unglamorous ordinary facets of life, like loving your family and serving your neighbor.

Based on the findings of my minimal research into Gospel music (less than four weeks in 1987), it appears that Gospel music contains many of the standard reversals that secular music does—messages that reflect on-going struggles within the Persona or the "Self," challenges that are normal for everyone. Reverse Speech simply details them in terms of structural metaphors, whatever belief system an individual professes.

Satanic messages don't seem to indicate demonic possession, nor do they necessarily reflect a sinful nature. To say that religious artists cannot have satanic reversals in their music simply because they're religious—an argument put forth by some fundamentalists who do not believe that backward masking exists in Gospel music—is to say that these people no longer have the inner challenges and struggles that are common to us all as human beings. The following quote from the Bible seems appropriate to end this section: "Though I speak with the tongues of men and of angels, and have not charity. I am become as sounding brass, or a tinkling cymbal." (I Corinthians 13:1)

Trends in Society: Singing the Deep Self

Music has long been considered a means of creative expression. Like poetry and literature, music helps people express their defeats and pain, their triumphs and joy, and their deep, inner struggles. Humanity details its life's journey, personal and historical, through music. We hear our beliefs and fears, our lessons, aspirations, and failures expressed in music. Music often describes the state of the world in which we live and may give prophetic warnings concerning what will come if we don't make necessary changes. And, sometimes, music is created simply for music's sake.

The very act of singing creates the necessary circumstances for right-brain hemisphere activity to peak. This enables the deep Self, or the collective unconscious, to surface. Music uses metaphors both forward and in reverse. In fact, we see the growth and development of society and the individual expressed in these metaphors.

Sometimes these metaphors use words such as "God" and "Satan" to describe the conflicts depicted. Other times, the reversals simply complement the forward lyrics. It all depends on the intent of the song and the depth of images that the forward lyrics use.

The complementarity that applies to speech also applies to music as the following examples depict.

- The song "Hotel California," by The Eagles supposedly tells a tale about the 1969 opening of the first Satanic church on California Street in San Francisco.[15] The reversal it contains is a simple complementary expression of the forward lyrics: **Satan organized his own religion.**

- We also find complementarity in Frank Zappa's song "Nanook Rubs It," with the reversal: **No man, no we never killed the nark. / There's no one except the sheikh that remembered we had the mumps.** What's the complementarity? The reversal is meaningless. As any avid Frank Zappa fan will admit, his songs are meaningless *forward*, as well. That's what attracts people. They are brilliant in their absurdity.

- "Baby, I Want You," by Bread is a short, gentle love song that seemingly reflects on a past or current lover. Right at the end of the song, however, a complementary reversal occurs that says: **You killed my baby. You stole my baby.** This appears to be a metaphor for hurt and anger in either this relationship or another.

Before the theory of Reverse Speech was developed and more direct research became all-consuming, I set out to trace themes that might appear in the spirit of reversals found in music as the decades progressed. During this task, I documented more than 2,000 reversals in songs. Not surprisingly, the themes I uncovered were similar to the general spirit and growth of developing musical trends and the events shaping the perspectives of the day.

The following list of songs is by no means complete. We can't consider the songs in depth without entirely analyzing each song, a task that would take more space than this entire book. The songs, however, do indicate trends: the reversals are complementary with the songs and the messages they project.[16]

Music in the 1920's

In the mid-1920's, as the world was introduced to a new and strange thing called "radio," the BBC put together a nifty little jungle, "Auntie Aggie and the BBC." It encouraged listeners to tune in, sit back and listen to Aunt Aggie. The reversal: **This is not a noose, no it's bleeding not,** probably addresses fears that people had concerning this new medium of radio.

Music in the World War II Era

In World War II, the Andrew Sisters released their song, "Rum and Coca Cola." It was a carefree, easy-going song about the oldest pastimes known to man: wine and women. The reversals reflected this and the spirit of the times, "Eat, drink and be merry for tomorrow we may die." The reversals are: **I look out for women. / I like it my lovely girl. / God, I'll lose you my Lord. / And I died the next morning.**

Music in the 1950's

"Love Sick Blues," by Patsy Cline contains a reversal that says: **Lucifer fuck off. / It was the Lord who saved me. / Jesus, he's the one.** This is not surprising because it reflects her Christian belief and the general spirit of society in the 1950's. Likewise, the song "Johnny be Good" by Chuck Berry, contains a reversal that reflects his Christian belief and society's state in general during the 1950's: **I would die for Jesus.**

In Buddy Holly's song, "It's Too Late," humanity's constant struggle between the positive and negative aspects of its nature is told in metaphoric terms: **Worship is nowhere. God is dead./ Now look Satan, now hear me. You have no hope. / I'm dead and thee worship, Lord Jesus. Now look Satan, now hear more. I'm sorry for I despise you.**

Music in the 1960's

"This Train," by Peter, Paul, and Mary captures the spirit of the 1960's with its reversal: **Lucifer. We rode with madness.**

As society became more confused and individuals became more frustrated by the dramatically intensifying rate of change, music became more aggressive and structural metaphors became more harsh, evident with songs like, "Satisfaction," by the Rolling Stones: **Worship Satan. Worship Satan's son;** and "Tell Mama," by Janis Joplin: **Lucifer now. He's in us. He's in all of us.**

Then, in 1968, the rock opera *Hair* opened on Broadway and signalled the end of an era with reversals like: **I'm the next Nazi and The Whirlwind. / Satan is Master,** on the song, "The Dawning of the Age of Aquarius."

A New Structural Metaphor Surfaces

A new structural metaphor began to appear that I hadn't located in any of my research that pre-dated the 1960's. This metaphor was **Nazi.** It continued to appear throughout the 1970's, and the Vietnam era in songs like, "Peace Train," by Cat Stevens: **Nazis will now take their revenge / Lucifer is dangerous./ Hebrew, he's a marked man. Now the Whirlwind.** And in the song, "The Monster," by Steppenwolf: **There's Nazis in the Whirlwind.** Creedence Clearwater Revival's song, "I Heard It Through the Grapevine," appears to typify the mood: **Ah, Jesus, no one wants him.**

It would be a more than fascinating exercise to convene a cross-disciplinary think tank to research the appearance of the metaphor **Nazi.** How long does it take, and what cultural impacts are required for images as devastating as those produced by WW II to sink to the level of the collective unconscious and re-emerge as a structural metaphor?

Music in the 1970's

As the 1970's turned into the 1980's, the spirit of reversals in music turned again with songs like: "Patch It Up," by Elvis Presley: **Gotta warn 'em. Evil is happening. Evil is here,** and "1984," by David Bowie: **Please hear me, man. Don't hear Satan.**

But the general trend in the 1980's, remained the same with songs like, "Miss Me Blind," by Boy George, **Hebrews! Satan smashed their faith. Oh shame Hebrew man,** and, "I Want to Make the World Turn Around," by Steve Miller, **It's an evil world we live. / Sad Satan's world we live in.** The metaphors found in the songs of Bob Marley seem to catch the struggle for transition with his songs "Trench Town," **Master. I'll fuck you bad, you're a Nazi,** and "Give Thanks," **Christ is the way.**

"What's My Scene" by the Hoodoo Gurus tells it all: **The Earth is damned, Armageddon. / You must receive his power. I makest war. Christ must come.**

What the future will bring is anyone's guess, but with the current dramatic turn around in the world's political system maybe there'll be something totally different.

So, are there satanic messages in rock 'n' roll? Yes, there are. Do they come from Satan? No, they don't. Are rock artists deliberately backmasking their songs? Not usually. Are the rock artists deliberately putting reversals in their songs? Never. The reversals are simply another facet of Reverse Speech and contain metaphors that depict humanity's struggle to come to terms with itself and with the world in which we live.

The Australian Bicentennial Song

In November 1987, national controversy raged over Australia's bicentennial song, "Celebration of a Nation." A 25-year old Army Corporal from Wagga Wagga, New South Wales, claimed that the song was backmasked with satanic messages.

Quoting Jacob Aranza on national television as the world's leading authority on the subject, this Army Corporal, and some of his associates, went into great detail as to how the writers of the song had placed these messages there, either through devious intent or unwitting satanic design.

The media ran with the story, and for the next few days radio and television stations around the country played sections of the song backward. Talk show hosts thrived with backward masking "experts" who appeared out of the woodwork to support the claims.

Naturally, my curiosity was aroused. I obviously would have refuted the notion that any reversals these records might have contained were satanically, or deliberately, inspired, but I also wanted to be able to explain them. I couldn't confirm or document, however, many of the alleged reversals by using the research criteria that I'd established (outlined in Chapter 7). Most of the reversals were extremely unclear.

The beginnings and endings of words were not sharply defined, there was a high degree of subjectivity regarding many of the vowel and consonant sounds, and even the syllable count was incorrect in some cases. I did, however, find three phrases that I felt could be quoted with confidence. Their meaning becomes obvious when you examine their complementary nature.

> Celebration of a Nation. [Give us a hand.] Let's make it grand. [Let's make it great] in '88. [C'mon give us a hand.] **How about Satan? / Can't make it stick / Has to be normal.**

It was stated many times on national television that the bicentennial celebrations were a big and, perhaps, ill-advised project (**Can't make it stick / Has to be normal**). Also, much controversy raged at the time regarding the desperate plight of Australia's Aborigines (their land rights, poverty, alcoholism, rampant glue sniffing, early deaths, etc.). In view of this, the phrase, **How about Satan,** becomes understandable viewed as a structural metaphor, a reminder of some of the darker aspects of Australia's history when the Aborigines were slaughtered by the thousands as the whites took possession of the land.

"Satan" and Reversals in Speech

We gain greater insight into the structural metaphor, "Satan," by looking at its occurrence in regular speech, in which we can connect the forward dialogue and behavioral patterns to its appearance. As discussed in Chapter Six, "Satan" often appears in situations in which people perceive that they're in danger, are emotionally distressed, or are describing harmful behavior.

"Satan's" appearance in music is broader than in speech, but the implications are the same. Here are some examples that I've found in speech.

- A man talks about someone who caused him severe emotional distress, following a betrayal of his trust. "I just can't understand why he did it. [I was pretty pissed off with what happened.]" **I hate Lucifer. See the bad man. What a bastard Lucifer.**
  (In this case, **Lucifer** is a metaphor for the emotional stress he felt.)

- A young man talks about his recent chronic weight gain. "I just kept putting it on all the time. [I couldn't stop. I'd do well for a couple of days and then pig out.]" **Used me Satan. My Satan. Still need that program. Servery was Satan.**

  (Satan here is described as the negative behavioral pattern that caused his eating problems—**MY Satan.** "Servery" is Australian slang for a food carrier, or server; its use has extended to some types of food service establishments, i.e. eatery. The man, for whatever reasons, must have needed the pattern.)

- A married couple, the recipients of an intense emotional attack, engages in a heated argument, in reverse, with friends. The husband supports his wife by using **Satan** as a metaphor for the emotions they were feeling.

  Husband: **Satan hasn't got any power.**

    (Or, nothing can be gained from this interaction.)

  Wife: **Help!**

  Husband: **All right. Take my cup.**

    (Husband offers help using the metaphor of the cup of Christ: "Take this cup of suffering away from me."[17])

  Wife: **Satan!**

    (Emotions still felt.)

  Husband: **I don't like it.**

- This example shows Satan in a different light, referring to deceptive business practices, as I'm discussing with a friend the merits of becoming involved in a get-rich-quick scheme. "Don't get involved. They don't follow through. It's [quick, sharp, a lot of con work]." **Unleash this earth from Satan.**

Satanic messages. The very name seems sinister. But, they're not really satanic messages. Rather, they're metaphors from the unconscious mind that describe emotions, concepts, and behavioral patterns.

Satan, which in reverse usually refers to intense, often negative emotions or almost unshakeable destructive behavior, appears frequently in music and speech because the *concept* of

Satan is rooted deeply in society with its legends, myths, and fables from centuries past.

Other comparable words also appear under similar circumstances. For example, **Lucifer** is more frequent and often refers to negative behavior. **Devil**, meaning mischievous or dormant negative behavior, and **demon**, meaning harm or emotional pain, also appear, but their implications in Reverse Speech are not nearly as strong as **Satan**.

I also found one reversal that referred to **Beelzebub** on a well-known, Australian woman television reporter who said, in reverse: **I'm not pure. I love you Beelzebub.**

Reverse Speech can help us exorcize the "demons" previously thought to be haunting our melodies. It sheds light on the fact that Satan, Lucifer, devils, and demons are most often used as metaphors that express only a small part of the vast human experience.

11

Personalities
and Politicians

Blessed is he whose fame does not outshine his truth.
—Rabindranath Tagore, *Stray Birds* (1916)

If you ever injected truth into politics, you have no politics.
—Will Rogers, *The Autobiography of Will Rogers* (1949)

We're often fascinated by all those charismatic characters who seem bigger than life on the giant movie screen, or those darlings of the airwaves who entertain and educate us, or the politicians who seem to direct events that change human history.

We know what these people *do* and what they *tell* us, but do we really know what they're *thinking*? Are they being honest with us? It might be quite enlightening to know—and, in some cases, crucial to know, especially where national security or the welfare of a society is at stake.

Let's listen in on a variety of celebrities and politicians: comedian and actor Steve Martin, entrepreneur Donald Trump, author and motivational speaker Tony Robbins, and current President George Bush and some of the "players" in the Persian Gulf crisis as it evolved into a full-scale war.

Steve Martin on *The Larry King Show*

The following is a partial transcript of reversals that I found when comedian and actor Steve Martin was interviewed on CNN's, *The Larry King Show*, in late 1990.

181

Interestingly, for about the first 20 years of his career, Steve Martin did stand-up comedy pretty much full time and earned an excellent reputation as one of America's most successful comedians. Then, in 1981, he began to explore his more serious side. In an interview for *Parade* magazine, April 1991, he was quoted to have said, "Today, I see myself as a comic actor who does serious."[1]

You might want to keep this career progression in mind as you read the following transcript.

> King: "Vinni Antonelli is in the witness protection program. His protector is Rick Moranis. [Here is a scene.]" **This is it.**

> Martin: "The screen play was written by Nora Efron who did *When Harry Met Sally* and [*Heart Burn* and many things]. It was so clever and the characters were so strong." **Now feel them. You got me.**

> King: "Who were [they thinking of] for that part?" **Oh, fellow funny.**

> Martin: "She said you should play [the other character]. I said I can't. I [just don't have any hint] on how to do this and I said I'll read it again." **Make that Goddess./ I love me near my heart.**

> King: "He was supposed to be with us tonight for the full [hour long show with you]. Was there some illness?" **Don't worry.**

> Martin: "You can say [it's a fabulous movie] it's got these stars. It appeals to these crowds and suddenly you just never know. [It's completely unpredictable] and every time the business thinks it can predict [what's going to happen] it doesn't." **Sea fucks evil./ Censored the nasty fellow. / Worse inside me.**

> Martin: "[So, you can't create] one unique thing that has a success and we thought, well, we'll create a unique and [have another success]." **You make it worse. / Source this mess.**

> Martin: (responding to the question why he left stand up comedy) "Well, [that was about ten] years ago and

Personalities and Politicians • 183

there were a lot of reasons. The headline is I had had it." **I'm not doing it.**

Martin: "You tell the [joke in February] and they laugh in December." **Mess in the filing.**

Commercial for hotel chain: "([song, cannot decipher forward lyrics)] . . . I mean [who wants to eat bait]?" **Why not give the devil his fuck. / Give me snow.** (Snow means purity, cleansing, positive affirmation.)

Commercial for vitamins: "An all new multi-vitamin made just for you and your changing needs. New Centrum silver ['cause you're over fifty] and you're out there swinging." **Is this a worry?**

Martin: "It's about [the effect that this character] has on the small town, and the effects that the small town on him." **Nice lonesome. Was I hurt?**

Martin: "They sort of have a relationship, but it's basically, er, [you know, fun and funny] and kinda romantic." **Enough. Enough funny.**

Martin: "Comedy [tends to deal with something] light and drama tends to deal with something, so called, serious." **It must weed its nest.**

Caller: "Thank you. [Steve, where did you get the idea] for the hilarious song, King Tut?" **I'm afraid I think, a little bit.**

Martin: "I enjoy anything from the *Tonight Show*, to *Wild at Heart*, is a [very funny movie, I mean it's tragic and, er,] kinda horrifying, but it has comedy." **I like this love. Sending evil.**

Caller: (old school friend) "I'm kinda sad to hear that you don't show up to the high [school reunions]." **They knew you.**

Martin: "[You were a] football player, weren't you Jim?" **Fuck off.**

Caller: "You do a lot of [funny dancing]. In a lot of your pictures I've seen you do some dancing [and I was wondering you had] any training." **You made me laugh. / You make Dad see your funny side.**

Martin: "Karl Reiner once told me he was once on, [er, show,] a [show of shows]. He did a fake German accent. He wasn't really saying anything and his mother phoned up and said I didn't know you spoke German." **Listen. / Get fucked.**

Caller: "Are there any look alike contests that one could enter for a person that [looks like you]?" **I suffer.**

King: (responding) "[Well, sir.] What do you do for a living?" **No sorry.**

Martin: (responding to question, what he would do if he lost a Steve Martin look alike contest?) "Well, [there'd be a lot] of investigating going on." **I'll leave it.**

Martin: "I never got a real [sense of rhythm]. I kinda have my own sense of rhythm." **I'm an Elvis.**

Caller: "The, er, [TV comic,] David Leisure, can you hear me, I think one of the reason he's so funny is because he looks, talks, and acts just like you." **They're mocking me.**

Announcer: "For live transcripts contact Journal Graphics, [Incorporated, 267 Broadway]. New York." **Now the message gets you.**

Martin: "[Seems like since I'm] on the show I should get one (a transcript) for free." **I was a selfish.**

So, it appears that everyone got in on the act: the personality himself, Steve Martin; the interviewer, Larry King; the caller, and even the announcer for the commercial. Reverse Speech includes everyone.

Donald Trump on *The Today Show*

This interview happened just days before a hearing was to be held in Atlantic City to decide whether entrepreneur Donald Trump could obtain a loan against his casinos to save his troubled empire.

Trump: (talking about three of his executives who were recently killed in a helicopter crash) "Life is very cheap. Because when you lose [three young strong fabulous] guys, happily married . . . It tends to cheapen life." **Silly love. Won't slow. Heal soon.**

Trump: "I think it hurt the [business psychologically] more than anything else. I have very talented people down there now." **Sign within a loan.**

Trump: (responding to the question, what would happen if the Atlantic City courts did not let him refinance?) "I don't want to [think about ruling against]. It's a very positive thing [for everybody]." **Not nervous. Snaking a new Whirl. / We love you both.**

Trump: "You have to go and restructure and change other deals so that [your debt gets reduced] and you have to survive at the top." **Soon you snake that new Goddess.**

Trump: "[You may sell percentages] of the Trump shuttle, which is now doing great." **The lesser force hear me.**

Trump: "[I think that I've become very resilient] over the years. It doesn't bother me perhaps like it should." **Why does the world mock about it?**

Trump: "I had the certainty of having a (pre-nuptial) agreement. When someone decides to challenge that, it takes out the certainty." **I must know.**

Trump: "I think that when someone signs an agreement [they should live by] that agreement. I've always thought that in business and I always will." **I build the shit.**

Trump: "[I'm not angry at Ivana.]" **I love her, dilemma.**

Trump: "I'll always love her. Ivana, again being the [mother of three very special children,] I'll always love Ivana." **The boss will help serve you through.**

Trump: "I never go back and say I wish I didn't because it can't be changed. [It doesn't help to think about it.]" **The love that give hath won.**

Tony Robbins' *Unlimited Power* Infomercial

Here are some reversals that I found in Tony Robbins' half-hour infomercial, selling his *Unlimited Power* tape series. The reversals were infrequent, with low clarity, and extremely robotic construction, which indicates a highly-scripted, rehearsed presentation. Since permission was not obtained to directly quote the original material, the forward text of the commercial has been paraphrased.

> Outlining the simplicity of achieving unlimited power: **Found Elvis.**

> Asking why people engage in negative behavior patterns: **Mask the slime. It must nude me.**

> Teaching that personal power is based on four lessons: **Shoot power. Sawn off sword.**

> Explaining that some people master one lesson, some master another: **They musn't sign it. / They musn't sign.**

> Commenting that our desire for freedom causes us to start making money: **Maybe you'll find some.**

> Encouraging people to condition themselves for persistent pursuit of their goals: **Sword wisdom exists.**

> Associating only pleasure rather than pain with the necessary action: **It must result in Jesus suing you.**

> Talking about highly publicized, big money, celebrity promotions: **You need money. / Why do we feed us?**

> Imploring people to do whatever it takes to make it work: **Don't want to go to house. / We make it more possible.**

While it may be entertaining to study celebrities' reversals, such as the personalities above, it ultimately may be more practical to study politicians' reversals, such as those below.

The Persian Gulf Crisis

Fortunately, the Persian Gulf war ended quickly. Unfortunately, it simply may have been "the war of the day." Given humanity's sometimes violent history, the Gulf war may not have been the last war that the world will see. This is why it's especially important to understand the part that reversal analysis can play in times of war.

In August 1990, the Arab nation of Iraq invaded its small neighboring country, Kuwait, and the eyes of the world were directed toward the Middle East as tensions, hostilities, and troop build-up escalated. Here are some illuminating reversals that I found in key press conferences and interviews during the first two weeks of this crisis. As you read these interviews, you might want to pay special attention to the following:

1. The completely different reversals found on Bush, the Ambassador for Iraq, and the Ambassador for Kuwait.

2. The word **Allah** on President Bush. This is the first time I've ever found it in reverse. It may have been adopted as a metaphor for the situation.

3. The word **Simone**, both on Bush and Secretary Baker, each time with forward reference to Iraq. A new word in reverse. I figured that Simone might be a code word or a metaphor, quite a "lucky guess," as you'll see below in the section, **Simone**.

4. The developing trend of Bush's reversals as the crisis evolved into a war.

5. The different frequency of reversals depending on the situation.

President Bush's Press Conference, August 8, 1990

The following are reversals that I found during President Bush's official press conference to the world since the invasion of Kuwait by Iraqi forces. Tape time was 10 minutes and 56 seconds with 22 reversals of "robotic" construction and moderate clarity.

The frequency was one reversal per 26 seconds, higher than average for this type of dialogue.

Bush: "Facing negligible resistance from its much smaller neighbor, [Iraq's tanks stormed in] blitzkrieg fashion through Kuwait in a few small hours." **The world was no game**.

Bush: "Iraq now occupies Kuwait. This aggression came just hours after Saddam Hussein specifically assured numerous countries in the area [that there would be] no invasion." **Evil with it.**

Bush: "My administration, as has been the case with every President, from [President Roosevelt to President Reagan,] is committed to the security and stability [of the Persian Gulf]." **They gave this Earth with power. / Fog this Earth with it.**

Bush: "The stakes are high. [Iraq is already a] rich and powerful country that possesses the world's second largest reserves of oil." **There was a power.**

Bush: "Our country now imports nearly half the oil it consumes and [could face a major threat] to its economic independence." **Game this Earth.**

Bush: "It's not an American problem or a [European problem or a Middle East] problem. It is the world's problem." **Sealed them all above me.**

Bush: "Both the Arab League and the Gulf Cooperation Council courageously [announced its opposition] to the Iraqi aggression." **She's a bastard slime.**

Bush: "The United Kingdom and France and other governments [around the world] have imposed severe sanctions." **Whirl with my wisdom.**

Bush: "I pledge here today [that the United] States will do its part to see that these sanctions are effective." **And I need it.**

Bush: "[Iraq has amassed an enormous war] machine on the Saudi border." **Simone, Simone in the sands.**

Bush: "Given the [Iraqi's governments history of aggression] against its own citizens, as well as its neighbors, to assume [that Iraq will not] attack again [would be] unwise and unrealistic." **Showed by your system. / I know power. / Not evil.**

Bush: "I sent Secretary of Defense Dick Cheney to [discuss cooperative measures] we could take." **Me the power, sex.**

Bush: "U.S. forces will work together with those of Saudi Arabia and other nations [to preserve the integrity] of Saudi Arabia." **I say, don't get me.**

Bush: "The mission of our troops is wholly defensive. Hopefully [they will not] be needed long. They will not initiate hostilities, but they will defend themselves, [the Kingdom of Saudi] Arabia and other friends in the Persian Gulf." **And I know it. / Soon be naked.**

Bush: "Secretary of Defense Cheney has just returned from valuable consultations with [President Mubarak] of Egypt." **A problem is left.**

Bush: "And he'll (Secretary of State Baker) then [consult with the NATO foreign ministers]." **Send 'em now forth in with the force.**

Bush: "Americans everywhere [must do their part]." **Off my wisdom.**

Bush: "As I've witnessed throughout my life [in both war and peace] America has never wavered when her purpose is driven by principal." **See if they'll fob me.**

President Bush at Kennebunkport, Maine, August 11, 1990

This press conference was held outside President Bush's holiday home in Kennebunkport, Maine. American troops had been sent in and the Arab nations had agreed to send troops to Saudi Arabia to assist in the fight against Iraq. Bush appeared to be tired during the interview and was surrounded by his aids. I analyzed 16 minutes and 51 seconds of tape time and located 32 reversals with an average of one reversal every 31 seconds. Third Level structural metaphor reversals were more frequent than in the previous section, which may confirm his weariness:

Bush: "We're pleased so far with the solidarity, [cohesiveness] of the economic actions that have been taken." **Sent the Seahawk up.**

Bush: (talking about when Egyptian troops will be there) "I don't have the [exact time on that, but, er,] they will do their share and so [will other Arab countries] and I think we've been saying all along that indeed this [would be a multi-lateral force] and it will be a multi-lateral force with some Arab components." **Hurt that man. My mark has given. / She'll not buy with Allah. / Suffer Allah. Come evil.**

Bush: (discussing the possibility of people in Iraq rising against Saddam) "I know that some countries around the world are [hoping that will] happen [in this situation]." **The pals will hurt them. / Hurt them. Shows this sin.**

Bush: "Well, General Schwarzkopf [is in command] of the United States forces." **I need a name.**

Bush: (talking about the effectiveness of sanctions) "Now with the Arab countries weighing in spite of Saddam's outrageous rhetoric and outrageous military action against Kuwait. I'd say [that's very promising]." **Mark Europe.**

Bush: (responding to question if he was optimistic about getting American citizens out) "I might ask Secretary Baker to comment on that, [er, but, er] some Americans have come out today." **We must hurt them.**

Baker: "We're hopeful that we're able to resolve the situation because it does run against all [international norms]. The fact that American citizens and other foreign nationals as well are [not permitted to leave Iraq or Kuwait]." **Simone won't shine. / They will feel it, our power. Feel it.**

Bush: (responding to the question as to whether there were 250,000 troops going to Saudi Arabia) "[You must have misunderstood me. I said I'm not going to comment on that.]" **I'm not going to come by the same. That's the lesson.**

Bush: "It's a difficult position that King Hussein is in, there's [no question of that,] and in my view he has [been a friend] of the United States for a long time." **I was in shock. / I need enough.**

Bush: "I said [there was a certain disappointment] factor there, [but now with] what the King was able to do yesterday perhaps we can find ways to move forward." **Satan verses the wind. / Find the weather.**

Bush: "My next step is to stay in touch with the situation over there and to implement the plan that is already in effect [and that is to do what we can] to guarantee the [total effectiveness] of the Chapter Seven sanctions." **I feel the wind with Saddam. / Soon be careful.**

Bush: "We'll guarantee the integrity of [Saudi Arabia] and by being there (we) offer some [moral support at least from countries] in the area who could be threatened in the future from this Saddam Hussein." **Very nice. / You not conceal that office slum.**

Bush: "The world is united [against him]. The action of the Arab Summit was very, [very important in this regard]." **They love me. / Guard you're sending. Help me.**

Bush: (responding to the question about what other countries will send troops) "[No, I can't tell you] what others, but I think you'll see others. I know you'll see others and I cannot prematurely say [who they will be] and in [terms of the United Nations] I think that there could be a role in the naval side." **We lost a gun. / Evil weather. / Ashamed that I need this.**

Bush: "We're not prepared to [support the overthrow, but I hope] that these actions we've taken will result in an [Iraq that is prepared to live] peaceably in a community of Nations." **Lord had a boss. The boy in office. / Feel the effort, Satan.**

Bush: "There's no use using different words that [may have, may have different] connotations [in different countries] and this one does in terms of legality." **Afraid by him, by him. / She's not afraid.**

Bush: "What we want to do is see that no oil comes out though the Strait of Hormuz and if it requires naval vessels to see if [that's that,] happens, fine." **Love's a bastard.**

Bush: "The export of oil is almost an impossibility now, but we've got some more diplomacy to make sure its a total [impossibility]." **Feel the love beside me.**

Bush: "Other countries can be helpful in making up the loss (oil) from Kuwait and the loss from Iraq [so to the American people I would say] that we are using every diplomatic channel we can." **Yes. I will beat the gun with the force.**

Interview with Defense Secretary Cheney

This is a brief interview with Defense Secretary Cheney taped as U.S. forces were being deployed to the Persian Gulf.

Cheney: "They used it [in their war with Iran] and Saddam Hussein has used chemical weapons on his own populous." **Now weigh the Whirlwind.**

Cheney: "Discourage [further] aggression is the commitment of U.S. forces to defend our friends in that [part of the world]." **Show our love. / Whirl with love.**

Interview with Iraqi Ambassador

In this interview with Iraqi Ambassador to the United States, Mohamed Al-Mashat, I located 12 English reversals in the 10-minute, 13-seconds recording, an average of one reversal every 51 seconds. This is a lower than the normal average located in other interviews concerning the Persian Gulf crisis.

I presume that other reversals occurred in the Ambassador's native tongue. I located specific tonal alterations, characteristic of reversal occurrence, but couldn't make sense of them. Among these suspected other language reversals, the single word, **Arafat**, occurred twice. Most of the English reversals occurred in an emotionally reactive section of conversation. They were low in clarity and disjointed, typical of the Ambassador's forward English.

Ambassador: "[Arabs, Iraqis] are concerned for all life. That is why we should work together." **God is mother.**

Ambassador: "There is no reason whatsoever [for the American build up,] particularly American offensive build up." **Problem. Making an Adolph.**

Ambassador: "There should be some kind of belt [tightening in the Iraq]. Naturally we are going to be affected. This is only normal." **You don't understand that power.**

Ambassador: "You should orient the American public [that we are passing] through a dangerous time." **It's our pride.**

Ambassador: "If it had not been for Iraq, the Khomeini forces would have [moved all over the gulf]." **Flog them from Allah.**

Ambassador: "We haven't done anything to touch your [interests, strategic] or otherwise." **Iraqis need boasts.**

Ambassador: "We are for peace. [Let us talk for peace.] Let us save life." **See prophets that kill.**

Ambassador: (responding to question when the Iraqis will leave Kuwait) "[We said that we will,] we set a general structure by saying that everybody should respect security council resolutions." **This evil will diverse you.**

Ambassador: "This is our peaceful initiative. That's why [the continuation of sanctions] and the continuation of the blockade illegally because there is a blockade illegally. The security council did [not authorize the United States] to make that blockade." **They shift for the show. / Big stand is Arafat.**

Ambassador: "(It is wrong) to bar Iraq with food [and this is, we,] I think this [doesn't go with the American] value system." **We fear you. / Make it another world.**

Interview with Kuwaiti Ambassador

This is an interview on CNN's _Crossover_ with Kuwaiti Ambassador, Shaikh Saud Nasir Al-Sabah. Twelve reversals occurred in this nine minute and 45-second interview, which was an average of one reversal every 48 seconds. The ambassador spoke in good English, the reversals were reasonably good, yet still low in clarity.

Ambassador: (referring to Iraq's war with Iran) "[Iraq got

stuck in this war.] We had to do something to get Iraq out of this war." **Wolf's in the guts. Don't doubt it.**

Ambassador: "We're not saying whether [Saddam Hussein indulged himself] in this conspiracy, but the whole range of conspiracies is surfacing now." **This Arab is mixing the force.**

Ambassador: "I don't think anyone could doubt the role Kuwait played regarding the [cause of the Palestinian people]. **We're beating this Arab.**

Ambassador: "[He's incapable of negotiating] any peaceful settlement to this. King Hussein already named himself [Sharib Hussein]." **They showed him for all faith to see. / There's a British force.**

Ambassador: "We're hoping that we can resolve this amicably and peaceably. We don't want to [see any further] bloodshed on the part of American boys or any multi-national forces in the area." **Died before you come. / They're stomping us.**

Ambassador: (answering question whether Saddam will pull out of Kuwait) "You want my frank answer. [I'm saying no.] [Saddam,] Saddam Hussein has to be stopped by the whole world." **Wow. He's nuts. / Help us.**

Ambassador: "The British and the Turks signed a treaty whereby they defined explicitly the borders of Kuwait." **Still has a Whirlwind.**

Ambassador: "Go to any international body. Ask them what Kuwait has been [doing for all the developing countries] through the Kuwaiti fund for economic development." **She's not yet in love with the war.**

Man Who Fled From Iraq

This is an interview on CNN conducted with a United States businessman who got out of Iraq before the Iraqis detained all foreigners. The reversals reveal his emotions and thoughts at the time the events happened.

Man: "We were told we should leave Iraq [whenever possible] and at that time it was not possible to leave Iraq. The airport had been closed." **It was awful.**

Man: "We heard from BBC reports that the [President, that is President Bush,] had authorized troops to go to Saudi Arabia." **Showed me love. They deserved it.**

Man: "[The five of us] decided to make the drive to the Iraqi border." **Don't be error.**

Man: (talking about crossing border) "Individuals were constantly brought back to the security people and they would go over [the visa again]." **Whirl was in shock.**

Man: "If you have any feelings at all for the people you are with, you [don't ask them any questions]." **That doesn't shock.**

Bush Addressing War Veterans

Here are two excerpts of President Bush addressing war veterans after Iraq detained all American citizens and they were declared hostages.

Bush: "When Saddam Hussein specifically offers to trade the citizens of many nations [he holds against their will] in return for concessions there can be little doubt that whatever these innocent people are called, they are in fact hostages." **This is a sword.**

Bush: "This is a crisis that we must and will meet if we are [to stop aggression]." **Show the bastard.**

Bush on Air Force One

This was a live press conference on Air Force One as President Bush traveled to Rhode Island. Note the high number of reversals and their clarity. This was because of the live, unrehearsed and relaxed setting, which allowed reversals to flow freely. Tape time was 50 seconds with five clear reversals, one reversal every 10 seconds.

Bush: "[It's only the last couple of days that these] demands have been made. Demands that are obviously totally unsatisfactory to most countries in the world. [His demands] for [allied forces] are of course included, [for U.S. forces] to get out and return to the States, Saddam Hussein having invaded Kuwait." **This man fucks Allah. / Hurt this man. / It's all for Allah./ Congratulate us.**

Bush: "The situation is about the same as [it was a few days ago]." **Saddam. Don't mess up.**

Interview with Iraq's Foreign Minister

This interview was with Iraq's foreign minister, Tariq Aziz, on August 21, 1990. It was a response to Presidents Bush's declaration that Americans in Iraq were hostages and the United States would not withdraw the troops as Saddam Hussein requested.

The interaction was live, spontaneous, and free flowing. The minister spoke excellent English and I detected reversals in a language other than English. These foreign reversals included references to the word "Allah."

Minister: "[The American administration] should know that it cannot dictate these conditions on this situation." **They shamed the devil.**

Minister: "They have to listen to the voice of the people in this region. [They have to know that there is a determined Arab nation] that wants to be free and be treated equally." **You feel it. The shamed Allah arises in the desert.**

Minister: "[The other allies, those people who] have put hundreds of billions of the Arab fortunes in the American banks. [Those people] who have ridiculed [the Arab nation]. He (Bush) [defends them]. **Who believes God. Allah arises / Believe God. / The shamed Arabs. / Hear me.**

Minister: "It has to [respect the feelings] of the Arabs nations, [of the Arab nationals]. It has to use standards, the [same standards] they use in other cases." **The Arab war. / You use standards the same. /**

God wants a sheikh.

Minister: "They (U.S.A.) have a different criteria according to their [special interest] and those of the capitalist countries in the world." **Arab meet. Worship war.**

Minister: "The Americans have left their country to come to a region where they have never been before. [And they have come there to wage war] against the Arabs." **Leave alone. Deal with my mud forever.**

Minister: "You have to react, to [export the acquisition] and to defend yourself." **Ashamed to get from Hitler.**

Minister: "[We want peace and they want a peaceful settlement of] all the problems of the region." **The evil rob the wars. The devil sleeps with Arab sheikhs.**

Minister: "Our provision is [to satisfy our concerns] before we start talking." **God divides the power.**

Minister: "Sometime [President Reagan called] the Soviet Union the empire of evil. He didn't want to talk." **God will give the deserts.**

Minister: "[Let us sit and discuss] all questions according to the initiative of my President." **God's in there. This evil.**

Minister: "[We are ready to discuss, we are ready,] let me answer the question. We are ready to discuss the situation in [the gulf and other situations in the region]." **The arrow. God will loose the arrow. / God is the one who shows the power.**

Saddam Hussein with Hostages

The following is a list of all the English reversals I found during a 47-minute television broadcast of Saddam Hussein with British hostages. I found a small number of reversals on the interpreter who was translating for Saddam Hussein. Of interest, however, was the greater proportion of clear reversals I found on him as the interview ended and he was talking casually to the hostages. I didn't find any English reversals on Saddam Hussein, although I found the following isolated words among the gibberish:

Allah (38 times)

Hebrew (7 times)

Ali (7 times)

Lenin (6 times)

Arab (6 times)

Hannum (4 times)

Harib (3 times)

Bosch (2 times)

Saddam (2 times)

Bush, Hussein, Iraq, Morocco,

British, Sheikh, Arabic, Islam

The hostages didn't talk much during the broadcast, but on most occasions when they did talk, I found reversals:

Child: (talking about playing volley ball) "Yes. [. . . mumbles . . . Yesterday]." **They're sick. Help us.**

Interpreter: "They thought that we were using people as a 'der-a' which means shield rather than as a 'der-r,' which we meant, [which means to prevent] war." **Never perceive you.**

Interpreter: "You have your own journals, your own diaries and you will jot down whatever you have as [feelings or as] recollections [or as impressions] of these days." **Help arrows. / Shout this arrow.**

Interpreter: "We wouldn't want to, [we would know how] you feel, but we are trying to prevent a war from happening." **We fear your hand.**

Interpreter: "(We want you to go) not because we are finding [your hospitality,] or your presence as guests here heavy on us." **He's the lad.**

Interpreter: "[For the first time,] God Almighty addressed his prophet through Gabriel." **I serve him.**

Interpreter: "[I pray] that your presence [here in this kind of situation] will not be long." **Allah. / Shows this, on our sin.**

Hostage: "We would like them (our families) [to know that we are fit] and well." **World will stiff you.**

Hostage: "At a guess, can, [what's the time scale] he thinks. I mean, he's got all his envoys and people who must be mediating." **He masks with snow.** (Note: the forward sentences are quoted exactly as they were said.)

Hostage: "There's been no negotiation [with the West]. [Can the East tell] whether there's been any contact with the Soviet Union?" **Sail with them. / I've seen Mecca.**

End of formal conference. Casual conversation follows:

Interpreter: "You could [have permission] for letters and perhaps have on [camera pictures, messages sent]. [This could, this could] be on television or it could be sent to your families." **This television. / I will leave a message. / Evil sin. Evil sin.**

Interpreter: "What's your name? That's [common here. It's an Arab name.]" **Promise. I promise no more problems arise.**

Hostage: "Can I shake the President's [hand having photographs]?" **Solve the problem.**

Child: "... mumbles ... **Help him. Help him.**

Interpreter: "... mumbles in background ..." **There's no danger.**

Guest News

On August 27, 1990, Iraqi television began to air segments that they called *Guest News*, which were interviews with hostages. The alleged purpose of this was to allow the hostages to send messages home to their families. Three of the hostages speak:

Myers: "Just like to say to our families [that we're all fine] ... [Look forward to a few] good sessions down the pub, Dad. Anyone else listening. [Hi. How ya doing?] We're okay." **I fob them off. / The beast was awful. / Media here.**

Female Student: "I'd like to say [hello to Steve and] all my friends back in London . . . Please don't worry about us, [you know, we're okay]." **I'm on a weird scholar./ Iraq help, promise.**

Barlow Woman: "We're being well treated and everything is fine and [we'll see you soon]." **We'll see you soon.** (NOTE: a rare occurrence, the Reverse Speech is exactly the same as it is forwards.)

Simone

It was apparent that there was special significance to the word **Simone** for it to appear suddenly in reverse only during the Persian Gulf crisis. Prior to the crisis, I had never heard this reversal. This led me to believe that it might have been a code word for the military operation in the desert or that it was a personal metaphor.

Curious to know the answer, I made some discrete inquiries through an acquaintance in Washington, D.C. A confidential letter was written by my acquaintance to his long-time friend, Dick Cheney, that explained Reverse Speech and **Simone**. One line in the letter sparked attention: "I mention this situation in case it is a code word that it would not be in the national interests to reveal."

Obviously, someone down the line thought that it *was* in the national interests because a copy of the letter found its way to the press and almost overnight, **Simone** made it to national news desks across the country.

CNN (Cable News Network) ran the story, implying that Reverse Speech was some new, secret technology about which the Pentagon was being very tight lipped. Newspapers across the nation ran the story with headlines like, *Is the President Hiding Secret Code Words Backwards in His Speech?* and, *What is Reverse Speech?*

In a radio interview that I conducted shortly afterwards, someone called in to inform me that "Simone" was actually an Arabic/African word spelled "simoom" or "simoon" which means "a dust storm in the desert." Further research revealed that it was a word that had been adopted in English. The *Contemporary Dictionary* definition is:

> *A hot, dry, dust-laden, exhausting wind of the African and Arabian deserts.*

The *Oxford Dictionary* goes a step farther and calls it "violent."

These translations were fascinating, especially considering their significance in light of the military operations in the Persian Gulf. My original thinking was that **Simone** described the way the Iraqis stormed Kuwait in a violent fashion in the sands of the Arabian desert. I theorized that **Simone** may have been a personal metaphor for the Gulf operations. I subsequently wrote an article about Simone for *Backtalk*, the Reverse Speech newsletter, but was advised not to print it due to possible military implications.

Here are a few excepts of the article, which I originally wrote in September, 1990, *three full months before* the crisis erupted into full-scale war and went from being called *Operation Desert Shield* to *Operation Desert Storm*.

> " . . . *Simone may be a code word for a military operation in the Gulf or a personal metaphor of some description . . . on a recent talk show a caller told me that it is the Arabic word for dust storm . . . other possible translations are desert wind or desert storm . . . ultimately, **Simone**, is another mystery in the new technology of Reverse Speech that may one day be explained.*"

Then, war broke out. Chills traveled up and down my spine when it was announced that Operation Desert Storm had begun. "Simone!" I exclaimed. I called some of my students and they had heard it, too. Excitement in the Reverse Speech analysts community and interest from every sector of society was suddenly intense. What better proof could there be for the profound importance of Reverse Speech?

The War Begins

Here is a collection of reversals found from the first 30 minutes of the war. These reversals were found on CNN reporters.

> Peter Arnett: "Now we're seeing a lot of activity in the area of this refinery. One thing after another. [One bomb, apparently,] coming down the area ..." **You must alert the bomb.**

> Peter: "Oops! Now there's [something on fire]. **I've known it**. That was an explosion fairly near our location at,

er, [near a mosque in downtown]. **I'm lonely. I'm worried.** We could sort of feel the report [from that]." **Damn them!**

John Holliman: "Tonight, [every bomb we have seen] land [seems to to have hit something]. They hit the refinery correctly . . . " **Now nuclear war. They are not invisible.**

John: "They seem to, they have [these, er, laser directed,] they, the, the, the guided [bombs systems] now." **They kill with a hardly sword. / Is this Simone.**

Peter: "[Well, the anti-aircraft] fire has died down and it seems to me that there's been [at least three waves] of aircraft so far. **Fucking Arab. / We fucked Arab.**

Peter: "[But, as I said, further out] in the city, on the outskirts of the city there seems to be [more explosions taking place, multiple explosions]!" **Hey, listen! / Shell with the bomb. Help me get results.**

Peter: "[Indeed. It's quiet over] there, too. But, I think it's probably just a lull [as President Bush follows] through his threat in an attempt to prove to Saddam Hussein that he should leave Kuwait." **They ousted Eden. / Don't shoot them. Nuke them.**

Charles Jaco: "[The war with Iraq] began early Tuesday morning as a squadron of U.S. [fighter bombers took off from] the largest U.S. air base in central Saudi Arabia." **Now with the Whirlwind. / Don't want to fuck with you.**

Charles: "Colonel Ray Davis said, 'This is history in the making.' [He said, er, watched a group of sombre] pilots board their aircraft, taxi down the runway] and take off." **You must remove the soul. We are at mercy. / You all know my disgust.**

Charles: "The military in Saudi Arabia has [no further information]. They say all briefings will probably come from Riyadh." **War is here. Ashamed of me.**

CNN Front Desk: "The liberation of Kuwait, in the words of the White House, has begun with Operation [Desert Storm]." **I know you monsters.**

Peter: "We have yet to see the bombs fall, but it's the same pattern of the previous [at least three raids,] that we have witnessed." **We're stupid. Get used to it.**

John: "The anti-aircraft [fire is now going toward the south]. We're looking [out to the west] and we [see the tracer bullets going]." **To hell with it. / The bastards don't know Fonzi. / Don't tell 'em it's yesterday.**

John: "The flames might be high, [but the tracer bullets are still going] up into the sky." **I know I'd waste it. Bomb Jerusalem.**

John: "[We've seen these bombs come down before.]" **Bomb them often. I must love in Hebrew.**

John: "We don't have any indication [at all that these] anti-aircraft guns are much success." **They use the Lord.**

John: "I'll give you another moment to [catch your breath]." **I'll respect it.**

The Persian Gulf War was unique in several ways. It was the first time that a war was so thoroughly monitored by public radio and television, it was unusually short, and it was the first time that people looked for reversals in the war broadcasts.

Reversals and the POW's

One of the terrible anxieties that plagues a nation in a time of war is the stress of seeing its captured military personnel paraded before the enemy and possibly coerced into delivering video-taped statements and confessions. Such public broadcasts raise many questions: Were the prisoners of war tortured into saying what they did? Were they reading from scripts or were they expressing their true feelings? How are they holding up? What's going on? What's going to happen? Will we ever see them alive again?

Even the few, short statements delivered by the POW's in the Gulf War yielded a number of reversals, seen in bold print below.

POW: "Lieutenant [Jeffery Morton Zaun,] United States Navy . . ." **Warn my home. You hurt.**

POW: "[I am from attack squadron 35] in the U.S. Saratoga . . ." **They don't have love there.**

POW: "My mission was to attack H3 airfield in [south western Iraq]." **Error, you still trust me.**

POW: "[I think our leaders] and our people have wrongly attacked the peaceful people of Iraq." **Do you know this hell.**

POW: "I would like to [tell my mother and my father] and my sister that [I am well treated]." **You know now my trouble. / Hurts to done it.**

POW: "And that [they should pray] for peace." **Ashamed in it.**

POW: "[For the children, please study hard at school.]" **Bush robbed your faith, Bush did.**

POW: "A large bang out the left wing and the [plane began to crash] . . ." **Serve this naked lesson.**

And, finally, this reversal found on an Iraqi speaking in Arabic: **Simoon.**

Reverse Speech gives new meaning to the phrase, "More than meets the eye"—or in this case, more than meets the ear.

More than Meets the Ear

In this rapidly changing and challenging world, we need to be well informed in order to make wise decisions and choices for ourselves and for those whom we love. We need to know where to spend our money, who to watch on television, who to listen to on the radio, who to believe in the media and, perhaps more importantly, who to vote for in our elections.

Reverse Speech can help us to determine the credibility and the reliability of the people who influence our lives.

12

Reverse Speech
and the Professions

Police Work, Law, Education, Insurance, Marketing, Sales and Advertising

Every calling is great when greatly pursued.
—Oliver Wendel Holmes, Jr. Speech,
Suffolk Bar Association February 5, 1885

Among the first professionals to step forward and be trained to use Reverse Speech, or to team up with Reverse Speech analysts, were psychotherapists, child psychologists, school counselors, attorneys, investigators, advertising and marketing specialists, and salespeople. Following suit have been educators, pastoral counselors, physicians, public speakers, and media professionals. Then, of course, there are all the people who want to explore Reverse Speech by working with an analyst to satisfy their curiosity or to resolve challenges in their lives.

Virtually anyone in any profession in which self-understanding and communication are necessary can benefit from what Reverse Speech has to offer. I've already discussed the use of reversals in work with children, therapy, relationship counseling, business, music, and politics. Now, I'll talk about the

205

use of reversals in police work, law, insurance, sales, marketing, advertising, and education—only a small portion of the professions in which reversals can be used.

A Word to the Wise

Much work with reversals involves increasing people's awareness of themselves, discovering the causes of their behaviors or problems, and introducing them to their deeper Selves—if they haven't already met. Professionals need to be careful, therefore, when they tell people what their reversals are. Some people who hear their reversals for the first time may feel nervous or physically unsettled, or may experience anger, denial, or restlessness. Some people sleep less than usual for the first few nights and others sleep better than usual.

The important thing is that this work be done under the auspices of certified Reverse Speech analysts. Professionals and analysts should also obtain signed release forms in which clients give their permission to have their sessions recorded and their reversals analyzed.

Investigations

The police record with video or audio many of their investigative sessions with crime suspects. A study of reversals can speed up these investigations or even prevent crimes by revealing details of a suspect's past activities—or anticipated activities. This can take much of the guess work out of an investigator's job.

In my experience, however, the police have been cautious about publicly admitting to the use of reversal analysis in their work. This is partially because they have to follow strict legal guidelines that protect citizens' rights. If they plan to use reversals in their investigations, when they read suspects their rights, they may some day have to include in the statement-of-rights that anything suspects say, both forward *and* backward, may be used against them in a court of law.

Reverse Speech has been used by the police in Australia and in the United States to uncover facts and information that has been relevant to case work. So far, however, they have been reluctant to talk about it, wishing to avoid publicity. Consequently, it's difficult for me to quote case studies. I have found some interesting reversals on television interviews that illustrate the usefulness of Reverse Speech in police work.

A Cry in the Night

The first case regards a much-publicized incident in Australia, which was the subject of the movie, *A Cry in the Night*, starring Meryl Streep. On the night of August 17, 1980, a nine-week old baby, Azaria Chamberlain, disappeared while her family was camping near the popular tourist spot, Ayers Rock. This is a large, natural outcrop of rock located in the outback, almost in the dead center of Australia.

The baby's parents, Lindy and Michael Chamberlain, claimed that they saw a dingo take the child. An extensive three-day search of the area, and examinations of the stomach contents of dingoes and wild dogs that were shot, failed to find any traces of the baby's body.[1]

Thus began the most notorious and protracted legal case ever witnessed in Australia. Lindy Chamberlain was charged with the baby's murder and, after numerous legal maneuvers, was found guilty and sentenced to life imprisonment. In 1986, a vital piece of evidence was found that proved her innocence. She was cleared of all charges and released from prison.

Had the police had access to Reverse Speech and been willing to accept its use, millions of dollars in legal costs and the virtual destruction of the Chamberlains' life could have been avoided. Here are portions of the transcript of Lindy Chamberlain's first television interview, which was recorded only four days after the event, well before any suspicion toward her had surfaced.

> "We think that someone there must have seen it happen. It's affected so many people's lives [and the letters that we're getting back now,] we know that other people's faith in God has been strengthened." **My man help me deal with this healing.**
> (Looking to her husband for support.)
> "I put the baby down and started to get my son into bed and [he said mummy, I'm still hungry is that all] the

dinner I can have?" **Now wish my mum had seen her.**

(Since her mother had never seen the baby, this was a natural reaction for her to have.)

"I [yelled at the dog and I thought] that's the baby cry, he's disturbed her." **Help us. God the warrior.**

(Her Christian faith shines through and she looks to her God for support.)

"I said [the dingo's got my baby and I was running] as I said this around the car and there was [the dingo standing at the back of the car]." **I was running. / I can forget an answer. I needed the wind.**

(Her reversals reflect her panic and are congruent with the forward story.)

"I chased it and there was nothing. It was all [shadows and I just, er,] Michael ran from the barbecue straight up into the dark and [I called out has] anyone got a flashlight?" **Slip on our shoes. / I needed shoes.**

(The reversals flash back to that night again, revealing other thoughts and events that transpired at the time.)

These reversals, and many others that appear in this interview, are totally congruent with Lindy Chamberlain's story. If she had been guilty, her reversals would have reflected that guilt.

A Murderer Confesses

Here are portions of a transcript of a video-taped interview with a man who was responsible for multiple killings in Melbourne, Australia. The video, shown on National Australian television in November 1988, was filmed only hours after the crime and after the man surrendered to police.

The video shows him making a full confession in forward speech, while he walked with police around the murder scene and described how he committed the crime. He was sentenced to 27 years hard labor with no parole and made no appeal against the sentence.

While the reversals use language typically associated with the Second Level, they are spoken in an experiential context, so they are in this case actually First Level. They give accurate insight into the man's mental state and into his motivations for the crime.

> Police: (live while the crime is in progress) "[He's just shot eight people!]" **Darn it. Don't shoot.**
> (Thoughts at the time.)
>
> Murderer: "[I was using the rifle.]" **The firing was easy.**
>
> Murderer: (referring to a passer-by whom he shot, but didn't kill immediately so he fired more rounds into him) "[I was about one or two meters in that direction.]" **Shoot them. I messed one up.**
>
> Murderer: "[I'd half] decided to go to my girlfriend's place, my ex-girlfriend's place, [and hand myself in]." **Murder. / Shot the folks down.**
>
> Murderer: "I heard the police car behind me so [I turned in the alley here]." **You know, I killed.**
>
> Murderer: "The mussel flash was so great [you could hardly see it anyway]." **I don't feel bad. I laugh at them.**
>
> Murderer: (talking about the arrival of the police) "I thought [they were outside behind the car doors]." **So annoyed. Must have more fun.**
>
> Murderer: "The policemen at that [stage were yelling]." **I don't feel bad.**
>
> Police: "Do you have any feeling of regret over these people dying?"
>
> Murderer: "[Yep.] I regret that it had to be civilians and I regret that I was [captured rather than killed]." **Hate. / They're all the same, shot.**

Guilty or Innocent?

Confidentiality forbids me to publish the forward dialogue of the transcript below, since this police case is still pending. These are reversals on a suspect whose business partner was shot the night before this recording and later died in the hospital.

Is this suspect guilty? Is he telling the truth? Did he have a motive to kill his partner? Could a lie detector test do any better in detecting guilt or innocence than Reverse Speech can? I leave that for you to decide.

> I wanna listen to murder. / Woman.
> We sure argue. / I killed him.
> I'm just an asshole with him.
> I rubbed him out, him. / I'm gonna lose the farm.
> I lost a deal with eight hundred. What happened.
> I need a gun. / I'll catch him that evening.
> Be careful.
> I'll phone and set him up. / I'll phone the signal.
> Gave them my signal. / I did panic. / I'll set this up.
> It's all bullshit. / Of course, I'm fed up.
> I'm nervous, money. / Rotten fellow, that person.
> They shot him. / I cursed, I shot, snapped, money.
> Power was the lover there. I'm sorry.
> I now seize the lover from him.
> It's time to shoot. / Time to set up this fuzzy war.
> Nothing in it. / I left the gun.
> Up the coast from now from memory. / The gun's there.
> Someone saw the weapon.

So, as you glanced through the murder suspect's reversals, do you suppose that he was he innocent—or guilty? Further investigation will tell.

Reverse Specch and the Law

For the legal and investigative community, Reverse Speech poses many thought-provoking questions[2] that must be addressed, a few of which follow:

1. In criminal investigations, once people relinquish their right to remain silent, can the content of their speech reversals be admissible evidence in a court of law? Who decides what the reversals mean? And, should they be treated as metaphors or as facts?

2. Can reversals be considered "subliminal" under current legislation? To outlaw the use of Reverse Speech

analysis or to bring litigation is pointless because reversals are beyond conscious control. What happens, then, when someone has an "undesirable" reversal? Can people be sued for defamation of character because of something they said in reverse?

3. Should rock 'n' roll groups be brought before the courts because of certain "unacceptable" reversals in their songs?

4. Should lawyers use speech reversals that they find in pre-trial, taped depositions to help them determine whether a witness is credible or not? Can the lawyers then use the reversals to decide which witnesses to use in a trial and which not to use? Is using reversals in this manner an ultimate invasion of privacy, an invasion on which the U.S. Constitution would frown?

5. Who owns the reversals on a tape recording? Can they be considered a derivative work and, therefore, protected under copyright law?

6. Does Reverse Speech pose a threat to national security? For example, if the President knows that his speech is going to be recorded and his reversals analyzed, might he be more reluctant to make public statements regarding international events? If he decides not to talk, is this denying citizens their right to know?

   Likewise, might politicians who fear that their reversals could endanger their chances of being elected, or re-elected, be more reluctant to make speeches or to give press conferences? Could this spell the end of the election campaign trail?

7. Could Reverse Speech lead to the increased use of wire tapping by authorities and, therefore, jeopardize the rights of citizens? Is this the dawning of George Orwell's "Big Brother" society? (Ironically, Reverse Speech was discovered in 1984.)

As Reverse Speech gains wide acceptance and credibility, special legislations will be required to govern its use.

Reversals in the Court Room

Here are portions of a case that I analyzed for an Australian lawyer. It is the transcript of a disciplinary hearing heard in the Adelaide, Australia, Department of Consumer Affairs, in which a public servant was alleged to have engaged in outside work activities. The reversals below reveal the strategies and the high emotions operative during the hearing.

> Lawyer: "The documents subsequent to that would be fairly important for him to check his diary to find out, if possible, to find out what he was doing on the various days so he can say what's happening. We'll be looking forward to having those documents so that we can actually have a reasonable opportunity." **It's a nuisance problem. It's a nasty problem.**

> Magistrate: "You've got a copy of everything, all the formal reports, which have been prepared in relation to this matter and there's no other documentation in existence." **You're a nuisance. / You should leave, you bastard.**

> Magistrate: "For an employee who is absent without reasonable excuse. Proof shall lie with the employee." **You help me and I'll like you.**

> Magistrate: "If he is denying that then what I'm trying to get you to say which you haven't said is that he did not engage in outside employment and he was always present here and if he was absent it was without reasonable excuse." **I see no reasonable wisdom. / Don't believe you.**

> Magistrate: "I think that any other argument along those lines quite frankly would not be acceptable to me." **I see you're careful.**

> Lawyer: "The charges only covered materials. Yes there were charges made, but that does not make remuneration." **Wisdom will fuck him up.**

> Magistrate: "Well what you're saying is that the charges made were in respect of pipes and all that sort of thing." **It seems not reasonable.**

Lawyer: "You have assumed that the charges included labor fees. You have therefore proceeded on an assumption of guilt and it seems to me to be quite clear that the investigator has not bothered to check the facts." **I can certainly fuck him.**

Lawyer: "The enquiry hasn't even checked out what was happening and why he may have been charging for things." **I must be careful.**

Magistrate: "Look, I think you're playing with words here. Did he or did he not charge for labor?" **I was nice. / Now he wants it.**

Magistrate: "It's not an assumption which is not without reasonable grounds given the extent of his business activities and with the number of people with whom he did business." **I'm a bit mad. This fellow wants it.**

Magistrate: "This particular man who your client did work for has known him over many years." **I want an answer.**

Lawyer: "I refer you back to the guidelines. Second clause, 'Without reasonable proof—without reasonable excuse, proof of which shall lie on the employee.' Now I think the first problem is to show absent of duty and we have not received the necessary documents to establish absent of duty." **I am a little bit careful.**

Magistrate: "Your client has had the last 14 days. The records are readily available if he wanted to do that, he's had plenty of time to do that and he's had reasonable opportunity." **Nervous. I wish it was done. / He's making this up. / They're selfish.**

Magistrate: "Your client was recorded as being on duty on the 11th of February '87, but it seems that he was also with Mr. Johnson on that day." **Messing me you people. My nerves are awful.**

Lawyer: "It says quite clearly he should be afforded a reasonable opportunity to question persons making accusations etc. Now we've not got most of the papers you're referring to." **There's an extra problem, error.**

Magistrate: "Yeah I know that. You keep coming back to that point. But what I'm saying, I'm just dealing with a very narrow point, what I'm saying is that if he wants to check anything in relation to the 11th of February 87, it's just a matter of him checking." **Don't worry I would not disturb his fun. / This man still is messy.**

Lawyer: "Someone could go now and do the photocopying for the remaining 28 pages so we at least know what's in there." **He fucked it up.**

Magistrate: "I think that we might adjourn the enquiry now for a few moments and you can check on the content of the material." **There's no reason.**

Lawyer: "How long do you get for morning tea." **That man. He's mad.**

Magistrate: (following recess) "We believe there has been admission in the relation of those two sub-sections for the following reasons. On page 5E of the interview between your client and the investigator, it seems to me quite clear from the material there that on the 22nd of August 1986, he did engage in outside employment." **Stuff this job. Don't deserve this. / Hey you're mad. / Be reasonable.**

Lawyer: "Excuse me. I have a page 5, but not a 5E." I **doubt that.**

Magistrate: "Your client is saying he was off sick on the 22nd of August. He felt he was better so he went to do some work on that day." **I'd love to fuck him up.**

Magistrate: "I don't know what sort of admission one would want in a case like this, but to me that is perfectly clear." **That's a fucking problem.**

Magistrate: "I seem to remember your comment that, referring to comments he has made to you directly, that in your opinion this is indicating guilt." **He's**

not careful. / The man is boring.

Magistrate: "We'll check on the procedure anyway." **Curse you.**

Lawyer: "We'd been seeking as adjournment." **He's done this. I kiss you.**

Magistrate: "They notify within 14 days after receiving notice of the finding or proposed action or recommendation of appeal to the disciplinary appeals tribunal, but we've made no finding." **Enough of this has been done.**

Lawyer: "You've found that he's had reasonable opportunity. That's a finding. We say it's not correct. He's not had reasonable opportunity." **Your response. We ask you. You've not established.**

Magistrate: "Well I can't find whether or not this appeal is valid 'cause I simply don't know and if you put an argument to me then I'll draw up a deposition to argue that point with you at this stage." **I've got a problem. That's a weird person. / I'm feeling bad. Don't argue.**

Lawyer: "I serve that copy on you now as the chief executive officer." **On cassette.**

Magistrate: "I will certainly accept service of it, but I can't admit whether it's valid." **What a problem. / Reversal of the Whirlwind.**

Insurance, Marketing and Sales, and Advertising

For insurance companies, analyzing reversals could save hundreds of thousands of dollars a year on fraudulent claims.

In marketing and sales organizations, studying salespeople's reversals can pinpoint their strengths, weaknesses, motivation, and belief in the product or service, which, in turn, can lead to more effective sales calls and presentations.

Reverse Speech can also verify the effectiveness of advertisements and identify which ads contain reversals that are counter-productive to selling a product or service. This in turn can lead to the development of more effective marketing strategies.

For example, here's a 60-second advertisement that I analyzed for a South Australian Lending Corporation whose product was home loans. The video scene shows a husband and wife looking for a house in the newspaper. The advertisement was an experiment using common abbreviations for extras in the house such as BIRs and UGPs, most of which meant nothing to the average viewer and created confusion, which resulted in the advertisement being ineffective. The reversals reflect this confusion and also show high, buyer resistance to the salesman.

> Woman: "Hey. This one looks good. 3BRs, [lounge, Sep DR,] AC, BIRs..." **I hate this smile.** (referring to the salesman).
>
> Salesman: "Tell him about the quality drapes, outfits, and WWCs throughout. Go on! You can afford it! . . . The Institution's loan at market rate. A fixed interest loan . . . Or, you can make a high start while you're both working with a lower repayment when the kids come along."
>
> Woman: "[Now you're talking.]" **He forced me on.** (buyer resistance).
>
> Salesman: "What do you think?"
>
> Woman: "[I think I'll put a pat stroke] perg at the side." **What's that? I don't want this stuff!**
> (Confusion, resistance high.)

The advertisement was subsequently taken off the air. My analysis of the reversals prior to putting the ad on the air might have saved the lending institution a significant amount of time and money.

Education

People who teach, instruct, or give group presentations can greatly benefit from reversal analysis of themselves, of the group, and of individuals within a group.

For example, teachers can increase their effectiveness by analyzing both their own reversals and the reversals of individual students, and they can obtain valuable insights into students who have behavioral difficulties.

Presenters can study their reversals in order to refine and polish their deliveries. In addition, they can monitor subtle attitudes or the disposition of a group. For example, just as an individual speaker uses particular voice patterns and inflections, a group of people, or an audience, has similar, but *collective* inflections, mumblings, and breathing patterns—fertile ground for reversals. An audience, in which the members are laughing and in high rapport with each other and with the speaker, sometimes chants words such as **Power, power, power** in reverse.

Businesspeople and professionals today are beginning to demonstrate more concern for global issues, to be more socially responsible, to view themselves and their companies in relation to the whole of humanity, and to cooperate instead of compete.

What an ideal setting for Reverse Speech analysis, which, by its very nature, helps encourage positive values, ethics and integrity. Reverse Speech can add a new, perhaps more honest dimension to the workplace, which, in turn, may make it a more productive environment—and, ultimately, a more rewarding experience for all involved.

13

Developing Areas
Of Research

*If the truth hurts most of us so badly that we don't want it
told, it hurts even more grievously those who dare tell it. It
is a two-edged sword, often deadly dangerous to the user.*
—Judge Ben Lindsey (1869-1943) *Revolt of Modern Youth*

*If you shut up Truth and bury it under the ground, it will but
grow, and gather to itself such explosive power that the day
it bursts through, it will blow up everything in its way.*
—Émile Zola (1840-1902) *J'accuse*

As with any new science, the various applications become
more evident as people experiment with the discovery. As
experimentation expands, anomalies emerge, creating new
possibilities for experimentation and growth. Even without
extensive background in many professions, the implication that
almost any profession could benefit from Reverse Speech
applications is obvious. It is also obvious that as expertise from
various professions is joined in the research, current articulations
will be clarified, 'old' wisdom will see new light, and additional
layers of 'new' wisdom will be unveiled. The opportunities for
research studies are virtually endless.

The only absolute certainty in the current process of discovery
is that more 'students' of the process are essential. Ideally, they

would come from every conceivable discipline to become certified graduates of the Reverse Speech Education and Research Institute's programs. For example:

- **Computer programmers** might be interested in writing programs to easily identify reversals in recorded speech.
- **Linguists** might want to compare the reversals found on English-speaking people with the reversals found on non-English speaking people, or on people who speak several languages.
- **Historians** might trace a certain reversal back through time to discover the impact of particular events.
- **Sociologists** might study and compare the reversals found on select groups such as members of a political party or a religious sect.
- **Psychologists** might analyze the reversals found on people under the influence of drugs or alcohol to discover patterns of readiness for change.
- **Physicians** might analyze patients' reversals to identify causes of disease and its state of progression/remission.
- **Theologians** might use the process of oral tradition to see if they can unravel the very words used by famous spiritual leaders.
- **Businesspeople** might study their competition's reversals in order to plot successful marketing strategies.
- **Futurists** might anticipate emerging trends and possible upcoming events by studying Future Tense reversals

Below are some other ideas and projects for enterprising researchers to explore.

Locating Reversals

Locating reversals quickly and efficiently requires intentional skill development.[1] Many people find it difficult to learn the new "language" and "accent" of Reverse Speech. This fact has been significant in preventing independent, controlled testing of the phenomenon. The frustration associated with a lack of training deters many from further study and research.

Deciphering reversed patterns is an acquired skill that one learns with practice, patience, and persistence. The pattern of growth in training classes is fairly standard.

1. Students who spend at least 10 hours a week studying and listening tend to interpret "gibberish" for the first 2-3 weeks. They tend to miss clear, obvious reversals.

2. Next, students begin to locate robotic, mechanical sounding phrases. Somewhere between four to 12 weeks, students begin to locate genuine reversals. Integral to this learning process is their ability to recognize tonal variation.

3. Students who relax and "experience" their way through the sounds, who approach the study of reversals from a more right-brain perspective, usually find learning the easiest. Playing music in the background, which stimulates right-brain activity, often improves the new student's learning ability.

As the patterns of learning are more clearly identified and the collective knowledge of reversal identification expands, the task becomes progressively easier. Future students of Reverse Speech will have cause to be forever grateful to those who have pioneered this learning curve.

Reversals and Other Languages

Currently, research indicates that if a forward language is English, the reversal will also be in English. Likewise, if the forward language is German, the reversals will be in German.

If people speak English, but have limited knowledge of English, their reversals mostly will be in their native tongue. People who've been speaking English for years and who say they think in English, even though English is their second language, have reversals primarily in English. The controlling factor seems to be whether they're *thinking* in their own tongue and silently translating as they speak. Proficient English speakers who have a native tongue other than English, however, still use scattered reversals from their native tongue.

Some tests have been conducted with people who are bilingual, but these tests have been minimal and the findings aren't yet conclusive.

Reversals in Sanskrit?

Some unconfirmed information, reported by Australian Reverse Speech developer and researcher Paul Von Stroheim, who speaks fluent German, complicates the above issue. Paul says that he's found a small proportion of German phrases on tapes exclusively in English—German spoken by people who didn't know how to speak German. He proposes that through the process of oral tradition, one might find other languages in Reverse Speech—all the way back to Sanskrit.[2]

Reversals from "The Dreamtime"

Australian researcher, Greg Albrecht, is currently conducting some exciting and well-documented studies. Greg, who's fascinated with the Australian Aborigines, speaks a little of their native dialect and is now the Aboriginal resource teacher for a large section of the Australian near-outback. This puts him in contact with many Aborigines and, with his trusty tape recorder and reversing machine in hand, he's come up with some amazing tapes and new theories concerning oral tradition and the nature of structural metaphors.

Greg has found numerous reversals on Aborigines in their native dialect—when they've been speaking in both English and their native tongue. In addition, he's found many structural metaphors that stem back to the legends of "the Dreamtime." Greg hopes that he may be able to trace these structural metaphors to their roots in "Dreamtime" and uncover some of the many mysteries that surround the Aborigines' appearance in the land of the hot sun.

English Reversals, Foreign Tongues

Here are some English reversals that I found on languages other than English during my initial research into music and public speeches.

- "Veraland," by Jim Reeves. The song was sung in Afrikaans: **Fuck off Satan. / Fuck off in the name of the Lord.**
- Hitler speaking in German during a pre-war speech: **There is no God. Armageddon, your Fuhrer. / Come**

to Fuhrer. **There is no oil.** (The phrase, **There is no oil,** is significant because Germany lacked the basic raw materials they needed for their war machine. They obtained these by plundering invaded countries.)

- "La Bamba," by Ritchie Valens. The song was sung in Spanish: **I am a believer are you? God gave us faith I know. I was lost but now am found.**

Reversal Control

Can reversals can be controlled? Studies have clearly shown that it is possible to consciously alter one's mind states. Is it possible to alter the state of the unconscious mind sufficiently to consciously control reversals?

In some initial experiments, hypnosis has been used to access the part of the mind responsible for the formation of reversals. Neurolinguistic Programming (NLP) "change" techniques have been used to request the unconscious mind to alter reversals accordingly.

Only minimal, relatively transitory success has been achieved with this so far. The major problem seems to be in the nature of Reverse Speech itself, which is a reflection of the unconscious mind. To change reversals, the unconscious mind must also be changed. Every evidence exists that this is possible and is being done in many other contexts. What works most effectively, exactly why it works and how long it takes seems to vary with every individual. Experimentation in many fields will need to be shared to test and verify this process of intentionally expanding consciousness.

In one experiment, however, reversals were "turned off," in that the rate of reversal delivery was extremely low. In fact, a reversal was delivered during this experiment that said, **Do not listen to my reversals.** On another occasion, a hypnotic suggestion was made to prompt sexual reversals. The ensuing reversals were so strong and phallic, that the initial suggestion had to be reversed. The "control effect" was adversely affecting those who were communicating with the subject. So far, reversal control appears to be temporary, lasting only a few hours.

Reversal Feedback

Experimentation has begun with the effects of using a person's own reversals in therapy, trance inductions, or conversations. In my own work, I've used a client's reversals, found in previous sessions, to induce a trance state in the client. I've also asked clients who were in trance what some of their reversed metaphors meant. The results have been fascinating—identifying personal metaphors, archetypal relations and more. This early research will be reported in a future volume.

I have also used an individual's reversals while speaking to them in casual forward conversation. On one occasion when I was travelling with my children from Adelaide to Brisbane, my daughter Symone was extremely upset during the overnight stopover. She'd been crying for several hours and I couldn't calm her. Knowing the high proportion of her reversals that used the word **help**, I held her in my arms and said repeatedly "Daddy's helping you. You have help." Within minutes she calmed down and drifted off into a sound, peaceful sleep.

Similarly, an Australian therapist reports that since she learned about Reverse Speech she has frequently used reversal language in her therapeutic techniques. She reports some interesting results and quotes one case in particular where a breakthrough was made with a client when she casually used the reversed metaphor, **another one.** Her client immediately responded with, "I wish I could," and the therapy took a major turn as the client began to discuss her desire to have another partner.

Consciously Hearing Reversals

Researchers have begun exploring the possibility of learning how to hear reversals consciously as they occur while someone is talking. Hypnotist and NLP practitioner, Graham Townsend, has done some initial work with me along these lines. In these experiments, Townsend gave my conscious mind instructions to reverse small sections of speech sounds as I spoke them, in the same fashion as a tape player is reversed to hear reversals.

Three instances of success were obtained in the final of six sessions. Personally, it was an eerie experience. All forward sounds suddenly disappeared from my mind, as though a tape player had been switched off, and a clear ghost-like voice reverberated in my head. Still under hypnosis, I reported the voice that I'd heard. When I came out of trance, we reversed the recording and the three reversals were located exactly as I'd reported them.

"Jason" Speaks

A second set of experiments were done with hypnotist Martin Stiles, that used a different method. In trance, we contacted that part of the mind responsible for the formation of reversals, and named it "Jason."

Jason was asked to relay to the conscious mind the reversals that he was hearing. No success was obtained under trance. Several days later, I had four separate experiences, similar to those we had attempted to set up in the Townsend experiments. Only one of these occurred while recording, so it was the only phrase we were able to confirm.

The others could not be confirmed, and the experiences haven't happened again.

Metaphor Restructuring

Effectively restructuring metaphors—that is, addressing those parts of a client's mind that have exhibited themselves in structural metaphor reversals such as **Wolf**, **Garden of Eden**, and **Lancelot**—requires image shifting throughout an individual's consciousness. Behaviors shift more rapidly if work is done at the level of images that support, sustain or encourage those behaviors. When a client is in trance, negotiations can be directly undertaken with that part of the mind where images reside in an attempt to achieve more desirable outcomes for the client. Monitoring the ongoing progress of reversals will reveal attitudinal changes occurring in clients. These deeper changes will be manifest in changes in the general spirit of their reversals.

The basic premise of metaphor restructuring is that the metaphors of Reverse Speech are universal. They have been adopted from the collective unconscious through the process of oral tradition as verbal descriptors of complex images within the unconscious mind. These images come together in a variety of ways to create, or reflect, the whole individual. To encourage positive behavioral change, one must reach and work with, the deepest causes of a problem.

Simply knowing the source of a problem, however, is, in many cases, insufficient to effect change. We unfortunately were not issued with blueprints for the mind when we were born and the webs and connecting patterns are complex to say the least.

Behavioral strategies can be deeply ingrained and very hard to shake. Many times, people's operational and structural metaphors have been etched into their psyches from early childhood. Children adopt parental metaphors, community or cultural metaphors and create some of their own. The building blocks of the mind are often so intermingled that a total unraveling and reweaving seems to be required for change.

For example, a person who has difficulty with serious relationships may run an unconscious sabotage program in which he or she falls rapidly in love, then becomes scared and instigates arguments that lead to the collapse of the relationship. This person may also have been hurt by a family member or a close friend, which further complicates their ability to sustain a relationship.

Reverse Speech analysis may reveal that he or she has a highly active **Wolf**, the part of the mind that is the primordial, instinctive hunter and protector. The Wolf, whose job it is to protect the psyche, is constantly on the prowl for situations that would hurt. Recognizing a potential love situation, the Wolf might switch off deep emotions or replace them with more superficial ones. The Wolf may then begin to test the new partner, most likely on an unconscious level, to see if the person is worthy. In the process of testing, the other person's Wolf is activated and a self-protection game is put into play. "War" has begun. Both wolves get hurt. The relationship is terminated.

But, the first Wolf knows that the person needs love, and allows the hunt for another partner to begin. The problematic potential of the ingrained metaphor becomes an established pattern.

The first step in unraveling behavior is to understand what each archetype, or structural metaphor, is trying to communicate. Structural metaphors are verbal descriptions of mental images.

For example, the Wolf is the hunter and protector, The Garden of Eden is the spiritual center, or source of knowledge and wisdom, Satan is that part of us that delivers intense, over-bearing emotions that can be destructive, and the Goddess is the healer. (See the Dictionary in Appendix II for a more complete list.)

Each part works together to make the whole human being. The Goddess without the Wolf lacks strength and becomes weak and insipid. The Garden without Satan becomes unprotected and, with too much Satan, becomes warped and perverted.

Briefly, to use metaphor restructuring, suppose a reversal was delivered that said, **My Wolf works with Satan** (**Satan** being the strong, destructive emotion that the **Wolf** uses to protect the person speaking). The basic principle of metaphor restructuring states that if the picture is inappropriate to achieve the desired outcome, change the picture that the metaphor describes and, in the process of changing the picture, the unwanted behavioral pattern may also change.

With metaphor restructuring we are, in effect, going in the back door. Rather than directly attempting to change the pattern, then monitoring the effectiveness of the change as revealed through the changing reversals, we change the basic metaphor, and watch the patterns change as a result. Amazingly, this can work *very* rapidly.

The Method

In an initial Reverse Speech session with a client, we locate the behavioral patterns that need or want to be changed. Locating the reversals the client uses is essential.

Next, the client enters a light hypnotic trance and is told to create a mental picture of the metaphor. Thus, a person whose **Wolf** works with **Satan** might picture a Wolf working with an image of Satan.

I then suggest that the client change the picture. For example, suppose elsewhere in the session the client said that **the Wolf has no sword to find the Garden**. I would instruct the person to create a picture of a sword and give it to the Wolf and let the Wolf go on a "walkabout," to use Aussie slang, to find the Garden. Satan would be dealt with in some other manner, depending on what had transpired in the client's speech reversals.

Metaphor restructuring sounds simple enough, but it actually takes great skill and should be undertaken only by well-trained, experienced Reverse Speech analysts. Among other things, in metaphor restructuring, reversal location and identification *must* be accurate to avoid working with pictures that don't exist, reversal interpretation must be exact, the light trance must be structured with the appropriate safety commands, and the behavioral patterns must be identified precisely.

Metaphor restructuring is well worth all the work that goes into it. Many people report immediate and powerful changes in their lives after working with this technique. Metaphor restructuring would be a excellent research project for a trained Reverse Speech analyst to pursue. I must restate, however, that this is an experimental technique that should NOT be attempted by untrained people.

Historical Research

Reversal analysis may prove useful to answering questions about historical events. For example, a short extract of reversals from President Nixon's retirement speech has already hinted that perhaps there was more to Watergate than what we've been told. Imagine analyzing all the available taped recordings of the Watergate scandal! Also, who *really* killed President Kennedy? And, just how involved was Colonel Oliver North in the Iran-Contra affair?

All this information and much more may be available on taped recordings of interviews with historical figures. An experienced researcher simply has to locate the reversals. The archives of many capital cities are gold mines of recorded information for the daring researcher, who may find himself or herself opening a veritable Pandora's box!

Or, speaking of Pandora's box, Reverse Speech may help illumine the evolution of consciousness by eventually revealing the "why?" behind the development of our brain's structure as a letter from Renee Tait, one of my first students in Australia, suggests:

> *I've given some thought to the remnants of the Reptilian brain cortex as discussed by Dr. David Suzuki, the environmentalist*

par excellence. Is it the operative impulse in reversals? Could well be. Putting some message forth for evermore. Basic and non-threatening, and that maybe our present forward speech is, and always has been, a mere corruption of universal truths. [3]

Controlled Experimentation

Reverse Speech continues to be confirmed by the growing numbers of professionals who use it, and I *always* welcome letters of endorsement. People who are involved in Reverse Speech are willing to take part in controlled experiments, provided the inquiring academic institution is accredited. Future experiments might include:

- Extensive EEG testing to determine what's actually happening inside the brain in connection with speech reversals. These tests should include the collection of appropriate, recorded data, the mapping of brain matrix patterns, and the preparation of results for publication.

- A statistical analysis that compares Reverse Speech patterns to the corresponding forward phrases responsible for them. This would involve the development of computer programming, the end goal of which would be to accurately verify the verbal content of reversals.

- A controlled experiment to further establish confidence in the existence of Reverse Speech. This could take the form of analyzing recordings of people from three separate groups: non-English speakers, people who have studied and spoken English for less than five years, and people for whom English is a native language. The tapes would then be analyzed "blind" to locate English reversals.

If Reverse Speech were merely a coincidence of sound, one could expect to find an equal number of reversals throughout the tape. Verification of the non-coincidental nature of reversals would appear as substantially different frequency rates for each group.

Greater Reliability

More work is needed to increase the reliability of locating and analyzing reversals. This might include:

- Collecting additional recorded data by competent professionals, particularly in the field of psychotherapy and police investigations. As of this writing, there are only a few people who are proficient in locating and interpreting reversals, and only a few therapeutic centers and investigative agencies using this technology.

- Extensive analysis of video-taped recordings to study the connection between body language with the appearance of reversals, which would provide an additional "control" factor. Some connections already noticed include lip movements synchronized with reversed phrases.

- Development of a computer program that uses voice-recognition chips and neuro-net circuitry to automatically locate reversals. Investigations already conducted show promise that this can be achieved, but the funds needed would be astronomical. Such a program, however, would negate the need for hundreds of hours of laborious, exhausting work; significantly reduce the human-error factor; and allow for analysis immediately following the recording session.

Speech reversals hold an important key to the secrets of the human mind and the nature of language. The question, therefore, is not, "Should research continue?" but rather, "How *quickly* can it continue?"

Historians answering age-old questions and solving ancient riddles . . . People who don't speak foreign languages speaking them in reverse . . . Wolves walking in the garden and changing behavior for the better . . . Futurists predicting upcoming events by studying Future Tense reversals . . .

Is this the "stuff" of science-fiction? Not necessarily. If at any point since you began reading, even a single question has come into your mind, or you've wondered what something you said might communicate in reverse, or if you think Reverse Speech might resolve a personal or professional issue, you already know we are discussing the possible.

Experiments that have been done, and which are currently being done, prove this is possible—right now. To the curious and the adventuresome: our work and our rewards are cut out for us.

Conclusion

Unlike many discoveries such as, "Time is relative instead of absolute," which unseat the old paradigms and throw us all back to square one and leave us wondering where to go from there, Reverse Speech *enhances* what we already know.

Reverse Speech unifies forward speech with backward speech and, *at the same time*, extends into the deep dimensions of metaphor and stretches into the past and the future.

Reverse Speech allows us to perceive, as never before, the gestalt of language and the wholeness of the human psyche.

Reverse Speech wouldn't exist without forward speech: its inflections, pauses and subtle exclamations. Together with forward speech, reversals communicate the exquisite texture and depth of language, gently unfolding the psyche, and exposing the very soul of humankind, united in the deepest realms of being.

Now that it's possible to consciously hear words that were always present in speech, but which were previously delivered and received unconsciously, humanity has the opportunity to revolutionize its understanding of itself, its heritage, and its future.

Reverse Speech is a scientific, reliable way to listen to and "read" human thought. It's a way to more fully understand human nature.

Welcome to the world of Reverse Speech.

Footnotes

CHAPTER 1 The Discovery of Reverse Speech
1. William Poundstone, *Big Secrets*, Corgi Books, London, 1985, p. 228.
2. Jeff Godwin, *The Devil's Disciples*, Chick Publications, Chino, CA 1985, p. 147.
3. U.S. Congress House, *A Bill to Require that Jackets in which Phonograph Records Containing Backward Masking Are Packaged Bear a Label Warning Consumers of such Backward Masking*. 97th Cong., 24th sess., 1982. H.R. 6363.
4. Poundstone, op.cit., p. 243, provided almost identical independent confirmation.
5. Ibid., p. 237.
6. Stan Deyo, *The Cosmic Conspiracy*, W.A.T.T., Perth, 1983, p. 73.
7. Also in *Jesus Christ Superstar* in the song "The Trial Before Pilate" the reversals **Idiot**, **Dimwit**, and **Get Fucked Master** exist.

CHAPTER 2 The Research Begins
1. *Rock and Roll—A Search for God*, Reel to Reel Productions, Washington, D.C. This video presents a Christian fundamentalist view of the role of rock music. The author viewed the video in Australia in 1987.
2. To date about 35 of these coincidental reversals have been documented. (See Appendix III.) "Another One Bites the Dust" by Queen created a great stir in some circles. 'Another one' is a coincidental phrase that consistently creates the reversal **Marijuana** whether spoken or sung.
3. Letters have been received claiming techniques for writing songs, forward and backward. Some examples quoted used phrases that were phonetic coincidences.
4. David Oates and Greg Albrecht, *Beyond Backward Masking: Reverse Speech and the Voice of the Inner Mind*, Jovamhaz Publications, Adelaide, 1987, presented the earliest research. The Theory of Reverse Speech as presented here has been dramatically revised and expanded over the last four years.

CHAPTER 3 The Source of Reverse Speech
1. "The NLP Center for Counselling and Training," brochure, Richardson, Texas, 1990.

2. Richard Bandler and John Grinder, *The Structure of Magic*, Science and Behavior Books, Inc., Palo Alto, 1975, p. 24.
3. John Suess, "Myndslink," NLP training course, Brisbane, Australia.
4. Dr. John Grinder, seminar held in Sydney, Australia, June 1988.
5. Don Holdaway, *The Foundations of Literacy*, Ashton Scholastic, Sydney, 1975, p. 13.
6. Tony Buzan, *Use Both Sides of Your Brain*, E.P. Dutton, Inc., New York, 1979, pp. 16-20.
7. Ibid.
8. Dianne Van Lancker, "Old Familiar Voices," *Psychology Today*, November 1987, pp. 12-14.
9. Martha M. Evans, *Dyslexia, An Annotated Bibliography*, Greenwood Press, London, 1982. p. 84.
10. This is explicit in many of Carl Jung's writing. Further recommended reading: E.A. Bennett, *What Jung Really Said*; C.G. Jung, *The Archetypes of the Collective Unconscious*, particularly pp. 275-354.; C.G. Jung, *The Structure and Dynamics of the Psyche*.
11. C.G. Jung, *The Structure and Dynamics of the Psyche*, Princeton University Press, New York, 1969, pp. 151-152. Also on page 185, Jung says: "The unconscious depicts an extremely fluid states of affairs: everything of which I know, but of which I am not at the moment thinking; everything perceived by my senses, but not noted by my conscious mind; everything which, involuntarily and without paying attention to it, I feel, think, remember, want, and do; all the future things that are taking shape in me and will sometime come to consciousness: all this is the content of the unconscious mind. . . . Thus far the unconscious is a fringe of consciousness."
12. Ibid., p. 151. Also on p. 148, Jung says: "Underneath [the unconscious] is an absolute unconscious which has nothing to do with our personal experience. This absolute unconscious would then be a psychic activity which goes on independently of the conscious mind and is not dependent even on the upper layers of the unconscious, untouched —and perhaps untouchable— by personal experience. It would be a kind of supra-individual psychic activity, a collective unconscious, as I have called it, as distinct from a superficial, relative, or personal unconscious."

CHAPTER 4 The Communicative Nature of Reverse Speech

1. *Illustrated Contemporary Dictionary, Encyclopedic Edition*, J.G. Ferguson Publishing Company, Chicago, 1978
2. Mr. John Hampel was a technical pioneer in Australia's early television days. He's now retired as an amateur radio operator (VK5SJ), designing antenna systems.
3. This is from personal correspondence with Mr. Hampel. AMPOL is one of the largest petroleum corporations in Australia. The distinction to be clarified here is that the direct command to BUY had a significant, measurable impact on PELACO sales. The less direct subliminal of only the well-known logo had no discernible impact on sales.
4. "Subliminal Advertising," Australian Broadcasting Tribunal, Sydney, 1984, p. 1.

5. Many resources are generally available that detail research on the structure and use of subliminals. These resources will enable the reader to distinguish the study of subliminals as a totally separate field of research with little or no relation to Reverse Speech as it is presented here.
6. Vincent Bugliosi, *Helter Skelter: The True Story of the Manson Murders*, W.W. Norton, New York, 1974.
7. Reversals sequentially in these songs: "Touch Too Much," "Shot Down in Flames," "Get it Hot," "If You Want Blood," "Love Hungry Man."
8. Compiled from various media reports in Australia, 1987, and the United States, 1990.
9. Reversals sequentially in these songs: "Exciter," "White Heat, Red Hot," "Better by You, Better Than Me," "Stained Class," "Savage," "Beyond the Realms of Death," "Heroes End."

CHAPTER 6 Reverse Speech Images

1. Paul Von Stroheim, personal correspondence, 1988: "Reversals may be coming from those parts of the mind that are being ignored or overlooked by other louder parts. For example, most people would have experienced times in their lives when they faced conflicts and two contradictory elements within them were fighting for control (e.g. you want to buy an ice cream but you know you shouldn't because you'll ruin your diet). If some part of the being is being ignored or 'gone-over-the-head-of' then that part may revenge itself in some way on the psyche. Speech reversals may provide a safety valve for those parts."
2. E.A. Bennett, *What Jung Really Said*, Schoken Books, New York, 1983, p. xii.
3. Jung, *The Structure and Dynamics of the Psyche*, op.cit. pp. 145-149.
4. Ibid.
5. Ibid.
6. This and all references to or quotes from *The Holy Bible* are taken from the King James Version, World Publishing Company, Cleveland, OH.
7. Jung, loc. cit.
8. C.G. Jung, *The Archetypes of the Collective Unconscious*, Princeton University Press, New York, 1969, p. 51. (Also recounted with additional details in, *The Structure and Dynamics of the Psyche*.)
9. The book was titled *Eine Mithrasliturgie*.
10. Jung, *Archetypes*,. loc. cit. (Taken from *Eine Mithrasliturgie*, p. 6ff.)
11. See also editor's note in *Archetypes*: "As the author (Jung) later learned, the 1910 edition was actually the second, there had been a first edition in 1903. The patient had, however, been committed some years before 1903."
12. Jung, *Structure and Dynamics*, op.cit. p. 151.
13. Jung, *Archetypes*, op.cit., p.52.
14. Bennet, op.cit., p. xii.
15. Jung, *Archetypes*,. op.cit., pp. 23, 30.
16. *Contemporary Dictionary*, op.cit.
17. King James Version, op.cit.
18. Chu Yuan, *Songs of the South: An Ancient Chinese Anthology*, Trans. David Hawkes, Penguin Books, New York, 1985.
19. Juan Mascsaro, *The Upanishads*, Penguin Books, Middlesex, 1965, p. 53.

20. *Encyclopedia of Mythology of All Races*, Marshall Jones Company, Boston, 1932, Vol. IV, pp. 9, 83, 179, 181, 182, 286; Vol. VI, pp. 233, 236; Vol. VII, pp. 81, 247; Vol. VIII, pp. 67, 70; Vol. IX, p. 274; Vol. XI, p. 323.
21. William James, "Frederick Myers' Service to Psychology," *Proceedings of the Society for Psychical Research*, London, 1903, p. 13.
22. *The Enchanted World, The Fall of Camelot*, Time Life Books Inc., Amsterdam, 1986.
23. This theory was initially developed by Greg Albrecht in an unpublished manuscript.
24. "Luther" was discovered by Greg Albrecht, who is currently conducting major research into oral tradition, structural metaphors, and their source. He claims to have located the exact conversation where **Luther** was first adopted as an structural metaphor.

CHAPTER 7 Intricacies of Speech

1. This category, first noted by Greg Albrecht, was the first of many common connections between the forward and reversed dialogue discovered. It eventually led to the formation of Reverse Speech categories.

CHAPTER 8 Sex

1. As heard through the headphone in my ear while being interviewed. Also confirmed during the commercial break by the commentator.
2. In this session, **Elvis** was frequently found on the reverse of the forward word "subliminal." It was initially thought to be a phonetic coincidence. It didn't occur every time she said "subliminal," however, nor did it occur when other speakers said "subliminal." To research this further, I conducted a quick test by saying the word "subliminal" into a tape and reversed it. "Elvis" did not occur in the reversed phonetics. With further testing involving numerous other subjects, this coincidental reversal proved to be peculiar to certain individuals only.

CHAPTER 10 Music

1. Jacob Aranza, *Backward Masking Unmasked*, Huntington House, Inc., Shreveport, 1984, p. 1.
2. Ibid., p. 12.
3. Jacob Aranza, *More Rock, Country and Backward Masking Unmasked*, Huntington House, Inc., Shreveport, 1985, p. 9.
4. Aleister Crowley, *Magick*, Samuel Weiser, Inc., York Beach, 1973, p. 482.
5. Aranza, *Backward Masking Unmasked*, op.cit., p. 4.
6. King James Version, op.cit.
7. Godwin, op.cit., p. 1.
8. Ibid., p. 158.
9. Stephen Davis, *The Hammer of the Gods*, William Morrow and Company Inc., New York, 1985, p. 335.
10. Raymond B. MacPherson, private letter, Melbourne, 1988.
11. C.R. Cammell, *Aleister Crowley*, New English Library, London, 1969.
12. Ibid.
13. Davis, op.cit.
14. Davis, op.cit. p. 146.
15. Godwin, op.cit. p. 152.

16. Much of the following section (music from the 1920's to the 1970's) was researched jointly with Greg Albrecht and myself and is documented in our initial, self-published book, *Beyond Backward Masking*.
17. A reference to Luke 22:42.

CHAPTER 11 Personalities and Politicians

1. Gail Buchalter, "It's Love That's Serious," *Parade Magazine*, April 1991, pp. 8-9. The interviewer notes in the article: "Most of those films have been comedies, but Martin is trying to change that. . . . Martin's point of view seems to include a profound discomfort with the recognition that goes with celebrity."

CHAPTER 12 Reverse Speech and the Professions

1. Ian Thurnwald, "The Chamberlain Case: The Anthropology of Social Dramas and Myths," dissertation, The Adelaide University, Adelaide, Australia, 1988, p. 10.
2. Paul Stewart, attorney. Partially compiled from a lecture given to the Reverse Speech Education and Research Institute, Dallas, TX, August 1990.

CHAPTER 13 Developing Areas of Research

1. My quest for reversal accuracy is intense. I'm approximately 80% accurate the first time I analyze a transcript and 95% accurate the second time through. My initial tapes, when I began my research, have been estimated to be 50% accurate, which increased as time progressed to my current level. This has been determined by checking old research tapes with other trained analysts. New students begin with approximately 60% accuracy (second analysis) to 80% accuracy after six months of intense study (second analysis). Figures are based on the monitoring of 50% of students over a two-year period.
2. Paul Von Stroheim has been involved with Reverse Speech since 1988. He regularly makes suggestions, conducts research and develops new concepts. He communicates through frequent correspondence.
3. Renee Tait, personal correspondence. Published in "Letters to the Editor," *Backtalk*, May 1990.

NOTE:

All otherwise unattributed initial chapter quotes have been taken from *The Illustrated Contemporary Dcitionary, Encyclopedic Edition*, J.G. Ferguson Publishing Co., Chicago, 1978.

Authors' Biographies

David John Oates was born in South Australia in 1955. He is married and has three children. In his early career years, he owned an insurance agency and conducted lectures in sales training and human communication skills. He also worked extensively with street kids and managed half-way houses and rehabilitation homes. At that time, he was also an active amateur radio operator.

In 1984, while running a half-way house, he first began his research into Reverse Speech. Since that time, he has pursued this career with fervor and has earned the unique reputation of founder and developer of the Reverse Speech technology.

David Oates now lives in Dallas, Texas, where he runs the Reverse Speech Education and Research Institute. He lectures extensively on Reverse Speech, conducts regular training programs, and is a popular guest on radio and television. To date, he has conducted in excess of 100 media interviews regarding Reverse Speech.

Kathleen Hawkins is the co-author of the popular book, *Time Management Made Easy*, and the best-selling audio-cassette programs, *How to Speed Read* and *How to Organize Yourself to Win*. She also wrote a column for *Success* magazine for five years. Her articles on how to increase personal and professional effectiveness have appeared in more than 200 magazines.

In addition, she has been a reading, writing, and management consultant for 15 years. More than 50,000 people have taken her courses.

Kathleen Hawkins was the second person in the United States to be awarded a Reverse Speech Developer Certificate. She made significant contributions to this book as a writer and editor.

Appendix I

Getting Involved with Reverse Speech

If you want to know more about Reverse Speech, and there is much more to know, we invite you to contact:

Reverse Speech Research, Inc.
P.O. Box 181862
Dallas, Texas 75218-9998
phone: (214) 324-3216 fax: (214) 324-1191

Reverse Speech Research is looking for enthusiastic people to become involved in further planning and development. We offer many services including tape analysis, informational brochures, training courses, lectures, and seminars.

If you want to use Reverse Speech yourself, you MUST receive professional training. This book only mentions, but does not detail, some of the many techniques that you need to locate reversals and interpret your findings. Reverse Speech Research in Dallas, Texas, is currently the only authorized training center in the world.

Training and Certification Programs

One of our highest aims is to ensure the integrity and the accuracy of the technology. Reverse Speech, by its very nature, is highly susceptible to abuse and misinterpretation. Consequently, to ensure the highest ethics of operation and to encourage the ongoing search for additional knowledge and understanding of the phenomenon, we offer several educational programs and standards of operation.

The Reverse Speech Process,^{SM} as defined and taught in Reverse Speech Training Manuals and partially detailed in this book, is protected by all available trademark, copyright, and intellectual property laws. These rights are owned by David Oates, the founder of the Reverse Speech technology, and are licensed to the Board of Directors who act as administrators for these ownership rights, operate within predetermined guidelines, and adhere to the prescribed code of ethics. All entrants into training programs must sign standard contracts and agreements.

Once graduates successfully complete various stages of training, they are issued certificates that testify to their expertise in the Reverse Speech process. Along with these certificates come various rights, including trademark use, commercial ventures, and other privileges.

The training and certification stage is regarded with the highest respect and honor. The technology associated with Reverse Speech is complicated and involved. The Institute Board maintains, based on experience, that it is extremely difficult to fully understand the implications of Reverse Speech and, therefore, to represent the technology accurately unless training has been undertaken. The Board, therefore, will not consider any applications for independent commercial or research ventures by anyone who has not taken some certification programs.

The Board will also take action to protect the technology should any breach be brought to its attention.

The first step, therefore, for anyone who wishes to participate in Reverse Speech is to undertake training and certifications.

The Analyst Certificate
Step One of "The Reverse Speech Process"

A comprehensive, six-month course, which consists of one weekend per month of intensive lectures and training, plus extensive homework assignments to be done between lectures.

Homework assignments are used to monitor new students' progress and to help the graduate. It's recommended that students spend at least 15 hours a week in private study in addition to class time. Homework results are used as a guide so that each person's strengths and weaknesses can be individually addressed.

The Analyst Course teaches all the basics of reversal location and analysis, including how to:

- Locate and document genuine speech reversals.
- Identify precise linguistic and syntax requirements for a reversal to be genuine.
- Determine the categories and structure of reversals.
- Prepare an accurate session transcript.
- Identify and interpret Reverse Speech metaphors.
- Discuss the unconscious mind and collective unconscious.
- Describe how people communicate.
- Discuss the sexual nature of human beings as exhibited in Reverse Speech.
- Conduct a session so that specific information appears in reverse.
- Discuss the history of Reverse Speech and the beginnings of reversed language in children.

Once successfully completing this phase of the training, graduates are given certain rights to represent Reverse Speech technology, conduct professional tape analysis, and instigate commercial ventures. *No rights are given for the use of the technology in a therapeutic setting, unless one holds an appropriate license in a therapeutic discipline.* No rights are given with the Analyst Certificate to train people or teach the technology in any form.

Participation in the course does *NOT* guarantee certification. This is earned through proficiency. Students who don't graduate may repeat the course at a reduced cost or receive private instruction in the areas in which they need strengthening.

Graduation consists of three requirements:

1. An initial examination after the second month, which includes a written essay on theory and techniques, plus a practical examination. Successfully passing this examination results in the issuance of a *Reverse Speech Trainee* certificate. No licenses come with this certification.

2. The completion of 70% of all the homework assignments.

3. A final examination, which consists of the comprehensive analysis of 30 minutes of tape, a written examination, and a "live" Reverse Speech session conducted with a fellow student on the final weekend and analyzed at that time.

Course fees are announced as each training class approaches. Fees include a comprehensive training manual, homework tapes, regular progress reports, and private instruction.

In addition to the course fees, students must purchase a reversing machine and become a member of the Reverse Speech Education and Research Institute. Other items not covered by the course are audio-cassettes other than the homework tapes, a stop watch for clustering reversals, miscellaneous electronic leads, and an extra tape deck for "dumping" reversals. Applicants for the training must also complete an application form and pay a non-refundable course deposit.

The Developer Certificate

This certificate is an honorary award, issued at the sole discretion of the Board of Directors, to encourage research and original thinking. It is awarded to anyone who has made a considerable contribution to the research and development of the Reverse Speech technology. This can be in any area such as providing new insights and information, finding a better way to do something, or making a significant advancement in the acceptance of Reverse Speech by society.

The prerequisite for a Developer Certificate is that the person hold a current Trainee Certificate.

The Advanced Analyst Certificate
Step Two of "The Reverse Speech Process"

Graduates of the Analyst Course may participate in the Advanced Analyst Course, also a six-month course of one weekend a month. The Advanced Analyst Course teaches advanced skills, including:

- Advanced theory.

- Detailed metaphor groups.
- Behavioral strategies and motivators.
- The building blocks of the mind and personality structures.
- High speed reversal location.
- Reversal intent.
- Detailed reversal staging.
- Double layered and over-lapping reversals.
- Reversal control.

Students must prepare a detailed thesis for their Master Analyst research project, exhibit intensive reversal location and analysis checking skills, recognize behavioral strategies and types through reversal understanding, and successfully complete extensive written examinations.

Graduates will have their licenses endorsed with permission to use the Reverse Speech Process for behavioral and personality analysis. The Advanced Analyst Certificate is required before any training certificates are issued.

The Associate Trainer Certificate

This course is usually held in conjunction with the Advanced Analyst Course. In addition to Advanced Analyst studies, students must also repeat an entire Analyst course and be trained in the techniques needed for student training and course preparation.

Additional studies include public presentation and training skills. Students must have also compiled research material and a reversal and session transcript library to facilitate public presentations. Holders of this certificate can train students up to Trainee Level in their own classes and issue Trainee certificates. They may also participate in student training during the entire Analyst courses.

The Trainer Certificate

Students for this course must hold both Advanced Analyst certificates and Associate Trainer certificates. Training includes conducting a full Analyst Course, under supervision, leading to the successful graduation of students. Students must be proficient in all aspects of reversal and metaphor theory and their applications as well as training techniques.

They must also have considerably expanded their library of reversal and session transcripts examples. Holders of this certificate can conduct full Analyst courses and issue Analyst certificates as well as participate in the training of Associate Trainers.

The Master Analyst Certificate
Step Three of "The Reverse Speech Process"

This is a 12-month course with extensive private homework, in which the "Masters" are born. The prerequisite is an Advanced Analyst Certificate. Students will learn:

- Super advanced reversal location and analysis skills on all levels and metaphor groups.
- The accurate recognition of personality types, behavioral strategies and physical appearances through reversal comprehension ONLY (no forward dialogue nor prior contact with, or knowledge of, the subject).
- Reversal feedback.
- Metaphor restructuring and other "change" techniques.
- Hearing reversals consciously and other techniques and topics.

Successful graduates will have also completed a major research project in which they have made a significant contribution to either the understanding and/or the applications of Reverse Speech.

Certification allows full use in commercial setting for Metaphor restructuring work. It is not necessary to have Training certificates and training is ONLY allowed if the appropriate training certificates are held.

The Advanced Trainer and
Master Trainer Certificates

This program is similar to the Trainer Program, except that all students must be studying for the Master Analyst Certificate. No Advanced or Master Trainer certificates will be issued unless Master Analyst certificates are held. Students must repeat the

Advanced Analyst course, plus complete other requirements, in order to receive the Advanced Trainer certificate.

They must repeat the Master Analyst course, plus other requirements, to receive Master Trainer certificates. This program will usually be held in conjunction with the Advanced and Master Analyst courses.

Holders of the Advanced Trainer certificate can train up to Advanced Analyst level as well as Trainer level.

Holders of the Master Trainer certificate can train up to Master Analyst level as well as Advanced Trainer level.

With additional training and studies, Master Trainers may be able to have their certificates endorsed so that they may also issue Master Trainer certificates. This is the highest level of certification currently available. It allows full commercial use of Reverse Speech in all situations, subject to the restrictions of the standard code of ethics of the Reverse Speech Education and Research Institute.

Reverse Speech Research Product List

Journal

Backtalk is a bi-monthly journal which reports on current research, breakthroughs and training programs in Reverse Speech. Six issues a year. If you are interested in following Reverse Speech developments, *Backtalk* is the only information source where advances in this rapidly changing field are pulled together. Order from Reverse Speech Research or from Knowledge Systems.

Reversing Equipment and Audio Cassette Tapes

Although Reverse Speech Research developed the following products for training purposes, we somewhat reluctantly offer them for general sale with the following caveat:

> *These tapes and recorders in no way substitute for the training process. Becoming proficient at discovering, hearing and analyzing reversals cannot be done on your own. It is much harder than learning a foreign language which can be learned from tapes alone.*

With that warning in mind, the following tapes are offered for informational value only; no certification is awarded with the acquisition of any tape series. Call Reverse Speech Research to confirm current pricing.

- Tape series of first weekend Analyst Course.
- Tape series of entire Analyst Course lectures.
- Analyst Course Correspondence Tape Series for Analyst Certification.
- Various other lectures and presentations.

Reversing Equipment

Please call for current prices. At present the following models are only available through Reverse Speech Research. Currently offered are:

- Playback only.
- High-quality recording with separate microphone.
- Superior audio and recording with external power.

Appendix II

Reverse Speech
Metaphor Dictionary

This dictionary lists the more common words that have been found in Reverse Speech. The meanings should be used as a guide only. A word can have several different implications depending on its context.

Metaphors vary in their significance depending on the context. The complementarity contained in the forward dialogue, subject matter of the conversation, the immediate circumstances of the individual, and that individual's background and experience can provide additional clues. For example, the word **whirlwind** usually means either personal or external energy. If **whirlwind** appears continuously when a person talks about depression, then it may be assumed that the person's personal energy system revolves around depression. If **whirlwind** often appears as a person discusses his or her work situation, then it can be assumed that the individual's personal energy system revolves around work.

What may be a metaphor in one context may also be used as a fact in another context. For example, the ·word **shoot** is a common metaphor that refers to intense emotional energy. If it is common metaphor that refers to intense emotional energy. If it is used in the context of a person shooting a gun, then it probably means exactly what it says.

This dictionary details common meanings that have come to be associated with these words in Reverse Speech. Different common explanations are separated in this text with commas. Again, the meanings listed should be used only as a guide. The entire dictionary is in a constant state of evolution. As the frequency of appearance of a word increases, the broadening reference base is used to clarify and update these definitions. Next to each word are italicized descriptions of their most common level of appearance in Reverse Speech:

1. Metaphors that can appear in all levels: First, Second, and Third Level reversals are designated (*multi*).
2. Operational metaphors or Second Level reversals (*operational*) indicate the behavioral effects of the root causes
3. Structural metaphors or Third Level reversals (*structural*) point to root causes of behavior.

ACID (*operational*) an instrument of harm or destruction, the opposite of water

ADAM (*structural*) as in Adam and Eve, the spiritual man, innocence

ALADDIN (*structural*) meaning imprecise, possibly charmer, the part of us that can achieve wonders

ALBUM (*operational*) memories of the past, may be affecting current behavior

ALEXIS (*structural*) meaning imprecise, possibly female seeking male characteristics, feminism

ALLAH (*multi*) as it says, another name for God

ALPHA (*structural*) shortened form of Alpha and Omega

ANIMAL (*structural*) a part of the psyche that is primordial and basic

ANOTHER ONE (*operational*) usually means another sexual partner, but can also appear in other contexts

ARMOR (*operational*) personal protection

ARROW *(operational)* to move toward a goal

BEAST *(structural)* primordial instinctive nature

BOOTS *(operational)* to move, instrument of movement, also Australian metaphor indicating the movement of truth

BOY *(operational)* a masculine and innocent part of the psyche, the "little child," also found in homosexual contexts

BOX *(operational)* phallic connotations, vagina

BRITISH *(operational)* a "proper attitude," organized, usually a descriptor rather than as a behavioral structure directed toward others, *See also:* London

BUST *(multi)* broken, damaged, faulty

BUY *(operational)* to secure, to convince to have

CAESAR *(structural)* white male dominance

CAMELOT *(structural)* from the Legend of King Arthur, the fortress, an ultimate goal of life's quest, usually appears in the context of that which is unattainable

CANCER *(operational)* disease, something that is destroying, uncontrollable

CASTLE *(structural)* the inner fortress, ultimate refuge or strength, the conclusion of life's quest

CELLAR *(operational)* a deep part of the mind, a place where things are repressed, a place to hide

CITY *(operational)* an active place, populous

CUM *(operational)* phallic connotations, to ejaculate

CURSE *(operational)* to insult, damage, reject

CYBORG *(operational)* half human, half machine, automated behavior, a sense of depersonification

DAME *(operational)* feminine counterpart of fellow, opposite of person, someone who has no real significance to the speaker

DEAD *(operational)* also refers to emotional death or death of energy, drive, or purpose in life

DEFEAT *(multi)* to overcome, to conquer, to fade away

DELIVER *(multi)* to deliver something, to be free of something

DEMON *(structural)* harm, emotional pain, negative behavior

DESERVE *(multi)* to have something for actions done

DEVIL *(operational)* usually treated as a soft word, mischievousness, sometimes has potential for destruction, uneasiness

DIE *(operational)* emotional death, give up, defeat

DINE *(operational)* spiritual connotations, to take in sustenance, to interact

DISEASE *(operational)* something that's destroying emotionally or spiritually, acute dis-ease

EAGLE *(operational)* meaning imprecise, possibly referring to strength and stamina, a visionary nature

EARN *(multi)* to receive as a reward

EARTH *(operational)* grounding, stability, strength, spiritual connection, relating to things of the earth

EDEN *(structural)* spiritual center, image of perfection

ELVIS *(structural)* superstar, well-known, king, potential for self-destruction in achieving greatness

ERROR *(multi)* fault, to come short

EVE *(structural)* as in Adam and Eve, the spiritual woman, innocence

EVIL *(operational)* wrong, inaccurate, harmful

EYE *(operational)* vision, insight, goals, dreams, intuition

FACE *(multi)* the essence of Self, the real "I," the Persona

FALL *(multi)* to come short of expectations, compromise resulting in harm

FANTASY *(operational)* something that's unreal, an ecstatic creation of perceived reality

FAT *(operational)* the essence of someone or indulgence— depending on context

FEATHER *(operational)* meaning imprecise, possibly to give subtly, to lighten a load

FEED *(multi)* nourishment, to give or receive nourishment or energy

FEEL *(multi)* kinesthetic predicate

FEET *(operational)* stability, movement, strength

FELLOW *(operational)* the masculine counterpart of dame, opposite of person, someone who has no real significance to the speaker

FIG *(structural)* from the Garden of Eden, to protect, hide from shame

FILM *(operational)* a life drama, life seen as a movie without personal connection, dissociation

FILTH *(operational)* personal inadequacy, emotional overload

FIRE *(operational)* high emotion, purify

FOB *(multi)* to ignore, to put aside, to procrastinate, to disregard

FOOD *(operational)* emotional or spiritual sustenance, energy source

FORCE *(multi)* male/female energies, personal power; sometimes meaning what it says, to persuade

FOUL *(operational)* severely unpleasant

FOXY *(operational)* desirable, perception of love, capable of fulfillment

FUCK *(multi)* harm, hurt, intercourse, damage, invasive

FUSE *(multi)* to join with, to work together

FUZZY *(operational)* unclear, not in good vision, a perception not yet sufficiently formulated

GARDEN *(structural) See:* Eden

GIRL *(operational)* the child within, sometimes an affectionate term for a partner, sometimes used with lesbian connotations

GOD *(multi)* usually as it says

GODDESS *(structural)* the perception of the perfect woman, desired but often unattainable, the ultimate dream or quest, sometimes the inner healer

GUARD *(multi)* to protect, to hide

HAND *(operational)* to relate, instrument of interaction, point of contact

HEAL *(multi)* to help, restore, bring together

HEAR *(multi)* auditory predicate

HEAVEN *(multi)* usually as it says, peace, source of wisdom

HEAVY *(operational)* painful, difficult, oppressive

HEBREW *(structural)* Christian, God's people

HELL *(operational)* an expression of displeasure, pain, suffering

HELM *(operational)* the control of one's life

HOME *(operational)* inner refuge, security, safety, belonging

HOUSE *(operational) See:* Home

HOWL *(operational)* a deep cry from within, usually agony

HUNGRY *(operational)* a need for emotional or spiritual sustenance

JERUSALEM *(structural)* someone's spiritual center, a source of teaching and wisdom

JESUS *(multi)* usually as it is, sometimes positive emotion

JUICE *(operational)* generally neutral, the essence of energy desired, more frequently found on males

KILL *(operational)* to cause harm, to keep quiet

KISS *(operational)* connect, interact, touch with significance

LANCELOT *(structural)* the perception of the perfect man, often unattainable, knight in shining armor sometimes with hidden dark aspects

LANTERN *(operational)* guidance, to be illuminated

LAW *(operational)* usually indicates rigidity, lack of compromise

LESSON *(operational)* as it says, usually a life lesson, spiritual lesson, karmic lesson

LICK *(operational)* to connect softly, to explore a relationship

LIGHT *(operational)* to understand, to perceive truth, motivation

LIP *(operational)* sexual connotation, to communicate, to connect

LIPSTICK *(operational)* meaning imprecise, possibly fancy surface projection

LONDON *(structural)* a "proper attitude," organized

LOOSE *(multi)* to free forcibly, to break free from a behavioral pattern

LORD *(structural)* sometimes as it says, area of importance, control factor in life

LOVE *(multi)* many meanings depending on context and level, usually affection or attachment, the key to interpretation of this word is complementarity

LOVELY BIT *(operational)* phallic connotations, sexual organs

LUCIFER *(structural)* sometimes as it says, negative behavior

LUST *(operational)* a strong desire or need

MAGICIAN *(structural)* enchanter, magic worker, enticing personality, the part that can overcome obstacles, also to transform

MAKE UP *(operational)* also a definition of self-structure, false or true depending on context, see lipstick; *See also:* Lipstick

MAN *(operational)* deep masculinity in its purest sense

MARK *(operational)* harm, damage to the psyche, to emphasize, scar or wounding

MASK *(operational)* a covering of the real self, a projected image

MAST *(operational)* phallic connotations, essential to life's movement

MASTER *(structural)* the one with control, organizer, teacher

MEN *(operational)* general description

MESSAGE *(operational)* an instruction usually from the unconscious

MIDDLE *(operational)* usually treated as the emotional center

MILK *(operational)* nourishment, closeness, healing, the essence of femininity

MISSION *(operational)* a quest, a goal, usually with religious-like fervor

MONEY *(operational)* exact meaning imprecise, usually associated with the sex/power metaphor group

MOVIE *(operational)* disconnection from life, non-attachment to event

MURDER *(operational)* to emotionally destroy, to harm, to suppress

MUSIC *(operational)* something pleasant, positive energy, opening of the heart

MUST *(multi)* insistence, dominance

NAKED *(operational)* willingness to be exposed, freedom, fulfillment

NAME *(operational)* the representation of the self

NAZARENE *(structural)* meaning imprecise, possibly defining religious attitude

NAZI *(structural)* strong evil, domination

NEED *(multi)* strong desire, essential for emotional survival

NERVE *(operational)* to be nervous, unsettled

NEST *(operational)* a place of safety and security

NIGGER *(operational)* a derogatory term, regardless of race

NIMROD *(structural)* the first king of Babylon, an insatiable quest for money and power

NOOSE *(operational)* an instrument of self-destruction

NUDE *(operational)* imposed, unwanted exposure; oppressed, fear, inhibited

OCEAN *(operational)* the waters of life, life's circumstances

ODIN *(structural)* meaning imprecise, usually false perception, can appear grandiose with deceptive hidden characteristics

OEDIPUS *(structural)* inappropriate sexual relations, perceived or factual depending on context

OWL *(operational)* false perception of knowledge or wisdom, self-made arguments, words with no substance, rhetoric

OXYGEN *(operational)* source of personal strength or energy, emotional nourishment or relief

PERSON *(operational)* someone of significance, an important person

PLASTIC *(operational)* false, shallow

PONY *(operational)* only found in children to date, security, stability

POWER *(operational)* high energy, protection, fulfillment

PROGRAM *(operational)* fixed behavioral pattern, to alter without consent

RAPE *(operational)* violate, forcibly intrude

RAYMOND *(structural)* a recently discovered word, meaning and origin are currently being researched

REEF *(operational)* an obstacle in life's journey

REFILL *(operational)* a desire for more energy

RELIEVE *(multi)* comfort, reduce

REFUND *(operational)* to desire something back and to not receive it, usually associated with loss

REPEAT *(multi)* refers to a repetitive behavioral pattern

REVERSE *(multi)* to alter, the opposite, often to alter behavior or emotions

ROCELIN *(structural)* from the tales of King Arthur, a deceptive person, one who drains strength from any available source: the opposite sex, someone's symbol system, etc.

ROCK *(operational)* strength, stability

ROPE *(operational)* a way out, an escape, a solution to a problem as in "throw me a rope"

RUSH *(multi)* intense excitement, adrenaline rush, to hurry

RUST *(operational)* to waste away, not used, loss of energy

SAIL *(operational)* to travel, to move through life

SALARY *(operational)* to receive for favor

SALE *(operational)* to give something for exchange, negotiation

SALT *(operational)* to preserve, keep, restore, possibly purify

SAM *(multi)* usually appears as a shortened version of Uncle Sam, or the United States

SAMSON *(structural)* a perception of strength that is easily weakened, something that looks nice and attractive, but which has weaknesses, one with a mission

SAND *(operational)* something shaky, non-lasting, insecurity

SATAN *(structural)* usually intense emotion, strong negative sense, powerful almost unshakeable destructive behavior patterns, strong power

SEAGULL *(operational)* meaning imprecise, possibly from "Jonathan Livingston Seagull," spiritual freedom, no boundaries to personal growth

SEAL *(operational)* to agree, protect, unbreakable bond

SEAT *(operational)* center of self, inactivity, stability

SEE *(operational)* very complex visual predicate inclusive of how one perceives, visions, dreams, establishes viewpoint and understanding; *See also:* Eye

SEED *(operational)* often appears in sexual context, semen, to create something new

SELL *(operational)* to persuade, convince, demand something in return, an unequal exchange

SERMON *(operational)* conditioning, imposed behavior

SERVE *(multi)* to help willingly, to assist without personal glory

SEX *(multi)* connection, union, power, fulfillment

SHACK *(operational)* home, refuge

SHADOW *(operational)* elusive, the hidden part of the self, alter ego, often refers directly to the unconscious mind

SHAFT *(operational)* phallic connotations, penis, an instrument of sexual energy

SHAKE *(multi)* to disturb, to bring to realization

SHEPHERD *(structural)* teacher, leader, spiritual guide, one to be trusted

SHERIFF *(structural)* meaning imprecise, possibly guardian of behavior or behavioral parameters

SHIFT *(multi)* to alter, to modify

SHIP *(structural)* the part that moves us, or the part of us that is moving, life's voyage, instrument of travelling through life

SHOT *(operational)* to receive high emotions

SHOOT *(operational)* to deliver high emotion

SHOW *(operational)* something put on, a performance, dissociation

SHOWER *(operational)* inundated, to be overcome, high energy

SICK *(multi)* not well, removed from normality; sometimes **SIC** as in "to attack"

SIGH *(multi)* to relieve, to release emotions, to let go

SIGHT *(operational) See also:* eye

SIGN *(operational)* to agree, unite, confirm

SILHOUETTE *(operational)* similar to shadow, elusive part of the self or of the unconscious mind

SILK *(operational)* fine outer protection of self, non-deceptive concealment, smooth

SILVER *(operational)* something precious, valued, refined, a fine outer protection or covering of self

SIN *(operational)* personal shortcoming, error, danger

SING *(operational)* charm, lure, to announce to those around you

SIT *(operational)* to take no action, inactivity, restrain

SKIN *(operational)* an outer protective appearance, personal protection

SLIP *(multi)* to give discretely, to fall short of expectations

SMELL *(operational)* to assess, to explore possibilities, usually sexual connotations, see sex

SNAIL *(operational)* lack of action, slow to decide

SNAKE *(multi)* meaning imprecise, deception, cunning, temptation, strategy

SNIFF *(operational)* to explore sexual possibilities, tease, ego indulgence

SNOW *(operational)* purity, cleanse, safe

SO *(multi)* adds emphasis

SORCERY *(operational)* a strong, enticing force, to charm or deceive

SORE *(operational)* damage to psyche, an unresolved issue, personal pain

SOURCE *(operational)* male/female energies, a means of attaining personal strength and power

SPEAR *(operational)* like sword with emphasis on harm

SPELL *(operational)* charm, deceive, entice

STIFFY *(operational)* phallic connotations, erection

SUCK *(multi)* to drain energy, to deplete, to improve ego at the expense of others, to control

SULTAN *(structural)* meaning imprecise, part of the self that would be king, leader, great and powerful

SUN *(operational)* a source of energy, spiritual power, source of light or enlightenment

SUNNY *(operational)* nice, pleasant, invigorating

SURF *(operational)* the movement of life, activity

SWEAT *(operational)* the scent of sexual attraction

SWORD *(operational)* personal strength and defense

SYSTEM *(operational)* personality, behavior, operating methods

THIRST *(operational)* emotional deprivation, need

ULYSSES *(structural)* meaning imprecise, possibly warrior, traveler

VESSEL *(operational)* meaning imprecise, possibly connected to "ship," also to hold or protect

WALRUS *(operational)* request for a story, metaphor, an analogy, a different perspective

WAR *(structural)* conflict, turmoil, struggle

WARHEAD *(operational)* instrument of destruction, delivery of emotions or ideas

WARRIOR *(structural)* a fighter, one with a mission, an intense desire or commitment

WASH *(operational)* to change, alter, cleanse

WATER *(operational)* means of fulfillment, to fill emotional need

WEATHER *(operational)* life's hazards, the movement of life

WHIRL *(operational)* softer version of whirlwind, also confusion, high activity

WHIRLWIND *(structural)* energy, power, empathy, activity

WIND *(operational)* softer version of whirlwind, also speed, haste, interaction with others, rapport

WINE *(operational)* spiritual connotations, something nice, refreshing

WISDOM *(operational)* deep knowledge, insight, universal truth

WOLF *(structural)* part of psyche that is hunter and protector, a prime mover behind behavior, also called (very rarely) "she-wolf" and "were-wolf" in its strongest form

WOMAN *(operational)* deep femininity in its purest sense

WOMEN *(operational)* general description

WORD *(operational)* spiritual connotations, divine guidance, wisdom from deep within

ZEUS *(structural)* meaning imprecise, another word for God, a sense of mystery

Appendix III

Coincidental Reversals

Certain words and phrases will sometimes reverse to say the same thing. The following list details some of the more common coincidences. They will not always reverse as shown (it depends on the tonality) but they may. Coincidental words should NOT be documented unless they appear in an entire sentence.

Reverse	Forward	Reverse	Forward
Dad	Dad	Sex	Discuss
Elvis	Subliminal	Shallow	Relationship
Firearm	My wife	Shock	Question
	My life	Shoot	Push
First	Surf	Shows this	Situation
Fuck	Confront		Emotion
I'm not	I'm not	Simone	Enormous
Love	Father	Sit	Just
Marijuana	Another one	Sleep	Its
Memory	Remember	Surf	First
Money	You know	You must	Tell me
Mum	Mum	Whirlwind	Well
My mum	Mother		World
Murder	I don't		Work
Say	Yes	Wolf	Forward
Serve	Reverse		Four
Sex	Discuss		Before

263

Appendix IV

Listening to the Voice of the Inner Mind

Hear reversals as they actually occur in speech. *Introduction to Reverse Speech: Listening to the voice of the inner mind* is a 45-minute audio-cassette tape narrated by David Oates.

The nature of Reverse Speech is explained with examples of reversals from Neil Armstrong's moonwalk, a reporter's commentaries during President Kennedy's assassination, babies communicating their needs, a conversation in which what people are saying is very different than what they are actually thinking, children talking about running away from home, U.S. POWs in the Persian Gulf War, a murder suspect declaring his innocence while his reversal states the opposite, President Truman announcing the decision to drop the atomic bomb on Japan, metaphorical and archetypal language of the mind, and more.

This tape is designed to be played on a standard tape player and is $12.95 (plus $3.00 shipping and handling for the first tape, and $.25 for each additional tape). Order from Knowledge Systems, 7777 W. Morris St., Indianapolis, IN 46231 or call toll-free with MasterCard and VISA orders at 1-800-999-8517.

Appendix V

Guidebook for the '90s

The Guidebook for the '90s: Resources for Effecting Personal and Social Change contains books, tapes and organizations screened from several hundred publishing sources to assist you in:

- coping with overload,
- engaging in sacred play,
- creating sacred time and space,
- making sense of the times,
- discovering high vocational adventure,
- catalyzing creativity in organizations,
- exploring the new consciousness,
- and much much more.

Write Knowledge Systems at 7777 W. Morris Street, Indianapolis, IN 46231 or call (317) 241-0749 for your free copy.

Index